JAZZ À LA CREOLE

American Made Music Series

ADVISORY BOARD

David Evans, General Editor
Barry Jean Ancelet
Edward A. Berlin
Joyce J. Bolden
Rob Bowman
Susan C. Cook
Curtis Ellison
William Ferris
John Edward Hasse
Kip Lornell
Bill Malone
Eddie S. Meadows
Manuel H. Peña
Wayne D. Shirley
Robert Walser

Jazz à la Creole

French Creole Music and the Birth of Jazz

Caroline Vézina

UNIVERSITY PRESS OF MISSISSIPPI / JACKSON

www.upress.state.ms.us

The University Press of Mississippi is a member
of the Association of University Presses.

Any discriminatory or derogatory language or hate speech regarding race, ethnicity, religion, sex, gender, class, national origin, age, or disability that has been retained or appears in elided form is in no way an endorsement of the use of such language outside a scholarly context.

Cover images: Lorenzo Tio Sr., photograph dated 1894, Hogan Jazz Archive Photography Collection, PH004098, Tulane University Special Collections, New Orleans, LA. Lizzie Miles, Hogan Jazz Archive Photography Collection, PH002762, Tulane University Special Collections, New Orleans, LA. Marchande de Calas, illustration by Edward W. Kemble in George W. Cable, "The Dance in Place Congo," *Century Magazine* 31 (February 1886): 527. The Original Creole Orchestra (Band), "Photograph taken in Los Angeles, summer of 1914." Reproduced with permission of Oxford Publishing Limited through PSL Clear. Gushee, *Pioneers of Jazz*, ii; Gushee and Carr, "How the Creole Band Came to Be," 84 (quote). "The 'Jelly Roll' Blues" sheet music, cover art by Starmer (Chicago: Will Rossiter, 1915).

Copyright © 2022 by Caroline Vézina
All rights reserved

First printing 2022

∞

Library of Congress Cataloging-in-Publication Data

Names: Vézina, Caroline, author.
Title: Jazz à la creole : French Creole music and the birth of jazz / Caroline Vézina.
Other titles: American made music series.
Description: Jackson : University Press of Mississippi, 2022. | Series: American made music series | Includes bibliographical references and index.
Identifiers: LCCN 2022038206 (print) | LCCN 2022038207 (ebook) | ISBN 9781496842404 (hardback) | ISBN 9781496842428 (trade paperback) | ISBN 9781496842411 (epub) | ISBN 9781496842459 (epub) | ISBN 9781496842435 (pdf) | ISBN 9781496842442 (pdf)
Subjects: LCSH: Creoles—Louisiana—Music—History and criticism. | Jazz—History and criticism.
Classification: LCC ML3560.C25 V39 2022 (print) | LCC ML3560.C25 (ebook) | DDC 781.62/410763—dc23/eng/20221011
LC record available at https://lccn.loc.gov/2022038206
LC ebook record available at https://lccn.loc.gov/2022038207

British Library Cataloging-in-Publication Data available

À Lucie

CONTENTS

Acknowledgments IX
Introduction 3

1. Creole, Creolization, the Creole State, and the Creoles. 8
   A (Very) Short History of the Creole State 10
   The Creoles of Louisiana 12
   Race Relations 19

Part I: The Precursors of Jazz

2. Black American/French Creole Folk Music. 27
   Characteristics of Black American Folk Music 27
   Plantation Songs 29
   Work Songs, Street Cries, and Voodoo Songs 33
   Congo Square 38

3. French Religious Music 49
   The Catholic Church in Louisiana 49
   The Ursuline Manuscript: *Nouvelles poésies spirituelles et morales* . . 52
   The *Cantiques* 54

4. European Music and Dances 60
   Balls and Dance Music 60
   Classical Music and Composers 63
   Military Music 66

Part II: Early Jazz

5. Early Jazz Creole Musicians 71
   The Tio Family 74
   Ferdinand Joseph Lamothe/Jelly Roll Morton (1885 or 1890–1941) . . . 77

Edouard/Edward "Kid" Ory (1886–1973) 81
Elizabeth Marie (Mary) Landreaux/Lizzie Miles (1895–1963). 84
Sidney Bechet (1897–1959) 88

6. The Early Jazz Revival and the Creole Songs 93
The Creole Songs 94
The Creole Songs and Early Jazz 98
The Revival Recordings of Creole Songs 104

Epilogue. 121

Appendices

1. More about Creolization and Creole Identity. 125
2. Chanson du Vié Boscugo/Michié Préval (Dansez Calinda). 129
3. *Cantique*: Tombeau, Tombeau Marie-Madeleine 134
4. *Cantique*: Dans un Jardin Solitaire. .141
5. *Cantique*: Marie-Madeleine, Laisse-Moi Passer. 151
6. *Cantique*: Grand Dieu Du Ciel/Paradis L'Aura. 158

Notes 163
Bibliography 194
Selected Discography 217
Index 219

ACKNOWLEDGMENTS

Like so many before me, I am facing the pleasant task of writing acknowledgments to the many people who have contributed in bringing this book to fruition. As they did, I fear I might forget some who believed in this project and helped me during my many years of research and writing.

I am grateful to former curator Bruce Boyd Raeburn and former associate curators Lynn Abbott and Alaina W. Hébert of the Hogan Jazz Archive at Tulane University; to Eric Seiferth, Molly Reid Cleaver, Jennifer Navarre, and their colleagues at the Williams Research Center of The Historic New Orleans Collection; and to Todd Harvey and his colleagues at the American Folklife Center at the Library of Congress, for their invaluable assistance and support that never failed over the many years I spent researching this book.

Also patient and supportive were former library technician Valérie Asselin and her colleagues at the Archives de folklore et d'ethnologie at Université Laval in Quebec City; Janet Harper, former librarian at the Center for Black Music Research of Columbia College in Chicago; the personnel of the Louisiana Research Collection of the Howard-Tilton Memorial Library and the Amistad Research Center, both at Tulane University; the Louisiana Division of the New Orleans Public library; the Earl K. Long Library of the University of New Orleans; the Cajun and Creole Music Collection of the Edith Garland Dupré Library of the University of Louisiana at Lafayette; the Institute of Jazz Studies at Rutgers University–Newark; the Schomburg Center for Research in Black Culture of the New York City Public Library; and the Warren D. Allen Music Library of Florida State University. To all these librarians, archivists and staff, I am grateful for lending their time and expertise.

Last but not least, I am indebted to Professor Matt Sakakeeny for inviting me at Tulane University to attend his seminar on New Orleans Music and Musicians; and to Professor Daniel Sharp, whose seminar on Music, Tourism, and Heritage I also attended during the spring semester of 2014. My thanks extend to Elizabeth Nazar from the Office of International Students and Scholars, for her help in getting through the maze of official paperwork. Their interest and work led to the realization of my project of going to New

Orleans while completing my MA in Music and Culture. I am also thankful to Dr. James Deaville, then graduate supervisor at Carleton University in Ottawa, for supporting this project.

To my friends, Lucie Kearns, who kindly took the time to read the first and last draft of the manuscript and helped in making the index, Patrice Lacroix and Mark Rowley who read the first draft of the manuscript, I extend my sincere appreciation. Finally, many, many thanks to Martha and David Grunning and their family, for their friendship and encouragement (even when I spoke too much about the book), and to the many friends and yoga teachers who contributed to make my time in New Orleans always joyful and inspiring.

JAZZ À LA CREOLE

INTRODUCTION

The title of this book is borrowed from the 1947 album of the same name. I bought the 2000 CD reissue a few years ago, while in New Orleans researching the music of the French Creoles.[1] My research grew out of a long interest in the many interactions between the *chanson française* and jazz. Somewhere in the early 1990s, I found out that Louis Armstrong recorded "La vie en rose" in June 1950, only five years after it had been written by French singer Édith Piaf.[2] This struck me because it created a direct link between the most iconic singer of the *chanson française* and the most iconic jazz pioneer and performer.

In 2011 (time flies), as I was considering going back to graduate school, I traveled to New Orleans for a week. During my first visit to some of the old plantations, I purchased the 1867 anthology *Slave Songs of the United States*, which—to my surprise and delight—comprised seven plantation songs in Creole French. From then on, my research shifted to focus on the Louisiana Creoles, their songs and music, and their contribution to the development of early jazz which deserves better recognition.[3]

In general, the narrative about the formation of jazz revolves around the idea of its emergence through the combination of African polyrhythms and the call-and-response structural form with European harmony and instruments.[4] Ring shouts, work songs, Negro spirituals, dance music (quadrilles, polkas, schottisches, and so on), and military marches (most famously from John Philip Sousa) are all frequently mentioned as being part of this musical blend. The blues, which brought its particular vocal timbre and melodic inflections, and ragtime, which brought its syncopated rhythms, stand as the direct forerunners of jazz, whereas Caribbean rhythms are mentioned only when the famous "Spanish tinge" of Jelly Roll Morton (himself a Creole) is discussed (see chapters 5 and 6).[5] Indeed, when the Creoles are mentioned, they are shortly described as a distinct cultural group descending from the unions between French or Spanish colonizers and enslaved Africans who retained the French language and culture, the Catholic religion, and European musical traditions, so that, "[f]or its part, Creole music contributed

French quadrilles and Spanish habaneras, and an insistence on high professional standards."[6]

The length of time over which these cross-cultural exchanges took place is just about overlooked, although it started long before the formative years of jazz, usually defined as being between 1890 and 1917. Indeed, the complex and multicultural nature of jazz suggests that it was born out of a process of creolization that took place from the early days of the French colony that was to become Louisiana. The Creoles have a long and complex history, and the music they played came from the musical traditions of the many people who formed or influenced their cultural identity. Thus, this book seeks to further document their contribution to the development of jazz in light of the music they played going back to the time of the arrival of the first enslaved Africans in *La Louisiane*.

As the word *Creole* is often misunderstood—partly because of changes in its signification—chapter 1 discusses its appearance to designate a group of people and then a specific cultural identity, eventually to become a free-floating signifier and convenient marketing tool. As a derivative, the term *creolization* (first used in linguistics) has come to designate both a concept and the model of a historical and sociological process that aims to describe and explain the formation of new cultural output—such as jazz. This process took place in the daily lives of the city's residents, among which jazz (not yet called jazz) started as a localized phenomenon—a versatile "micromusic" played by musicians of varied cultural background—in New Orleans and its vicinity.[7] Consequently, a brief overview of the history of Louisiana and some clarification about the Creoles in the specific context of this state constitute the second part of this chapter.

Grouped together as "The Precursors of Jazz," the next three chapters explore the rich and dynamic musical life of the French Creoles who, whether enslaved or free, all danced, sang, and played music on multiple and diverse occasions. As soon as they arrived, enslaved Africans sang to accompany their work and gathered to dance during the leisure time they were allowed on Sundays and holidays, both in New Orleans and on neighboring plantations. Considering that the first anthology of plantation songs was published in 1867, most of the information available was collected years after the abolition of slavery and the end of the Congo Square—first known as *Place Congo*—Sunday gatherings.

However, two largely unknown interviews—one conducted in 1960 with Creole Alice Zeno (1864–1960), the first twenty minutes of which are in French, and the other made in 1939 with Jeanne Wogan Arguedas (1886–1969), who grew up on her grandparents' plantation (Labranche Plantation)—add valuable insider knowledge about the music on Franco-Creole plantations and Congo Square after the Civil War. These interviews are presented for the first time in chapter 1.[8]

As the propagation of the Catholic faith was primordial in France's colonial project, the Church's musical traditions came to Louisiana with the first explorers and colonists. Masses were sung in parish churches; as of 1754, the Ursuline nuns owned a book of *chansons morales*; and *cantiques* were sung both at church and at home. Fortunately, some forty "*cantiques nègres*"[9] were recorded in the 1950s, part of the effort to preserve the declining French culture of Louisiana. Since they have been scarcely documented, the few discussed and analyzed in chapter 3 present new information about their provenance and the process of their appropriation by the Creole Catholics as the French counterpart of the Negro spirituals.

Not surprisingly, the performance of European classical and military music can also be traced back to the establishment of the colony. As seen in chapter 4, the center of *La Nouvelle-Orléans* was soon occupied by the *Place d'Armes* (parade ground, now Jackson Square), and two musicians, a fife player and a drummer, are listed in the 1727 census. A few years later, a clerk from the Company of the Indies, himself a player of the hunting horn (the ancestor of the French horn), wrote the account of his 1730 Carnival celebrations while serving in the colony. This marked the beginning of the long-lasting tradition of the now very famous New Orleans Mardi Gras.

During the eighteenth century, balls—private, semiprivate, or public—were held almost every day, catering to all, regardless of color or social status. The Franco-Creole population's legendary passion for balls and Carnival, eventually shared by the Anglo-American newcomers, not only provided plenty of employment for Creole musicians but also became fertile ground for multicultural interaction. Whether or not people approved, the fact that Creole musicians played for a White audience, or that the audience itself would sometimes be mixed—thanks to masked ball and Carnival celebrations—would be enough to facilitate such interaction.

The Creoles viewed French art and culture as a form of refinement and strongly valued musical education. They frequented the opera and as early as the 1830s, they formed a *Société Philharmonique*. A few became renowned musicians and composers in their own right, such as Basil Barès, who achieved the extraordinary feat of having one of his compositions published while enslaved. In regard to jazz history, the pioneering work of composer Louis Moreau Gottschalk (a White Creole) stands out for his use of Creole melodies and rhythms and is now considered one of the precursors of ragtime.

Part II, "Early Jazz," comprises the last two chapters of the book. Chapter 5 briefly describes the life and music of a few musicians whose careers demonstrate the Creoles' significant contributions in all aspects of the development and diffusion of early jazz, whether as outstanding instrumentalists or singers, teachers, bandleaders, composers, and/or arrangers. At the same time, the history of the Tio family and the careers of Jelly Roll Morton, Kid Ory, Lizzie Miles, and Sidney Bechet provide interesting examples of creolization in the making over generations or in the lives of gifted musicians.

Finally, chapter 6 considers the early jazz revival of the 1940s and 1950s, during which several Creole songs were (finally) recorded by jazz musicians. This is really fortunate, for many interviews clearly indicate that these songs were an integral part of the music-making of the whole Creole community, as well as part of the repertoire of early jazz musicians.[10] Combined with those recorded or collected by other musicians or scholars at the time when the Franco-Creole culture was declining, the Creole songs, of which I have gathered approximately one hundred, form a repertoire that belongs to both Black American and Franco-American folk music. As such, they reflect both the creolized nature of jazz and the cultural heritage of the Creoles of Louisiana, for they are still being played and recorded to this day.[11]

Three years after my 2011 "investigative" trip to Louisiana, I completed a Master of Arts in Music and Culture, during which I spent a semester as an invited scholar at Tulane University in New Orleans, the first of many other sojourns in the city as I decided to pursue this research on my own. Consequently, I have consulted many written sources, such as memoirs of the first French settlers, French administrative documents, old travel diaries and letters, and unpublished theses and dissertations, as well as listened to recorded material such as oral history interviews, field trip recordings, and old 78 rpms and LPs. Thanks to the pioneer jazz historians who had the foresight to interview and record early jazz musicians and other witnesses, we can hear their stories in their own words. This is why I have chosen to quote from many of these conversations: to once again let these people speak for themselves. Most of the primary sources are kept at the Hogan Jazz Archive at Tulane University, the Williams Research Center of The Historic New Orleans Collection, and the Archives de folklore et d'ethnologie at Université Laval in Quebec City. Some hidden gems were found at the American Folklife Center at the Library of Congress in Washington, DC, the Center for Black Music Research of Columbia College in Chicago, and the Warren D. Allen Music Library of Florida State University. Finally, this research also led me to the Louisiana Research Collection of the Howard-Tilton Memorial Library and the Amistad Research Center, both at Tulane University; the Louisiana

Division of the New Orleans Public Library; the Earl K. Long Library of the University of New Orleans; the Cajun and Creole Music Collection of the Edith Garland Dupré Library of the University of Louisiana at Lafayette; the Institute of Jazz Studies at Rutgers University–Newark; and the Schomburg Center for Research in Black Culture of the New York City Public Library.

Chapter 1

CREOLE, CREOLIZATION, THE CREOLE STATE, AND THE CREOLES

Although the word *Creole* is now commonplace in the English language, its meaning was, and often still is, not always clear because it has varied with time and location. Nonetheless, it is generally agreed that it first appeared in Portuguese as *crioulo* and in Spanish as *criollo*, both derived from the verb *criar* (to create, nourish/nurse, raise), from the Latin *creare* (to create). It was either first used to designate the enslaved Africans born in the colonies and then applied to the Spaniards born in the colony, or the reverse—applied first to Spaniards and then to Africans.[1] First spelled *criole* in French, it appears in the 1690 *Dictionnaire Universel*, where it is defined as "the name that the Spaniards give to their children born in the Indies," which is to say in the colonies.[2] Virginia Domínguez retraced the first use of the word in French Louisiana in baptismal, marriage, and death registers kept in Mobile (now in Alabama) and New Orleans. On several occasions, newborns, brides, grooms, or the deceased are referred to as *Creoles*, and she argues that it was used only to designate people of European parentage born in the colony. On the contrary, historian Joseph Tregle argues that in the French colony of Saint-Domingue, "*creole* meant simply native-born, again without reference to color, and it was this tradition which took root in colonial Louisiana as early as the beginning of French settlement at Mobile."[3] Other examples found in the literature exemplify this variation of meaning during the seventeenth and eighteenth centuries.[4]

First applied to the formation of new languages themselves called *Créoles*, or Creoles, the notion of creolization now refers to both a concept and the model of a historical and sociological process that aims to describe and explain the many facets of contact, exchange, and cross-fertilization between cultures in colonial and postcolonial societies as people adapt to new environments.[5] As such, it has been used to study the creation of new cultural products or practices, as in Daniel Usner's essay on the "Creolization of Agriculture in the Lower Mississippi Valley."[6] But, as noted by sociologist Robin Cohen, "a variety of similar terms—creolization, hybridity, syncretism, métissage, mélange and others—are frequently used interchangeably. . . . I prefer creolization (because of its links to existing and historical examples and its cultural reference points). . . ."[7]

I also prefer *creolization*, for it better represents the intricate, multilayered, and dynamic aspect of the process during which various elements of diverse cultures get intertwined as people adapt to new or changing environments in which creolized products or practices can themselves be part of a new process of creolization—making it a rather appropriate tool for studying the formation of jazz in New Orleans. Cohen also outlined a few areas where creolization occurred in popular culture, such as religion, food, and music: "Jazz emerged as a fertile dialogue between black folk music in the USA, often derived from the plantations and rural areas, and black music based in urban New Orleans. The field hollers met parlour music. . . . In the parades, the funeral dirges, the popular songs for picnics and parties, jazz developed as a Creole music *par excellence*."[8] This sentiment is echoed by Joseph Logsdon and Caryn Cossé Bell: "Drawing from this peculiar creole-American cultural interchange, black New Orleanians added many new features to the city's vibrant folk culture—none more famous than the new musical form of jazz."[9]

However, the complex and multicultural nature of jazz suggests that it was born out of a long process of creolization that started right from the early days of the colony, in the daily activities and interactions of the diverse cultural communities living in New Orleans and its vicinity. (See appendix 1.) Indeed, before becoming a new and global genre, jazz started as a localized and varied micromusic—a term used (and maybe coined) by Mark Slobin following his observation that "[e]verywhere [he] went, [he] noticed small musics living in big systems"—produced by subcultures that can be defined using different parameters such as ethnicity, social class, religion, and/or gender. Subcultures are also formed by individual choices, relationships, or memberships often closely linked to specific locations (such as urban neighborhoods). Slobin postulates that micromusics (the music of subcultures) always develop in relation to a superculture, while an interculture, a phenomenon that penetrates and influences various communities, can also be at play.[10] In Louisiana, the superculture was that of the White elites, Creoles or Anglo-Americans, and the subcultures were those of the Creoles of Color, free or enslaved, and other ethnic groups. However, after the Purchase (1803) and especially after the Civil War (1861–65), the Anglo-American culture gradually became the sole superculture, whereas the French Creole culture, whether White or Black, became more of an influential subculture.

The impact of racial prejudice and segregation on the (lack of) civil rights of African Americans and the (regulated) interaction among socio-racial groups are certainly intercultural phenomena that have to be reckoned with. But a shared passion for dancing, the Mardi Gras tradition, and the rich musical life of the city might also be said to be components of intercultures that came into play in the development of jazz. In this framework of analysis, families, bands, and musicians (professional or not) are themselves dynamic agents making choices based on personal taste, particular affinities and sense of belonging, in the day-to-day aspect of the creolization process. Indeed, even as a micromusic, jazz was not homogenous, as it emerged in a cosmopolitan city rich with the cultures of diverse socio-cultural communities.

Following a trend initiated in the 1850s—as French culture was becoming more influential rather than dominant—the word *Creole* slowly morphed into a "free-floating signifier" ascribed to products or places (such as food, hair treatments, a market, and even a racing course) rather than the marker of a cultural identity, the knowledge and understanding of which faded away after the Civil War, especially outside Louisiana.[11] As jazz was first recorded in the late 1910s (starting in 1917) and 1920s mostly in New York and Chicago, and gained in popularity and recognition, *Creole* was used as a convenient marketing tool: "blackness" became associated with authenticity when speaking about jazz, and the word *Creole* also implied some (attractive) exoticism.[12] The most famous examples would be King Oliver's Creole Jazz Band (although not a Creole, Oliver had some legitimate cultural claim for he spoke the French "patois," and he had studied with, played with, and hired Creole musicians) and songs such as "Creole Love Call" (1927) and "Creole Rhapsody" (1931) from the Duke Ellington Orchestra.[13]

A (VERY) SHORT HISTORY OF THE CREOLE STATE

To better appreciate the complexity and length of the creolization process as it happened in Louisiana, it is necessary to review its history and development as a cosmopolitan, but asymmetric, three-tiered Creole society under the French and Spanish Empires, closely tied to the Caribbean, mostly to Saint-Domingue (Haiti) and Cuba. As the French Creole culture persisted until the turn of the twentieth century, it provided a propitious environment for intricate cross-cultural exchanges as various waves of immigrants and Anglo-Americans came to New Orleans and its vicinity before and after Louisiana was sold to the United States in 1803 (the Louisiana Purchase).

Although it is no longer apparent, France once had a vast empire in the Americas. Samuel de Champlain founded Port Royal in Acadia (Nova Scotia) in 1605 and Quebec City in 1608. In the following decades, French and

French Canadian explorers and missionaries led many expeditions, mapping the waterways and founding missions. In 1682, René-Robert Cavelier de La Salle reached the mouth of the Mississippi River and took possession of a vast territory reaching from the Great Lakes to the Gulf of Mexico on behalf of Louis XIV, king of France—hence calling it *La Louisiane*. Pierre Lemoyne d'Iberville initiated the colonization along the Gulf of Mexico with the construction of Fort Maurepas (later called Vieux Biloxy, now Ocean Springs, Mississippi) in 1699 and Fort Louis de la Louisiane (now Mobile, Alabama) in 1702. In 1718, Jean Baptiste Lemoyne de Bienville founded New Orleans. Along with becoming the capital of the colony four years later, the city also stood as a continental expansion of the French Caribbean colonies—Saint-Christophe (St. Kitts), Dominique (Dominica), Guadeloupe, Martinique, Sainte-Lucie (Saint Lucia), and Saint-Domingue (Haiti)—while under the authority of the Diocese of Quebec for its religious administration.

Following the Treaty of Utrecht (1713) and the Treaty of Paris (1763) that respectively ended the War of the Spanish Succession and the Seven Years' War, France ceded Acadia and St. Kitts, then Canada and the territory east of the Mississippi to Great Britain; New Orleans and the territory west of the river had already been ceded to Spain a few months earlier (Treaty of Fontainebleau, 1762). In 1803, after a short retrocession to France (Third Treaty of San Ildefonso, 1800), Napoleon sold *La Louisiane* to the United States.[14]

A Multicultural Population

Needless to say, Louisiana was inhabited by many First Nations—the Natchez, Choctaw, Chickasaw, Houma, Natchitoches, and others—long before the arrival of the Canadians, the French, and the few German families that came during the first decades of colonization. Adding to this ethnic diversity, a few enslaved Africans were brought from the Caribbean islands, and from 1719, thousands were forcefully transported from West Africa to help build the city and work on the plantations.[15] As in Canada, the French made alliances with the First Nations. Native American women, some of whom were enslaved, helped both Africans and Europeans survive in the wilderness and isolation of the early years by providing food through their agricultural work and company as concubines.[16] Native Americans maintained a "marked ... presence" in the city that was noted by many residents, visitors, and authors up to the beginning of the twentieth century.[17]

According to historian Jerah Johnson, *La Louisiane* "represented an extension of the French experience in Canada" where the "eighteenth-century French ethos" and "assimilationist ideal" (rather than segregationist) had been carried and adjusted, and then transferred to Louisiana a century later. This particular French ethos "offered far greater freedom for individuals to associate not only with members of their own corporate group but, more important, with members of other groups as well."[18] If we also consider the difficulties of colonization and the harshness of frontier life, which certainly acted as powerful stimuli for maintaining peaceful relations, colonial Louisiana fostered a social organization generally tolerant toward encounters and exchanges between people of different cultures or social classes, despite the imperialistic position of one over the others and periods of war and revolt.[19]

Under the Spanish regime, French continued to be the prevalent language and culture of the colony, despite the arrival of Spanish-speaking Isleños (from the Canary Islands) and Malagueños (from the city of Málaga in Spain). In an effort to populate the territory, Spain also accepted thousands of French-speaking Acadians who settled mostly in the bayou country southwest of New Orleans, where the Native people and early German immigrants and planters already lived in villages or on small farms or plantations.[20]

From the 1790s to the mid-1810s, before and after the independence of Saint-Domingue (1804), thousands of people sought refuge in Louisiana, a significant number coming via Cuba or Jamaica, where they had lived for a few years. Most notably, the population of New Orleans doubled in 1809 with the arrival of ten thousand migrants divided in thirds among White plantation owners, Free People of Color, and enslaved Blacks.[21] The city also attracted French citizens fleeing the revolution (1789) and the rise or fall of Napoleon (1804, 1814–1815). Thanks to the influx of these "foreign French," the Creole society prevailed for a few decades after the Purchase (1803) and the coming of Anglo-American settlers and their enslaved workers. In the 1830s, the arrival of a large number of Irish and German immigrants led to a decrease of the relative importance of the French-speaking population.[22] Finally, at the end of the nineteenth century, Eastern European Jews and Italians, mostly from Sicily, also immigrated to New Orleans in significant numbers.[23] By then, New Orleans was a very cosmopolitan city with a highly stratified society where the diverse socioeconomic and cultural communities interacted on a daily basis.

THE CREOLES OF LOUISIANA

After the Purchase, the French-speaking population vigorously claimed its *Créole* identity to differentiate themselves from Anglo-American Protestant settlers. They shared the Catholic religion and the French language and culture as important defining factors of their cultural identity, although they were divided by skin color, wealth, rights and privileges (or lack thereof), occupation, and education; the *Gens de Couleur Libres* stood between the Whites and the enslaved, which granted them access to a middle-class status and associated economic and social privileges. Nonetheless, through their distinct but shared history, the enslaved, Free People of Color, and Whites all left their mark on the cultural landscape of Louisiana.

The Enslaved Creoles

In 1724, five years after the arrival of the first Africans "shipped in" to New Orleans, the *Code Noir* was introduced in Louisiana. It was a revised version of the 1695 *Code Noir* enacted by the king of France to regulate the conditions of slavery and race relations in the Caribbean colonies. The *Code Noir* prescribed baptism, marriage, and religious instruction in the Catholic faith, as well as minimum food and clothing allowances, and the right for the enslaved to complain if mistreated. It also decreed Sundays and Catholic holidays as days of rest, forbade the sale of children without their mothers—and fathers if from the same plantation—and prohibited interracial marriages and concubinage.[24] Women and men brought both their labor potential and, more importantly, their knowledge of the cultivation of rice, indigo, and tobacco. A small number became apprentices with French tradesmen, merchants, and craftsmen (such as carpenters, joiners, blacksmiths, or ironworkers), paving the way for "Black artisanship," whereas others, mainly women, were employed as domestic servants.[25]

The first documentary evidence of the presence of enslaved people in the colony dates back to 1709, when Governor Antoine de Lamothe Cadillac reported that a ship, *La Vierge de Grâce*, had embarked a few enslaved during a stopover in Havana. "In one way or another a black from time to time was procured," and, by 1712, there were ten of them in the colony.[26] However, under the French regime, most of them arrived between 1719 and 1731, mostly from Senegambia, the Bight of Benin, and Congo/Angola. Despite their different origins, their dehumanizing ordeal, and many deaths, they formed "a particularly coherent, functional, well integrated, autonomous, . . . self-confident," and rather homogenous cultural community, the majority being from the Senegal River Basin.[27] The small number of new arrivals between 1731 and 1763 (the end of the French regime) led to "a period of considerable creolization and stabilization" of the "slave force."[28]

The community grew more diverse during the Spanish regime with the arrival of many thousands of Africans of various origins. Thomas N. Ingersoll and Ibrahima Seck give a rather similar list of regions of origin that include Central Africa, Bight of Biafra, Bight of Benin, the Gold Coast, Sierra Leone, and Senegambia. Ingersoll adds the Windward Coast, and Seck adds Mozambique, but both agree that Central Africa (the Congo and Angola) provided the largest number of people.[29] Finally, thousands of enslaved people arrived with the various waves of refugees fleeing from Saint-Domingue.

After the international slave trade prohibition took effect in January 1808, the growth of the enslaved population depended on natural increase, the domestic slave trade, or the illegal smuggling of people, some of whom came from Africa and others from the Caribbean.[30] In one of the few articles dealing with the life of the enslaved after the Purchase, Michael Picone presents evidence that Francophone planters purchased enslaved Anglo-Americans, so much so that eventually Francophones, Anglophones, and Creolophones worked together in the fields and in the households.[31] He conducted his research in the Cane River Valley, in northwestern Louisiana, but as Laura Locoul Gore's memoirs (which Picone quotes) clearly show, such multicultural encounters between the enslaved also happened in southwestern Louisiana. Indeed, Paul Lachance estimates that

> [s]laves were probably the first caste to cease to be predominantly French. . . . In January 1831, [a refugee from Saint-Domingue] wrote that over the two preceding years more than twenty thousand slaves had been introduced into the state and complained that "everywhere one only hears English spoken, for in every house there are a number of old servants who have become fluent in this idiom."[32]

But even if the Anglo-American enslaved population grew bigger, there were enslaved French Creole up to the Civil War. After emancipation, people who had been enslaved downtown (the French district), some of whom had free relatives, often remained where they were and joined what had been the Free People of Color community.[33] (See table on pages 16–17.)

The Free People of Color/Creoles of Color

From the early days of the colony until the first years of the American period, Africans enslaved in Louisiana had several avenues to freedom that allowed for the creation of a middle class of Free People of Color similar to that found in the French West Indies. The 1724 *Code Noir* included the right to manumission (*affranchissement*), providing freed Blacks with the same rights as other subjects of the king while carefully endorsing and protecting White supremacy. Although the *Code Noir* did not permit self-purchase, Jean-François Benjamin Dumont de Montigny wrote that some enslaved Blacks were able to earn enough to buy their freedom. Finally, children born to free mothers were also free, and if a free manumitted man of color married an enslaved woman with whom he had children, they would all be freed. Others were granted their freedom as a reward for military service.[34] Under the Spanish regime, the *Code Noir ou Loi Municipale*, which included the old French *Code Noir* along with *Las Siete Partidas*, an ancient code of Spanish laws, ruled the lives of the enslaved population. The latter included the right of *coartación*, the guaranteed right to self-purchase, that had become judicially recognized in Cuba a few years earlier. According to Jennifer Spear, almost two thousand people took advantage of this new opportunity to buy their freedom.[35]

As Kimberley Hanger points out, "the libre population grew to assume the 'critical mass' needed to establish a distinct sense of identity." But as she also notes, the Creoles were not a monolithic group: some maintained a closer association with the enslaved society, such as the newly freed or those with enslaved relatives or spouses, and others with the White society, such as second-generation freed people, those with appreciable wealth, or those with White relatives.[36] Manumission remained legal after the Louisiana Purchase, although on shakier ground and under increasing restrictions.[37]

During this time, the number of Free People of Color increased due to the unions between White men and free Quadroon women. Although usually referred to as *plaçage*—as a short-term relationship in which a White man maintained an "official" Quadroon mistress—many of these interracial unions were rather similar to common-law marriages as both Kenneth Aslakson and Emily Clark—who provided a more accurate portrait of the lives of, and fiction about, the Quadroons—have clearly demonstrated.[38] The *Gens de Couleur Libres* also benefitted from the arrival of thousands of St. Dominguan immigrants, allowing the community to "remain preponderantly French-speaking as late as 1840."[39] (See above.)

Like its predecessor, the 1806 Black Code was careful to protect White supremacy, as Free People of Color were enjoined not to "conceive themselves equal to the white; [and] to yield to them in every occasion."[40] Nonetheless, they enjoyed some of the civil liberties and economic rights of the Whites up to the Civil War, although the rising tensions leading to the conflict had already started to challenge their special status. The US Census of 1860 numbered 18,647 Free People of Color in Louisiana, with 10,689 living in New Orleans.[41] (See table on pages 16–17.) Despite their relatively small number, they played an important role in the economic and cultural development of the new state. Many were skilled artisans: women were often

The New Orleans Population of Color: 1721–1970

Census Year	Total pop. of New Orleans	Pop. of color	% Colored of total	Free-colored	% of colored	Slave	% of colored
1721[a]	472	173	36.7				
1732[a]	893	258	28.9				
1769[b]	3,190	1,387	43.5	99	7.1	1,288	92.9
1778[c]	3,659	1,507	41.2	353	23.4	1,154	76.6
1785[d]	5,028	2,194	43.6	563	25.7	1,631	74.3
1791[e]	4,816	2,751	57.1	1,147	41.7	1,604	58.3
1803[f]	8,056	4,110	51.0	1,335	32.5	2,775	67.5
1805[g]	8,475	4,671	55.1	1,566	33.5	3,105	66.5
1810[h]	17,242	10,911	63.3	4,950	45.4	5,961	54.6
1820	27,176	13,592	50.0	6,237	45.9	7,355	54.1
1830	46,082	25,953	56.3	11,477	44.2	14,476	55.8
1840	102,193	42,670	41.8	19,222	45.0	23,448	55.0
1850	116,375	28,029	24.1	9,961	35.5	18,068	64.5
1860	168,675	24,074	14.3	10,689	44.4	13,385	55.6
1870	191,418	50,456	26.4				
1880	216,090	57,617	26.7				

1890	242,039	64,491	26.6
1900	287,104	77,714	27.1
1910	339,075	89,262	26.3
1920	387,219	100,930	26.1
1930	458,762	129,632	28.3
1940	494,537	149,034	30.1
1950	570,445	181,775	31.9
1960	627,525	233,514	37.2
1970	591,502 (city proper)	267,339	45.2
	1,045,809 (SMSA)	323,973	40.0

Notes:

ᵃ See Beer 1911: 92.

ᵇ See the O'Reilly Census, cited frequently (cf. Wood 1938).

ᶜ See Wingfield 1961 (Table I, *n* 4). He cites documents in *Archives of the Indies*, Seville, 1717–1820, prepared by the U.S. Survey of Federal Archives, document 42,70A.

ᵈ See Berquin-Duvallon (1803), translated by John Davis in 1806, p. 136 of 1806 ed.

ᵉ See Wood 1938.

ᶠ See Berquin-Duvallon (1806 ed.), p. 33.

ᵍ See the New Orleans City Council 1805 census, published in 1936.

ʰ U.S. Bureau of the Census, census years 1810–1970.

Table 1. The New Orleans Population of Color: 1721–1970. Virginia R. Dominguez, *White by Definition: Social Classification in Creole Louisiana* (New Brunswick, NJ: Rutgers University Press, 1986), 116–17. Copyright © 1986 by Rutgers, the State University. Reprinted by permission of Rutgers University Press.

seamstresses, *modistes* (dressmakers), or hairdressers; men were often in the building trade, but also tailors, shoemakers, cigar makers, coopers, and so on. Others were entrepreneurs, business owners, real estate developers, or real estate agents, and some worked as clerks or had a profession, among them architects, physicians, nurses, and midwives. Some became writers, musicians, or artists—lithographers, engravers, marble sculptors, and ironworkers. In southwestern Louisiana where the *Gens de Couleur Libres* were among the "first families," some became slaveholding planters, and others landowner ranchers or farmers. The less fortunate were tenant farmers or agricultural laborers.[42]

Generally speaking, Creoles of Color formed a close-knit and protective community that promoted respectability through proper education, good manners, and formal musical training. When the family means permitted, many received a "European" education, either at home or in France. Indeed, they valued the French language and French art and culture, which were seen as cultural refinements and which they claimed as a defining part of their identity. (See appendix 1—"Identity Politics and *Créolité*," p. 128.)

The White Creoles

As the descendants of French, Spanish, and French Canadian colonizers, White Creoles occupied the top of the social ladder—the Creole aristocracy, as they came to be called with the emergence of the plantation economy during the Spanish regime and its coming to maturity during the antebellum period. Johnson argues that it is only from then—the late eighteenth century—to the Civil War that the inclusion of Louisiana as part of the "circum-Caribbean plantation society . . . can be applied most effectively."[43] However, the social status of the first White settlers was more modest.

Some had been granted land concessions where they started to operate small plantations (*habitations*), but many were military officers and soldiers, sailors, artisans, laborers, and indentured servants (*engagés*), along with missionaries and young women of marriageable age. Others were smugglers, convicts—both women and men—or the wives of convicts. In the early 1720s, dozens of German families came under the auspices of the *Compagnie des Indes* to farm the land and eventually assimilated—mostly through marriage—with French settlers.[44] Acadians born in Louisiana didn't come to be designated as Creoles. Through a complex history—of immigration, cultural exchanges, assimilation (of other groups into their community), and upward or downward mobility—they maintained a separate cultural identity now known as Cajun, although this would not be true for an elite of Acadian planters who aimed to associate with their Creole or Anglo-American counterparts.[45]

By the time of the Purchase, many of the first settlers had become planters. Some were quite wealthy, owning big estates on which they cultivated sugar cane through the labor of enslaved workers.. They enjoyed a rich lifestyle, often living on their plantation during the spring and summer until the harvest, and in New Orleans during the winter. Such families often sent their sons to be educated in France, while their daughters were educated at the Ursuline Convent in New Orleans. In their leisure time, White Creole families attended the opera and frequented society balls, masked or not. But even if they maintained close ties with France and were very attached to their distinct cultural identity, some married their daughters—and less frequently their sons—to the children of rich Anglo-American planters, creating alliances that maintained their social status and privileges after the Louisiana Purchase.[46] The Civil War, and the desolation it brought, spelled the end of the French Creole aristocracy.[47]

RACE RELATIONS

In the first decades of the nineteenth century, the lasting struggle for political power between the White Creoles and the Anglo-Americans led to the division of New Orleans into three semiautonomous municipalities from 1836 until 1852. The First and Third municipalities were under the control of the Creoles, while the Second became the American sector. This arrangement allowed both communities to maintain schools, do business, and pass regulations in their own language to preserve their culture and traditions. However, even though the various Black Codes endorsed White supremacy, the difference between the social position deemed appropriate for Blacks and Creoles of Color to occupy led to the continuation of the French Creole three-tiered society, alongside the growth of the Anglo-American racial classification as either Black or White. Relations between White Creoles and Free People of Color could be tense even if they had become used to living side by side, sometimes sharing family names because of common-law unions. In one case, a dispute arose when the White heirs of a White Creole man attempted to disinherit the mixed children he had had with the Free Woman of Color with whom he had lived for fifty years, until his death in 1845.[48] In contrast, a few years earlier (in 1841), St. Augustine Parish and Church had been founded, whose congregation and services were mixed. (See chapter 3.)

Following the Civil War and the emancipation of the enslaved, Whites appropriated the term *Creole* to designate only White native-born people, in an effort to hold on to their class privileges and differentiate themselves from the Free People of Color and the newly freed Blacks. As "Northern newcomers . . . and other non-Creoles" insinuated that they all had "a touch of the tarbrush," the White Creoles also actively argued for the purity of their ancestry, denying miscegenation and strongly excluding people of mixed heritage from this new definition of the Creole identity.[49] Among other things, this required putting aside their rivalry with Anglo-Americans for the sake of protecting their belief in White supremacy. As Tregle observed, "[u]nchallengeable white supremacy, in short, had made it possible to accommodate a pan-racial creolism. The Civil War changed all that."[50]

Thereafter, the *Gens de Couleur Libres*, wanting to hold to their middle-class position and privileges—which implied differentiating themselves from the freed slaves—started to designate themselves as Creoles of Color. Nonetheless, the Constitutional Convention held in 1867–68 brought together a group of ninety-eight elected delegates divided in "nearly equal numbers" between "men categorized as white and [men] categorized as black or of color," representing both the English- and French-speaking electorate. Reflecting the "anticaste thinking" of the Free People of Color, and the "aspirations of former slaves . . . to a place in the politics and public culture of the state,"[51] the Constitution (adopted on March 7, 1868) clearly indicated that "All persons, without regard to race, color, or previous condition, born or naturalized in the United States . . . are citizens of this State." . . . They [the citizens] shall enjoy the same civil, political, and public rights and privileges, and be subject to the same pains and penalties."[52] This clause was of particular importance for people of African descent. Not only did it protect their rights but also their dignity, which was linked to the way they were treated in public spaces. Required acts of "self-dishonoring" public deference to Whites—as before the Civil War—or other signs of subordination were seen as an affront to their dignity. Not surprisingly, however, proponents of White supremacy felt threatened by this very same clause and managed to have it removed from the State Constitution in 1879.[53]

Moreover, following the end of Reconstruction, the removal of the federal troops in 1877, the rise of the Redeemers, and the 1879 and 1898 Louisiana Constitutions, all African Americans faced increased segregation with the application of Jim Crow laws and the one-drop rule, which stipulated that one drop of Black blood made a person legally Black.[54] This new rule hit Louisiana's three-tiered society at its core, and little by little, the Anglo-American bipartite White and Black social order and the "separate but equal" ideology took over, but not for lack of resistance against it.

In 1892, Homer Plessy, supported by the *Comité des Citoyens*, a Creole activist organization, challenged the 1890 Separate Car Act by sitting in a Whites-only car. In the 1896 decision of the *Plessy v. Ferguson* case, the Supreme Court ruled against Plessy, stating that the Louisiana Segregation Act was constitutional. Rebecca J. Scott argues that the 1890 Separate Car Act was not only enacted to ensure public segregation but also "to make clear the formal repudiation of the egalitarian guarantees of the 1868 constitution." Indeed, race relations in Louisiana slowly but surely became very much like the rest of the southern United States: segregation, violence and lynching, and political exclusion. The struggle to maintain White supremacy rose and lasted well after the turn of the twentieth century.[55]

This new and institutionalized segregation was particularly harsh for the Creoles of Color, who were stripped of their antebellum middle-class privileges. As a result, the community isolated itself, maintaining exclusive practices with regard to education, occupational patterns, social relations, and marriages. Markers of their Creole cultural identity—family background, French language and culture, professional trade work—became important signs of distinction from the larger African American population. However, they lived in multicultural neighborhoods where Irish, German, Jewish, Spanish, Italian, and Creole families "interact[ed] with each other in a variety of ways, [and, even if they did not become] socially intimate, . . . sincere and genuine patterns of neighboring developed in downtown New Orleans' racially mixed neighborhoods" in the last and first decades of the nineteenth and twentieth century.[56]

As mentioned above, even if the society was highly stratified, the boundaries of social interactions and exchanges were fluid and frequent enough to create the propitious conditions for cultural cross-fertilization—a situation reminiscent of colonial New Orleans. (See note 36.) The lives of two women, Alice Zeno (1864–1960) and Jeanne Wogan Arguedas (1886–1969), offer concrete examples of the complex integration and daily contacts of the many cultures and social classes in the city and neighboring plantations. Both women were Creoles, one Black and the other White, and they both spoke French as their first language.

Alice Zeno was born in New Orleans on June 7, 1864. At the time, her mother was working as a maid, and "as soon as she could go back on the job she took me. And the Miss Mazureau—they had me in the house like a child, a white child; they didn't want my mother to have anything to do

1.1. Alice Zeno. Ralston Crawford Photography Collection, Box 16, number 2, Tulane University Special Collections, Tulane University, New Orleans, LA.

with me. And they spoke nothing but French to me."⁵⁷ When she got older, Ms. Zeno worked as a maid for various prominent Creole families and was exposed to the cultural life of the city's elite. For instance, while employed by the family of W. W. King, a lawyer and the father of the author and historian Grace King (1852–1932), she learned some Spanish and German through the ladies who were having lessons with native private teachers, making the language of the day the only one spoken in the house, herself included.⁵⁸ She also kept a very good memory of Judge Renshaw and his family: "Oh, I liked the Judge very much. Stayed with him 'till he left this earth." Similarly, one of his daughters, Gladys Renshaw, who had a successful career as a language teacher, continued to visit Ms. Zeno as she got older, a habit that suggests a long and warm relationship between the two.⁵⁹

Ms. Zeno was very fond of her grandmother, who had been enslaved and died in 1900 at 101 years of age. Her grandmother was the daughter of a Senegalese woman who "was stole[n] from her country" when she was only eight years old, and she passed down her story and some of her language to her granddaughter Alice. At the time of the interview, Ms. Zeno still remembered some words and expressions from Senegal, but none of the songs. However, she still could sing a song from the Haitian Revolution she had learned from her grandmother, who had learned it from her mother, reflecting the influence of the Saint-Domingue enslaved refugees.[60] She also remembered meeting "real Indians" at her grandmother's house, who would come to pass the night after attending "La halle sauvage, Indian market." She said that they did not speak a lot, but the few examples she gave by imitating their speech indicate that they spoke Creole French or at least a little of it.[61] As a child, she also understood Creole, because other children used it to speak to her, but she said she began to speak it only when she had her own children, in the 1890s. Later—it is not quite clear when—she learned English "with everybody."[62]

Toward the end of her life, Alice Zeno was interviewed three times by early jazz and Louisiana French music researchers Bill Russell, Richard Allen, and Harry Oster. She caught their attention not only because of her age and family story, but also as the mother of early jazz clarinetist George Lewis (1900–1968). Her memories are invaluable, for they also shed light on the religious practices, Carnival, balls, and Congo Square dances at the end of the nineteenth century. Ms. Zeno died in 1960 at age ninety-six, at her son's home in the city of Algiers, right across the Mississippi River from New Orleans.

Jeanne Wogan Arguedas (1886–1969) was born in an old family of planters who could trace ancestors in both the Louisiana and the Saint-Domingue White Creole elites. Not surprisingly, her Dominguan family escaped the island at the time of the war of independence, coming to New Orleans via Cuba around 1804. Most notably, her great-grandmother Mélazie Labranche bore the name of the plantation where Ms. Arguedas spent most of her childhood, as the Labranche Plantation then belonged to her grandparents. In 1939, she was interviewed by Herbert Halpert, who was then working for the Federal Writers' Project. Part of the interview focused on her recollection of the time she spent on the plantation from ages three to fourteen, from ca. 1889 to 1901.

> It was located on [sic] St. Charles Parish about twenty-five miles from the city. It faced the river. There was the river in front, then the wide levee, the dusted road, a pretty garden—flower garden—then the house. Like all plantations, with high columns, a big gallery all around,

bricks downstairs, a hall in the middle and rooms—four, five rooms. The house was square shaped. Further out was the sugar house [sugar mill], then the Negro houses, called the Negro camp. Very often, in the afternoon, my grandmother would take me with her to bring some remedies to the Negroes who were sick. It consisted of Vaseline and cod liver oil. Then, in thankfulness to the help my grandmother gave them, they would sing old songs [from] slavery time. That's how I learned most of them.

She recalled hearing the workers singing in the field or in the sugar house or "at night [as] they used to have meetings in the camp, light a big fire and ... they'd sing songs and sometimes Voodoo songs too. I could hear them at a distance while I was in bed. And this had an impression in my mind, I've never quite forgotten," adding she would have been "about six years old ... 'till I was fourteen" when she heard most of these songs.

She also had vivid memories of her "mammy," who, as she explained, had been given to her grandmother as a wedding gift back in 1853 and had raised all of her grandmother's children before taking care of Ms. Arguedas and her brothers and sisters, and from whom she also learned a lot of songs. French was the language spoken in the family, and communication with the servants was done in "Creole French." Ms. Arguedas became fluent in English around the age of fourteen (ca. 1901).[63] She also learned many Creole songs, through the accounts of her great-aunt who "lived nearby [Congo Square] and went with her mother and father to hear the Negroes sing and dance" and from hearing "the Negroes who worked around the house" when living in New Orleans later in her life. Ms. Arguedas died in the city in 1969, at the age of eighty-two.[64]

Because both women liked singing, their interviews are enhanced by the performance of several songs they learned during their childhood, which will be discussed throughout this book.

Part I

The Precursors of Jazz

Chapter 2

BLACK AMERICAN/FRENCH CREOLE FOLK MUSIC

The years between 1890 and 1917 are generally agreed to be the time when the development of jazz took place.[1] One of the major musical components involved in the formation of early jazz was Black American folk music, which comprises work songs and boat songs—whose texts were not always related to the work itself, but were sometimes "insult songs" or "songs of derision"—field hollers, cries from street vendors, prison songs, and play songs for both children and adults, as well as spirituals, ring shouts, and eventually the blues.[2]

However, Creole songs and their variants, such as street cries and work songs, and the *cantiques* (more in chapter 3) sung in the Catholic Church, as well as Voodoo songs, also belong to the Black American folk music that led to the development of jazz, as they were part of the soundscapes of New Orleans and southwest Louisiana well into the early twentieth century.

CHARACTERISTICS OF BLACK AMERICAN FOLK MUSIC

Although the discussion about the African origins of jazz varies among scholars, jazz historians and musicologists have constantly described several African-derived features that were crucial in the development of jazz:[3]

1. A complex approach to time involving syncopations and polyrhythms, often transcribed using three-over-two figures in Western notation, that eventually evolved into the rhythmic "swing" of jazz that emphasizes the second and fourth beats of a measure in 4/4;
2. A strong and regular rhythmic pulsation that serves as the foundation over which a melodic line can be played in more or less improvised free rhythm and phrasing;
3. Common use of blue notes—microtonal alterations of the third, seventh, and sometimes fifth, so that the actual note falls in between the notes of the diatonic scale;[4]

4. The use of various vocal and instrumental techniques to alter the timbre and/or pitch, such as slurs from note to note, guttural tones and rasps, and melismas;
5. Musical forms relying on call and response and collective or solo improvisation.

These characteristics have always proved to be a challenge when attempting to transcribe them into European musical notation, a challenge that remained true when transcribing Afro-French music. For instance, the Creole songs from the Good Hope Plantation (described below) published in 1867 in the first collection of *Slave Songs of the United States* were "as peculiar, as interesting and, in the case of two or three of them [out of seven] as difficult to write down or to sing correctly, as any [of the songs in English] that have preceded them." Editor William Francis Allen commented on this in his introduction to the book:

> The voices of the colored people have a peculiar quality . . . the intonations and delicate variations of even one singer cannot be reproduced on paper. . . . [They] abound in "slides from one note to the another and turns and cadences not in articulated notes." "It is difficult," writes Miss McKim [Garrison], "to express the entire character of these negro ballads by mere musical notes and signs."[5]

In her 1932 thesis, Camille Nickerson noted "the difficulty of notation . . . owing to the Negro's oddity of intonation and his ingenuity for complicated rhythms."[6] And in his 1950 PhD dissertation, Dr. Alfred Pouinard's transcribed "Joé Férail" (which he had collected the year before) using a "binary rhythm in 2/4 with syncopation on the second beat following an irregular triplet that could give the impression of a 'Negro rhythm,'" which also demonstrates the challenge of notating the Creole songs.[7]

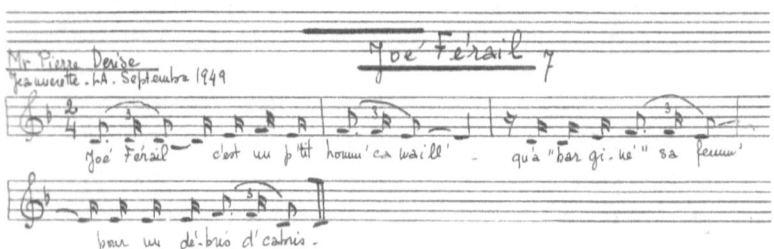

2.1. Alfred A. Pouinard, "Recherches sur la musique d'origine française en Amérique du Nord, Canada et Louisiane," PhD diss., Université Laval, Québec, 1950, vol. 2, 157.

In 1934, John and Alan Lomax also recorded a version of "Joe Féraille" [*sic*] and two related songs. In his thorough research about these recordings, Joshua Clegg Caffery asserts that "the character of 'Joe Féraille' relates directly to Louisiana and Haitian Creole song."[8] Indeed the three-over-two approach to rhythm characterizes rhythmic cells of Caribbean dance music, such as the habanera and tresillo that were developed by the enslaved dancing and singing in the Caribbean and in New Orleans. Further research is needed, for it is hard to say whether these cells were transplanted to New Orleans or their arrival reinforced rhythmical units already in use, since enslaved people arrived in the very early days of the French colony both directly from Africa and via the Caribbean, not to mention the influx of refugees who came from Saint-Domingue, sometimes via Cuba. (See chapter 1.)

2.2. The habanera.

2.3. The tresillo.

The habanera eventually made its way into the European classical music of nineteenth-century Creole composers such as Louis Moreau Gottschalk (a White Creole) and Basile Barès (see chapter 4). Described as the "Spanish tinge" by Jelly Roll Morton, these rhythms also appeared in the blues, early jazz, and Creole songs. (See chapter 5.)

PLANTATION SONGS

Africans began to gather to dance and sing early under the French regime. In 1726, Antoine Simon Le Page Du Pratz, who had come to the colony in 1718, accepted the position of "manager of the Company's plantation that became the King's plantation shortly after," on the south shore of the Mississippi River, across from New Orleans. Le Page Du Pratz goes on to describe Sunday gatherings of "at least four hundred 'Negroes,'" adding that "he agreed with the other planters on what needed to be done to prevent these meetings." In 1758, in his *Histoire de la Louisiane*, largely based on the sixteen years he lived in the colony, from 1718 to 1734, he explained: "In a word, nothing is more to be dreaded than to see the negroes assemble together on Sundays, since, under pretence [sic] of Calinda or the dance, they sometimes get together to the number of three or four hundred, and make a kind of Sabbath, which it is always prudent to avoid; for it is in those tumultuous meetings that they ... plot their rebellions."[9] Indeed, a fair number of planters could have feared such meetings. Marc-Antoine Caillot, a clerk for the Company of the Indies (*La Compagnie des Indes*), who was posted in New Orleans from July 1729 until May 1731, wrote that there were thirty-five plantations—of which fifteen to twenty were "quite substantial, both for the number of slaves as well as cattle"—downriver from New Orleans, and "going upriver two hundred leagues, there are as many plantations as concessions—one hundred fifty—among which twenty to twenty-five are very rich, ... who together hold more than 560 Negroes, 1,000 cattle, and many Indian slaves."[10] In the city, informal meetings took place in private houses or taverns. "The *affranchitte* Jeannette held suppers at her house in the 1740s. [And], [i]n 1755, the merchant-planter Pradel complained that his slaves met at houses in the city owned by free blacks where plantation and town slaves met to eat and drink and dance all night to the sound of a fiddle."[11]

Enslaved African Americans continued to dance and play music on the plantations until the Civil War. Ms. Francis or Frances Doby was 100 years old when she was interviewed in 1938 as part of the Federal Writers' Project in Louisiana. Hers is a rare narrative about enslaved children. She remembered having come on a boat and being sold with her mother on a plantation in Opelousas (St. Landry Parish), most likely in the early to mid-1840s, although another interviewer wrote that she had been born on the plantation in 1845.

> So, one day de old man dey call Antoine—he was so old dat dey keep him in de camp to amuse de chilens ... "Watch me make dat drum." So he take a big barrel—empty barrel—and tack dat [cow's] skin right-tight, tight, tight. Den he done straddle dat drum and beat on it. And first thing you know we was a dancin', a beatin' de flooh wid de foots—boom, boom, boom, boom—and de drum keep on a-beatin'. Chile, [sic] we dance till midnight. To finish de ball, we say, "*Balancez, Calinda*" (Turn around, Calinda), and den twist and turn and say again "*Balancez, Calinda*," and just turn around. Den de ball was over.
>
> Den old Granma come along and sing dis for us to go to sleep:

Sizette, te ein bell femme	Sizette is [you're] a beautiful woman
Mo chere amie-aie	Ah dear one-aie
Mo achete ban-ban	I buy pretty things
Ce pou nou marie.	For us to get married

Den we used to play Ti Balai (Little Broom). We used to pick an old broom dat lay around in de camp, and all de chilens sit on de grass in a circle. One of dem take de little broom and sing, going around outside de circle of de chilens:

Tringue, Tringue ti balai	I drag, I drag a small broom
Ti mouton la queu coupe	Lil lamb wid its tail cut off
Cha po ti bam bail	Lookin' for its tail all around
Cha po ti bam bail	Lookin' for its tail all around

Den dey drop dat piece of the old broom just back of someone, and keep on a-goin', saying, "Cha po ti bam bail. Cha po ti bam bail." When one of dem chilen notice like dat, dat de gal goin' around had done lost de broom, all de chilen begun to look around in de back. And de one who find de broom got to get up quick, and take de broom and chase de gal doin' de runnin', and hit her with it. Den everybody sits on de ground again, and de one what find de broom, den its her turn to be goin' around and around.[12]

Slaveholders or their friends also witnessed singing and dancing in the quarters where the enslaved lived. However, their music was not given much consideration. For instance, on June 11, 1856, in a letter from Hore Browse Trist to "My Dear Bringier," Trist condescendingly wrote, "Then again, such is the peculiar temperament of the woolly heads, but [unclear in text] bountifully are they endowed with animal spirits that after working all day, just scrape the cat gut or twang the banjo [and] they will dance all night, but enough on this subject."[13] A few years later, William H. Russell described a ball in the sugar house during a visit in the quarters:

> As we passed the back of the mansion some young women . . . who were, the Governor told me, the domestic servants going off to a dance at the sugar-house [sic]; he lets his slaves dance every Sunday. . . . The scraping of the fiddles attracted us to the sugar-house, . . . a large brick building, with a factory-looking chimney. In a space of the floor unoccupied by machinery some fifteen women and as many men were assembled, and four couples were dancing a kind of Irish jig to the music of the negro musicians—a double shuffle in a thumping ecstasy, with loose elbows, pendulous paws, angulated knees, heads thrown back, and backs arched inwards—a glazed eye, intense solemnity of mien.[14]

Dance Songs

Most of the pieces included in *Slave Songs of the United States* were Negro spirituals, with the exception of the last seven songs, all secular, that were "obtained from a lady who heard them sung, before the war, on the 'Good Hope' plantation, St. Charles Parish, Louisiana." A short explanation informs the reader that they were sung in a language that is "evidently a rude corruption of French [as] spoken by the negroes in that part of the State." Despite their small number, they are still very informative: four of them—"Belle Layotte," "Rémon," "Aurore Bradaire," and "Caroline"—were

> sung to a simple dance, a sort of minuet called the *Coonjai*; the name and the dance are probably both of African origin. When the *Coonjai* is danced, the music is furnished by an orchestra of singers, the leader of whom—a man selected both for the quality of his voice and for his skill in improvising—sustains the solo part, while the others afford him an opportunity, as they shout in chorus, for inventing some neat verse to compliment some lovely *danseuse*, or celebrate the deeds of some plantation hero. . . . and the usual musical accompaniment, besides that of the singers, is that furnished by a skilful [sic] performer on the barrel-head-drum, the jaw-bone [sic] and key, or some other rude instrument.

The next song was based on a "sort of contra-dance" called the Calinda—hence the name they gave to the song—which, according to the authors, had then passed entirely out of use. The melody and lyrics indicate that this is the satirical song also called "Michié Préval" (more below). "Lolotte" provided Gottschalk with the theme for his "Ballade Créole" called "La Savane." Finally, the last song, "Musieu Bainjo," is described as an original composition from an "enterprising negro" who successfully wrote a "French song."[15]

After the War and Reconstruction, sugar remained an important industry, and plantations continued to operate with low-paid Black workers who still lived on site, some on the same plantation where they had been enslaved. Songs that were collected on postwar plantations included work songs, street (vendor) cries, Voodoo songs, and dance songs. However, considering the movements between plantations and New Orleans—a lot of planters had a city home both before and after the war—it has to be understood that "plantation songs" were not sung only on plantations.

WORK SONGS, STREET CRIES, AND VOODOO SONGS

Work Songs

In April 1886, New Orleans–born novelist and historian George W. Cable (1844–1925) published an article, "Creole Slave Songs," in which he included two (work) "Songs of Woods and Waters," as he classified them. "From the treasures of [an] old chest" he wrote, "comes to my hand, from the last century most likely, on a ragged yellow sheet of paper, written with a green ink, one of these old songs." He called it "Rowers' Song." Indeed, as rivers and bayous were useful means of transportation, "[t]here was a time, [when] every planter [had] his boat and skilled crew of black oarsmen." Cable gave only his translation of the five verses, prior to which he noted "[t]he throb of their song measured the sweep of the oars . . . their strong voices chanted" in praise of their master who might have been sitting in the stern, but also in praise of their beautiful lovers. Unfortunately, Cable didn't include the lyrics of the other, a hunting song of which

> [e]ach stanza begins and ends with the loud refrain: "*Bomboula!, bomboula!*" . . . However, the dark hunters of a hundred years ago knew, [the meaning of *bamboula*] and between their outcries of the loud, rumbling word sang, in this song, their mutual exhortation to rise, take guns, . . . to find game for master's table and their own grosser [*sic*] *cuisine*, . . . that make "*si bon gumbo.*" . . . The lines have a fine African ring in them, but—one mustn't print everything.[16]

As mentioned in chapter 1, Jeanne Wogan Arguedas lived on her grandparents' Labranche Plantation (also located in St. Charles Parish) from ca. 1889 to 1901. She recalled learning many Creole songs from her old Mammy Cavie and when accompanying her grandmother during her regular visits to the sick workers to bring some remedies.[17] She also recalled hearing the workers "s[inging] while they were cutting the canes. They sang bringing the canes back on the big wagons with three mules, they sang putting the canes into the carrier and they sang doing other kind of work."[18] Of all the songs Ms. Arguedas sang during the interview, "Moulin Grillez di Cannes" is one of the most interesting. She sang it twice in a somehow-classical head voice, adding vibrato and a blues-ish ending most likely reflecting the vocals she still heard in her memory.

We could hear the voices [of the cutting women] way at a distance, because sometimes they were about six or seven city blocks away from us. . . . it was slow and the movements of cutting the cane were sharp and quick, so [the song] didn't cooperate with their movements. It was rather, more of plaint, a complaint than anything else. But it was very picturesque and very pretty. . . . very unusual, as a rule, the music accompanies the movement [sic].[19]

The lyrics of her second rendition were slightly different, suggesting that multiple variations existed, as the women most likely sang it over and over again during their long hours of hard work in the field. In answer to the interviewer's question about the rhythm of cane cutting, Ms. Arguedas demonstrated by clapping her hands at the speed of the cutting while singing the first two verses. This very short rendition seems to indicate that the slow melody fits with the movements by holding notes over a few cutting beats.

Found in *On the Trail of Negro Folk-Songs*, "Tout Pitit Négresse" is a short, repetitive "Creole song from Louisiana" of two ABCC four-line verses about washerwomen and washermen working down by the bayou. They are sung over a very simple eight-bar ABCC melody mostly moving stepwise down the major scale, with only a few leaps to and from the fifth degree and few accentuated beats in the fifth and seventh bars.

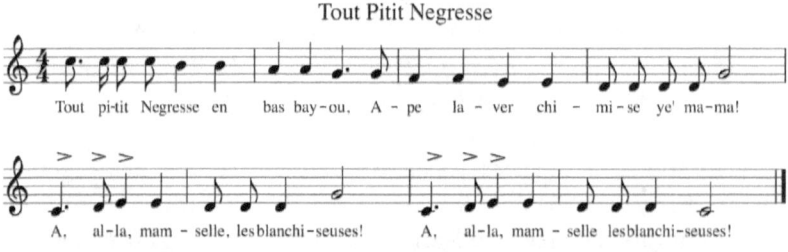

2.4. Dorothy Scarborough, *On the Trail of Negro Folk-Songs* (Cambridge, MA: Harvard University Press, 1925), 212.

Tout pitit Negresse en bas bayou,	A very little Negress down on the bayou,
A-pe laver chimise ye' mama!	Washing shirts, oh, mama!
A, alla, mamselle, les blanchiseuses!	Oh lady, the washerwomen!
A, alla, mamselle, les blanchiseuses!	Oh lady, the washerwomen!
Tout pitit Negre en bas bayou,	A very little [Negro] down on the bayou,
A-pe frotter culotte ye' papa!	Scrubbing underclothes, oh, papa!
A, alla, monsieur, les blanchisseurs!	Oh man, the washerman! [sic]
A, alla, monsieur, les blanchisseurs!	Oh man, the washerman!

The simplicity of both the lyrics and the melody allowed plenty of room for improvisation (and vocal melisma or pitch alteration) as noticed by the author, who specified that "[t]he rhythmic possibilities of the washboard in the hands of a Negress are all but illimitable." It was given by Mrs. George Deynoodt and Mrs. J. O. La Rose from New Orleans, whose names suggest that they were White women who would have overheard the washerwomen singing. This could also explain the melody's simplicity and the absence of any ornamentation. It is described as one of many "rubbing songs, but one example will serve." That's unfortunate considering the interesting use of the washboard as a rhythmic instrument. It was collected somewhere between 1915 and 1925, for when the book was published (1925), the author, Dorothy Scarborough, had been collecting songs for about ten years.[20]

Street Cries

Ms. Arguedas also remembered "Louisa who used to catch shrimps in the river" while singing "Mo Marché sur Grand Chemin," which is not about shrimps at all, but is a sad piece about a child telling her mother and father that they must come to her funeral when she dies. She recalled Louisa wearing a black straw hat, on top of which she was carrying her "bucket full of shrimps," crying out to sell her merchandise: "Her voice was very deep, she was always smoking a pipe and she come [sic] to my grandmother in the morning and said, 'pour les chevrettes [crevettes] Madame, pour les chevrettes. Pour les chevrettes Madame.' For 10 cents, perhaps 5 cents, we bought a great large bucket of delicious river shrimps."[21] Rarely reported by visitors or diarists writing about plantation life, street cries were an ever-present feature of the New Orleans soundscape (see fig. 2.7, p. 42). According to James R. Creecy, who visited the city in the mid-1830s,

> [m]any of the female slaves are *marchandes* during the week, and their shrill cries never cease from morning's dawn till *"le milieu de la nuit"*—Marchande de tait [sic]; *marchande des patés, tous chauds*; marchande des oranges, douces tres [sic] douces; marchande des ooufs [sic], Creoles, *tous frais*; marchande des galettes chauffe [sic] marchande des plants [sic]; marchande des figues, douces et frais [sic], and marchandes in everything to eat and drink or use in a *small way*, for the Creoles buy everything in that way.[22]

Many decades later, Danny Barker (1909–1994) also recalled the calas vendors outside the church after Mass:

They have a basket on their head, and they wouldn't hold the basket. It would be the blackberry lady or the strawberry lady or the pie lady. . . . Old ladies used to sell . . . I can't think of them things. Calas. . . . Each church you see these old women standing there with a basket. Have on 'em slave clothes. Big skirts. . . . One particular . . . I'd go and stand and look at her, and she would look at me, and I wouldn't say a word. She would shake her head. "Pauvre. Pauvre petit."[23]

In 1925, Emmet R. Kennedy published *Mellows—A Chronicle of Unknown Singers* in which he included the cry of a "Pam Patat" [sic] vendor with a short eight-bar melody. In her thesis, Cora Sadler cleverly introduced it with Edward Larocque Tinker's (1881–1968) vivid description of New Orleans street vendors, dressed with "bright guinea-blue dresses, and starched white aprons, wander[ing] through the Vieux Carré crying the wares. . . . Each chanted her own individual call in a rich, mellow voice. The 'marchande de pan patat' sang . . . a haunting melody."[24]

2.5. R. Emmet Kennedy, *Mellows: A Chronicle of Unknown Singers* (New York: Albert and Charles Boni, 1925), 21.

Once again, the simplicity of the call allows plenty of room for improvisation, vocal melisma, or pitch alteration. In fact, this transcription arguably represents an attempt to notate a melody with microtonal variations, of which the nearest Western scale would have been C minor with a raised seventh (harmonic minor). Borrowing again from Tinker, Sadler also added the chimney sweep, "Ramoné la Cheminée," described by Scarborough as a "weird cry, half wail and half chant, which can scarcely be imitated, but which is very impressive: *Ramonee* [sic] *la chemine* [sic] *latannier!*[25] Despite their common use, few New Orleans street cries have been preserved, with the notable exception of "Belles Calas" and "Les Oignons," which were combined to form the popular song "Les Oignons." (See chapter 6.)[26]

Voodoo Songs

There seems to have been some exceptions to the rule of secrecy of the Voodoo ceremonies, for on June 24, 1884, an article was published in the *Times-Democrat* describing the "Voudou dance" held the night before—St. John's Eve—on the shores of Lake Pontchartrain. Although in a rather condescending tone, the reporter described an old man playing a "two-stringed sort of a fiddle … [with] a long neck, and [a] body … not more than three inches in diameter [and] littles drums made of gourds and covered with sheepskin" played "with their thumbs." A man started singing eventually joined by all for the refrain, and then by two women at the "fourth stanza" as they "began a march around the room."[27]

Still on the plantation, Ms. Arguedas heard the workers singing around the fire camp at night, and sometimes they would sing Voodoo songs. She was also very impressed by stories and songs from her old mammy, other servants, or the cook, all of whom she believed "belonged to the Voodoo." She only recalled a short song whose first verse would be best described as spoken words backed by an accentuated rhythm, in which one phrase could be considered the refrain, because it is repeated a few times. The second verse consists of a short, wordless melody repeated three times—that surely allowed for improvised vocal embellishments—punctuated by the insertion of the spoken refrain repeated twice. She sang it twice, first accompanying herself with a gourd and foot stomping, and then with hand clapping and foot stomping, somehow imitating a drum, and with a different arrangement of the verses.[28]

In "Creole Slave Songs," Cable devoted a lengthy section to the Voodoo—in which he included a summary of the 1884 celebration—that he concluded with "a genuine Voodoo song" only nine bars long, with two verses, the words of which "are rendered phonetically in French."

2.6. George W. Cable, "Creole Slave Songs," *Century Magazine* (April 1886): 820.

"And another phrase: 'Ah tingouai yé. Ah tingouai yé. Ah ouai ya, Ah ouai ya, Ah tingouai yé. Do sé dan go-do, Ah tingouai yé,' etc."[29] We can only speculate, but its rendition during a Voodoo ceremony might have implied multiple repetitions—varied or not—with musical accompaniment that would most likely have included at least some drums and maybe other instruments. Isaac Holmes in 1821, Théodore Pavie in 1829–30, and Alcée Fortier in 1888 all wrote about various dances, indicating that the enslaved had similar practices whether they gathered on rural plantations or in New Orleans.[30] Their descriptions of the musical instruments, songs, and dances bear close resemblance to the descriptions of Sunday gatherings held at Congo Square, or *Place Congo* as it was then called.

CONGO SQUARE

New Orleans's Congo Square is a very important location in the cultural history of the United States. Before colonization, the area was already sacred ground for Native Americans who celebrated their annual *Fête du Blé* (Corn Feast) there. Later, as it became the *Place Congo*, African cultures and traditions, having come directly from Africa or through the West Indies, not only were commemorated but interacted and eventually merged, creating a unique Afro-Creole culture—a fact largely overlooked since the African cultures transplanted to the colonies are often perceived as one uniform culture, rather than the diverse cultures of the many communities of enslaved people that eventually formed a rather homogenous cultural community. (See chapter 1.)[31] In *Congo Square*, Freddi Evans also stresses its importance "on the perpetuation of African cultural traditions in North America":

> As time passed, songs with a combination of African and Creole words, those in Louisiana Creole, and those in English joined and basically replaced songs of African origin. Although examples of songs representing each of these categories appear in [her book], Louisiana Creole constitutes the majority of those included here as well as those documented in general.[32]

The Black Code adopted in 1806 maintained Sunday as a day free from work, as prescribed long before in the French *Code Noir* (see chapter 1).[33] In 1817, following an ordinance by the City Council to limit assemblies, Congo Square was designated as the only place allowed for the Sunday gatherings, which continued throughout the 1830s and 1840s. They were so impressive that numerous Whites and tourists gathered to listen and watch. In 1846 an article appeared in the *Daily Picayune* advising that "[n]o stranger in this city ... should fail to visit, of a Sunday afternoon, the square in Rampart street [*sic*], commonly called 'Congo Square.'"[34]

Almost three decades earlier, in 1819, architect and engineer Benjamin Latrobe "accidentally stumbl[ed] upon an assembly of negroes . . . on the Common in the rear of the city" [the future Congo Square], where he observed "a crowd of five or six hundred persons [who all] seemed to be blacks" dancing, singing, and playing instruments of African origin such as various drums, a stringed instrument (the ancestor of the banjo), and other percussive instruments.[35] Another visitor, James R. Creecy, went to see the gatherings in the mid-1830s:

Groups of fifties or hundreds may be seen in different sections of the square, with banjos, tom-toms, violins, jawbones, triangles, and various other instruments from which harsh or dulcet sounds may be extracted. . . . The dancers are most fancifully dressed, with fringes, ribbons, little bells, and shells, and balls jingling and flirting about the performer's legs and arms, who sing a second or counter to the music most sweetly . . . and in all their movements, gyrations . . . the most perfect time is kept, making the beats with the feet, heads, or hands, or all, as correctly as a well-regulated metronome![36]

Congo Square was also chronicled by George W. Cable in "The Dance in Place Congo," published in February 1886. It is not clear if Cable ever witnessed the gatherings as a child, but his sequencing and comments in the descriptions of the songs and dances give the impression that he might have once seen some. After describing the Bamboula that "grew everywhere more and more gross. No wonder the police stopped it in Congo Square," and the Counjaille, Cable continues: "There were other dances. Only a few years ago I was honored with an invitation, which I had to decline, to see danced the Babouille, the Cata (or Chacta), the Counjaille, and the Calinda."[37] In any case, that doesn't mean Cable didn't have other occasions to hear or see the songs and dances somewhere else. Indeed, in "The Scenes of Cable's Romances" published in 1883 in the *Century Magazine*, Lafcadio Hearn describes real locations and houses—mostly on and around "*Rue Royale*"—used by Cable as models for the short stories included in *Old Creole Days*, first published separately in *Scribner's Monthly* (later to become the *Century Magazine*) starting in 1873, and published as a book in 1879. Most importantly, Hearn describes a "Congo dance" that took place in the yard of an old house on Dumaine Street:

Until within a few years ago, the strange African dances were still danced and the African songs still sung by negroes and negresses who had been slaves. Every Sunday afternoon the bamboula dancers were summoned to a wood-yard on Dumaine street [*sic*] by a sort of

> drum-roll, made by rattling the ends of two great bones upon the head of an empty cask: and *I remember* that the male dancers fastened bits of tinkling metal or tin rattles about their ankles, like those strings of copper gris-gris worn by the negroes of the Soudan. Those whom *I saw* taking part in those curious and convulsive performances—subsequently suppressed by the police—were either old or beyond middle age. The veritable Congo dance, with its extraordinary rhythmic chant, will soon have become as completely forgotten in Louisiana....[38]

If Hearn actually saw such a "Congo dance," then Cable could also have seen one, different from the Babouille and other dances he had declined to see. Indeed, according to Johnson, Cable "saw" and "observed" the musical instruments he described without actually saying where he would have seen them. Evans argues that Cable's date of birth (1844) would have precluded him from actually seeing the dances in Congo Square, although he could have seen them "at other times or locations." On the other hand, S. Frederick Starr opines that Cable didn't see the dances at all, but instead relied on his interviews with Clara Gottschalk Peterson—whom he thanked in his article—and prior writings about dances in Saint-Domingue to substantiate his article. But, if it seems plausible that, as a novelist, Cable used his imagination to recreate the Congo Square gatherings—based on dances he might have seen, interviews, or previous written material—it should be noted that, at the end of "The Dance in Place Congo," he specified that Henry E. Krehbiel provided a "much valuable collaboration" before withdrawing from the project of writing the article as a "joint work." He also listed a number of friends to whom he was indebted; the names of some were "attached to the musical scores," while others were acknowledged for their contributions in "earlier steps—for the work of collection has been slow."[39]

In any case, Cable's description of what he called the "Grand Orchestra" is consistent with the description of early observers: he mentions two drums, one "large, the other much smaller," "huge wooden horns," a gourd (an "important instrument"), triangles, jew's-harp [*sic*], a jawbone, empty barrels or casks, the Marimba brett—which according to his description seems to have been a mbira (thumb piano)—and the banjo, adding that "for the true African dance,... there was wanted the dark inspiration of African drums and the banjo's thrump and strum.... To all this there was sometimes added a Pan's pipe ... called by English-speaking negroes 'the quills.'"[40] In "The Dance in Place Congo," Cable focuses on the main dances and some of the songs with which they were associated, for which he included lyrics and musical transcriptions. The dances were the Bamboula (also the name of the drum used to accompany it), the Counjaille, and the Calinda.[41] Describing the slow beginning of the Bamboula, Cable reproduced a song that consists of a simple four-note melody that showed the "emphatic barbarism of five bars to a line," which he once heard on the cane field.

> The singers almost at the first note are many.... They swing and bow to right and left, in slow time.... Among the chorus of Franc-Congo singing-girls is one extra good voice, who thrusts in, now and again, an improvisation.... The measure quickens... the female voices grow sharp and staccato, and suddenly the dance is the furious Bamboula.[42]

A song of the same name accompanies this Bamboula. Commonly known as "Quan Patate La Cuite," it was used by composer Louis Moreau Gottschalk for the beginning of "Bamboula: Danse des Nègres." (See chapter 4.) The next song, "Musieu Bainjo," is simply described by William Francis Allen, Charles Pickard Ware, and Lucy McKim Garrison as an original composition, whereas Cable classified "Miché Bainjo" as a Bamboula.

> Suddenly the song changes. The rhythm sweeps away long and smooth ... with a louder drum-beat.... I could give four verses, but let one suffice; it is from a manuscript copy of the words, probably a hundred years old, that fell into my hands through the courtesy of a Creole lady some two years ago. It is one of the best known of all the old Counjaille songs.[43]

Four songs are classified by Allen, Ware, and Garrison, as well as by Cable, as Coonjai/Counjaille: "Belle Layotte," "Rémon," "Aurore Bradaire/Aurore Pradère," and "(Aine/Inne, dé, trois) Caroline," which seems to be the song appearing on the old manuscript copy that was given to Cable.

The last dance described by Cable is the "bad enough" Calinda, whose "song was always a grossly personal satirical ballad" that "ended these dissipations of the summer Sabbath afternoons" adding that "[a]ll this Congo Square business was suppressed at one time; 1843, says tradition." Similarly, Lyle Saxon wrote that "the Calinda was a voodoo dance ... Considered indecent.... it was officially banned throughout the State in 1843, but continued to be performed for many years afterward." Nonetheless, Cable (who was born in 1844) recalled that, as a child, he heard a street merchant—a *marchande de calas*—singing the Calinda song mocking "Miché Preval," also compiled by Allen, Ware, and Garrison under the name of "Calinda."[44] And, as the story told by Frances Doby attests, the Calinda also survived longer on plantations (see above).

2.7. "A Marchande des Calas." [sic] Illustration by Edward W. Kemble in George W. Cable, "The Dance in Place Congo," *Century Magazine* 31 (February 1886): 527.

The lyrics published in the January 6, 1858, edition of *Le Villageois/The Villager* under the title "Chant du Vié Boscugo," led the authors of *Textes anciens en créole louisianais* to conclude that "Michié Préval" "represents one of the oldest texts published in Louisiana Creole [language]."[45] The same lyrics were included in Will H. Coleman's 1885 *Historical Sketch Book and Guide of New Orleans and Environs* as the "Chanson du Vié Boscoyo." It comprises sixteen verses, all followed by the chorus "Dansez Calinda, Boudoum, Boudoum." In "The Dance in Place Congo" (1886), Cable wrote that "[t]he number of stanzas ha[d] never been counted" and presented only "a few of them," including one that hadn't appeared in the *Le Villageois* or Coleman's book. In "Bits of Louisiana Folk-lore" (1887), Alcée Fortier, commenting on Cable's remarks, explained that "[i]t often happened that many stanzas were added to a song or to a poem, when it was very popular." Similarly, Krehbiel, who collected sixteen verses from various sources, sometimes only in their English translation, also found some not included in Coleman.⁴⁶ This abundance of verses—along with those that might have been lost, or improvised and never written down—allowed singers to artfully tell the story in their own way. Nonetheless, of all the notated or sung versions that I have found, spanning from 1867 to 1957, the melody remains pretty much the same, with some minor variations that do not alter its character, apart from Mina Monroe's version notated in 3/4 rather than in 6/8. (Appendix 2 contains a comparison of the various versions.)

The song is about judge Gallien Préval, listed as Associate Justice of the New Orleans City Court in 1834, the year that he bought a lot to build a livery stable on *rue de l'Hôpital*—now Governor Nicholls Street—and another one on Royal Street where the Préval house still stands today.⁴⁷ As the story goes, Judge Préval lent the stable to, and allowed, his coachman Louis to give a ball, but failed to obtain the required permit to organize such an event. *Satire oblige*, there is a verse about the horses that must have been really surprised, and another one about "the old Jackass [who] came in to dance," while many who showed up were wearing fine clothes apparently stolen from their masters and mistresses. Finding the situation rather funny, the jailkeeper said he too would throw a ball, and went to arrest and jailed the judge. The song ends with the judge having trouble gathering the money to pay the $100 fine, and indeed, both the house and stable were sold in 1841, as Judge Préval filed for bankruptcy.⁴⁸ Attesting to their importance, Cable noted that "satirical songs of double meaning . . . readily passed unchallenged . . . beguiled the hours afield or the moonlight gatherings in the 'quarters,' as well as served to fit the wild chants of some of their dances." As a matter of fact, two of the seven Creole songs published in *Slave Songs of the United States*—"Calinda"/"Michié Préval" and "Musieu Bainjo"—were satires.⁴⁹

Cable's remembrance of the *marchande de calas* singing this song also points to the fact that, not surprisingly, Creole songs were performed not only in Congo Square, but also in the streets of New Orleans.⁵⁰ Indeed, regardless of the city's 1817 resolution mentioned above, dances also took place outside the square. Timothy Flint, who visited New Orleans in the early 1820s, wrote, "[e]very year the negroes have two or three holidays, . . . in New Orleans and the vicinity . . . The great Congo-dance [sic] is performed. . . . Some hundreds of negroes, . . . follow the king . . . I have seen groups . . . following these merry bachanalians [sic] in their dance through the streets."⁵¹ In 1843, the *Daily Picayune* published an article about the Congo dance, "this favorite dance of our servile population," depicting a public "black ball . . . held in the capacious yard of a house in the Third Municipality." Although it says that the "orchestra was full," it seems that there were only four musicians:

> The leader strummed a long-necked banjo, . . . another of the musicians beat the jaw bones of an ass with a rusty key; a third had . . . a kind of a *la petit tambour* [sic], on which he kept time with his digits, and a fourth beat most vehemently an old headless cask that lay on its side, ballasted with iron nails. To these instrumental efforts were given a general vocal chorus.

They were accompanying three dancers, two women who "move[d] their feet rapidly, but still with the least possible visible motion," and one man who "had on a pair of leather knee caps from which were suspended a quantity of metal nails, which made a gingling noise that timed with his music."[52]

As the tension rose before the Civil War, restriction on movements and assemblies of both enslaved and Free People of Color increased, leading to an 1858 ordinance making it unlawful for them to assemble. An 1864 *Daily Picayune* article titled "Memory Types of New Orleans" indicates that the Congo Square gatherings were over.[53]

Congo Square after the Civil War

Alice Zeno's memories clearly indicate that some gatherings did resume in the square—*La Place Congo*, as she called it—after the Civil War. She called them *danses Créoles*:

> You see, the colored people would go there whenever they get ready to get their dance, they'd go. And, and put the *bière Créole*, Creole beer, they'd make it with the pineapple hull, you know, and apple, they sell that cider that I believe they call it now. . . . They'd go, at the Congo Square, then they put the little table there, and they'd give you, sell you a glass for a nickel. . . . It really was nice to see them people dancing with the guinea blue dress and the checked apron . . . and the tignon, you know, they wore head handkerchief.[54]

It is not clear whether Ms. Zeno actively participated in these dances, but she spoke about the Calinda as both a song and a Creole dance, and the Bamboula as an African dance, which she explained as follows: "They hold their dress, . . . it's just the foot and they had the horse jawbone, that's how they made music out of. . . . Well sometimes, they'd have 'em, and if they didn't have that, they'd take tin plates and spoons and make music out of that. But most of the time, it was the mouth."[55] Making music with the "mouth" seems to indicate that they would sing, but she might also have tried to convey the idea that the dancers were also accompanying themselves with voice percussion—or else why not say that they were singing? During the same period, People of Color also met at dance halls or theaters in the vicinity of Congo Square. A notable example is the Globe Hall, located in the back of Congo Square since the 1850s until it was demolished in 1920 for the construction of the Municipal Auditorium.[56]

Ms. Arguedas knew about Congo Square through stories and songs recounted by her great-aunt, who used to visit the square with her own mother and father. She actually learned the songs very well, either from her great-aunt or from hearing them sung by the "Negroes who worked around the house," as her precise renditions, with self-accompaniment using a gourd, or with hand clapping and foot stomping, demonstrate.[57] She provided three "Bamboula songs," as she called them because they were performed in Congo Square with the accompaniment of a Bamboula drum: "Chère, Mo l'Aimer Toi"; the "Calinda"; and "Tan Patate La Cuite." The latter she remembered "as a child, sung on the street . . . everybody sang it around me, and it belonged to the song [sic] of the Congo Square like the two others that I have given."[58] The "Calinda," also called "Mesieur Mazureau," is the same song—with some melodic variations—as "Michié Préval" discussed above, but mocking other people. This adaptation reflects not only the popularity of this satirical song but also its lyrical flexibility and its improvisational storytelling nature. (See appendix 2.)

Mesieur Mazureau	Mister Mazureau
Dans son vieux bureau	In his old office
D'ici semb' crapeau	From here, looks like a frog
Dans un baye do lo	In a water tub
Dansez Calinda, Boudjoum, Boudjoum (2x)	
Mesieur Carondelet	Mister Carondelet
Gagné deux mulets	Won two mules
Té courri su parade	He ran to the parade
Sur la rue Esplanade	On Esplanade Street
Dansez Calinda, Boudjoum, Boudjoum (2x)	
Mesieur Delachaise	Mister Delachaise
Prends tout mon des fraises	Took all my strawberries
Pour son vieille milâtresse	For his old Mulatto woman
Qu'était son maîtresse	That was his mistress
Dansez Calinda, Boudjoum, Boudjoum (2x)[59]	

As with "Michié Préval," these three verses might have been based on real events. Étienne Mazureau (1777–1849) was attorney general of Louisiana three times during the nineteenth century. Ms. Arguedas explained that "[h]is office was on the riverfront. And one night, when he was working, the river began to rise, water came in his office." Mazureau then put his feet in a bucket to keep them dry while working all evening by the candlelight. As he leaned forward, rounding his back and "writing arduously," people passing by found that he looked like a bullfrog in a tub, so "they improvised that song." Cable, who mostly discussed "Miché Preval," also remarked that "[n]o official exaltation bought immunity from the jeer of the Calinda. Préval was a magistrate [see above]. Stephen [sic] Mazureau, in his attorney-general's office, the song likened to a bull-frog [sic] in a bucket of water."

François Louis Hector (or Francisco Luis Hector), Baron de Carondelet, was governor of Louisiana and West Florida from 1791 to 1797. According to the enslaved, he was too "stingy to buy horses . . . and one day, he went on a big parade on Esplanade Street driven only by his mules." Ms. Arguedas wasn't sure if this was a true story, suggesting that the French word *mulet* (mule) was used just to make the verse rhyme. Indeed, when Carondelet was governor, Esplanade Street didn't exist yet, but there was an esplanade—a grassy area—along the fortification, to which people were referring to. As it eventually became the name of the street laid out in this area, it could also have easily become "rue Esplanade" in a song being passed from one person to another. Finally, Mesieur Delachaise, a "very prominent" man, was ridiculed for having stolen strawberries in somebody's ward, and gave them to his "sweetheart who was a Mulatto girl." Again we don't know much about this story, but there is a Delachaise Street in New Orleans named after the family of the same name who once owned this plantation land before its subdivision, as Faubourg Delachaise, in 1855.[60]

When asked to repeat them, Ms, Arguedas sang the verses in a different order and with minor changes in the lyrics, tapping her foot lightly on the beat throughout the first verse, and more heavily on "djoum" for all the choruses. She also explained:

> The Calinda was come of [sic] women forming a circle. In the center were two women *improvising songs* in a loud and piercing voice. They usually took names of well-known public officials or sometimes names of their masters and mistresses *and said a few words ridiculing their shortcomings or sometimes telling little stories about them.* It was their way of having a *little revenge* sometimes when they thought that they were ill-treated or . . . without any kindness or encounter duration. [She probably meant duress.]

They were not afraid to do so because it was "not very serious and mostly something funny and amusing." To the contrary, the song was apparently very well known as "[t]he chorus 'Dansez Calinda' was taken by everybody around the square."[61] Finally, Charles D. Warner described how singing and dancing to the chorus "Dansé Calinda, boudoum, boudoum" played a significant part of a Voodoo ceremony he witnessed when visiting New Orleans in 1885.[62]

Another song, "Cadja, Ma coupé ça," was associated with a contest-game played by men only, during which they had to carry "something like a jar" full of water on their head while dancing and without spilling water on the ground. Ms. Arguedas said it was taught to her by her old maid Cavie, but that the game was usually played in Congo Square.[63] Alice Zeno recalled a similar Congo Square dance, "Zoli Pon. . . . They'd hold their dress. [Singing] . . . And then, they'd put a bottle, and they'd throw, they'd pour over it like that. They say 'Çaya, m'a coupé ça. Çaya, m'a coupé ça.' That was some African song I suppose."[64]

In a letter to H. E. Krehbiel written from New Orleans in February 1884, Hearn very briefly mentioned a similar dance which he describes as:

> the negro-Creole bottle-dance, danced over an upright bottle to the chant—
> "Ça ma coupé—
> Ça ma coupé—
> Ça ma coupé—
> Ça!" [repeated twice][65]

Unfortunately, he didn't say where he saw it, but the similarity is so striking that it is most likely the same dance—or a close variation—of the dance described by Ms. Zeno. As she indicated, she saw the dances when she was old enough to "run off and go see *danses Créoles*"—which, according to a later answer, means that Ms. Zeno would have been thirteen or fourteen years old—after which they faded away as "things got so modern, so modern, so modern." In any case, this implies that the dances were held until 1877–78. As with their antebellum counterpart, they continued to be a popular attraction for White people and tourists, and Hearn, who arrived in New Orleans in 1877, could have been among them.[66]

Cable's declined invitation to see the Babouille and other dances a few years prior to 1886, Hearn's visit to a "wood-yard on Dumaine street [*sic*]" (see above), and Ms. Arguedas's and Ms. Zeno's vivid recollections well demonstrate the survival of some of the Congo Square's traditions after the Civil War both in New Orleans and in the countryside until (or almost to) the end of the nineteenth century. This implies that some early jazz musicians—such as Kid Ory, born on Woodland Plantation in 1886 (the same year as Ms. Arguedas), in the parish adjacent to Labranche Plantation—might have witnessed remnants of the Sunday gatherings in their childhood.

Chapter 3

FRENCH RELIGIOUS MUSIC

THE CATHOLIC CHURCH IN LOUISIANA

As a French colony, Louisiana was fashioned by the Roman Catholic Church, which regulated the lives of the inhabitants, whether natives or settlers, free or enslaved. Moreover, religion and politics were often intertwined: missionaries traveled with the early explorers, and religious orders established missions in the colonies. In doing so, they brought music with them: "At sea the chaplain led the ship's company in morning and evening prayer, which would include the chanted versicle 'Domine, salvum fac regem,'... Mass was announced by drums, its beginning signaled by the firing of a cannon, the elevation acknowledged by the roll of drums and the triple lowering of a pennant."[1]

Soon after its founding, New Orleans was ministered to by missionaries and Capuchin priests—they arrived in 1722—who celebrated Mass in various places such as company warehouses, private residences, or quickly built sheds, until the completion of the St. Louis Parish church in 1727.[2] That same year, a group of Ursulines crossed the Atlantic to found a convent in the new colonial capital. Madeleine Hachard, known as Sœur Saint-Stanislas (Sister St. Stanislaus), chronicled the Ursulines' six-month journey to Louisiana in letters written to her father and family back in France. She recounted that the nuns found comfort in the daily Mass, the singing of the High Mass and vespers on Sunday and holidays, and the celebration of Easter while on board.[3] Soon after their arrival, the Ursulines started to provide instruction to girls and women, regardless of social status or color. In a letter dated April 24, 1728, Hachard described how their little community had grown to include "seven enslaved boarders to instruct for Baptism and First Communion, besides a large number of day students, and Negresses and Indian women coming for two hours each day for instruction."[4]

In a letter dated April 24, 1728, Hachard proudly described their latest Easter celebrations:

This Reverend Father gave us and our boarders a retreat during Holy Week. Several ladies from the city attended assiduously, sometimes they numbered to almost two hundred for the Exhortations and Sermons. We had the *Leçons des Ténèbres* in music and a *Miserere* accompanied with instruments every day; our Mother assistant, Mme Le Boulenger, distinguished herself on this occasion. On Easter Sunday, during Mass and the Benediction of the Blessed Sacrament, we sang motets in four parts and, on the last day of the Easter Feasts, we sang the entire Mass with instruments. The convent in France, with all their splendor, do not do as much.[5]

Because the *Code Noir* required slaveholders to baptize and instruct their enslaved workers in the Catholic faith, the Church maintained a "universal ideal," so that Black and White Catholics worshipped together as members of the same congregation.[6] The presence of enslaved boarders and of African and Native American women among the Ursulines' day students, or servants at the convent, and of enslaved people on the Ursulines' and Capuchins' plantations—together they owned 123 enslaved workers in 1766—as well as the registries' entries of "slave baptisms" in the St. Louis church and other rural parishes, are a clear indication that African Americans were exposed to the musical practices and traditions of the Catholic Church from the early days of the colony.[7]

Spain being Catholic, the Ursulines and the Capuchins, who were joined by Spanish confrères, had no difficulty continuing their evangelizing and educational work after the change of regime (1763). In fact, as historian Emily Clark points out, "[o]ver the course of the eighteenth century, people of African descent came to dominate the congregational ranks of the Catholic Church in New Orleans." By the mid-nineteenth century, Free People of Color took an active part in maintaining parish churches and even sang in interracial choirs.[8] Following the creation of St. Augustine Parish in 1841, they raised part of the funds to construct the church of the same name that eventually served the racially mixed (and then) mostly French population of the Faubourg Treme.

In an unprecedented, political and religious move, the colored members also bought all the side aisle pews. They then gave those pews to the slaves as their exclusive place of worship. This mix of the pews resulted in the most integrated congregation in the entire country: one large row of free people of color, one large row of whites with a smattering of ethnic folk, and two outer aisles of slaves.[9]

3.1. The music room at St. Mary's Academy, circa 1900. From Sister Mary Bernard Deggs, *No Cross, No Crown: Black Nuns in Nineteenth-Century New Orleans* (Bloomington: Indiana University Press, 2001), insert.

Around the same time, the congregation of *Les Sœurs de la Sainte-Famille*—The Sisters of the Holy Family—was founded by three Free Women of Color (Henriette Delille, Juliette Gaudin, and Josephine Charles) with the mission of evangelizing "their people"—New Orleans People of Color, free or enslaved—and to "instruct the ignorant, assist the dying, and care for the needy." Historians Virginia Meacham Gould and Charles E. Nolan have credited the Ursulines for their "influence [that] led directly to the formation in the 1830s of Louisiana's first religious community of women of African descent."[10] The community officially became *Les Sœurs de la Sainte-Famille* in 1842. Ten years later, the Sisters founded a school for girls, and in 1870, they opened St. Mary's Academy (for girls), which included a high school, and moved it to Chartres Street in 1881, where they had a nice music room (see fig. 3.1). As for the Ursulines, music was an important part of the Sisters' teaching and activities:

> Beginning every day during the month of May, Mother Josephine would have the girls and their mothers come and sing at night when their duties were over.... Our dear mother [Mother Marie Magdalene Alpaugh] had many troubles during the administration of Rev. Father

DeCarriere. One reason was that our singing at Sunday benediction was so superior to that of the nearby church that its congregation completely abandoned the parish church to come over to our chapel to listen to the lovely singing of our sisters. That was true, because our dear mother was a very holy person and loved sacred music. She took great care in having the sisters' voices carefully trained so they could sing for God at mass [sic] in our chapel.[11]

During the 1870s and 1880s, they reached out and opened branch houses and schools in Baton Rouge, Donaldsonville, and Opelousas that contributed to the continuing presence of the Catholic Church—and its music—in southwest Louisiana. Eventually, with the rise of segregation at the end of the nineteenth century, the universal ideal of the Church slowly eroded, and in 1895, St. Katherine Parish became the first Black parish in New Orleans.[12]

THE URSULINE MANUSCRIPT:
NOUVELLES POÉSIES SPIRITUELLES ET MORALES

A unique source about the Ursuline music is the 1736 hand-copied manuscript (given to the congregation in 1754) *Nouvelles poésies spirituelles et morales sur les plus beaux airs de la musique françoise et italienne avec la basse*,[13] for it consists of religious songs in French (and not in Latin, like music for the Mass and Catholic liturgy). The songs highlight the eighteenth-century musical practice of spiritual or sacred parody (*parodies spirituelles* or *contrafacta*), according to which popular secular songs or instrumental pieces were given spiritual or moral lyrics (*chansons morales*).[14] The nuns already—and beautifully—sang motets in four parts and the Mass with instruments, so clearly they had the ability to perform these songs.[15] Conductor Anne-Catherine Bucher described her experience in the performance of some of them:

> I brought together a little group of "Ursulines" with young voices, alternating passages for semi-chorus with solo *récits*: it is easy to imagine that this was the practice in the New Orleans convent that held the manuscript. The more difficult *récits* must have been sung by the most experienced sisters, whilst the novices formed the semi-chorus.[16]

Unfortunately, little is known about how the Ursulines used the manuscript. Considering their work as teachers and the popularity of the Easter retreat and musical celebrations described above, the book would most likely have been valuable for instilling moral values in their pupils and the community, therefore exposing Africans and people of African descent to a vernacular religious repertoire, easier to understand and learn (than Latin).

The expert textual and musical analyses in the opening essays of *French Baroque Music of New Orleans* deserve to be quoted at length for the old performing practices they describe. Discussing the psalm "Tandis que Babylone," Jennifer Gipson writes:

> [It] provides an example of complementarity between music and poetry.... The music, marked *lent* [slow] and punctuated with mournful melismas, reinforces the poetic content of this lament about the impossibility of singing in a strange land. These melismas, which prolong syllables over several notes of mostly stepwise motion, essentially stretch the text to fit the music. But they also highlight a more complex formal problem of contrafacta, that of making the rhythm of the music and the rhythmic conventions of poetry work in tandem.

About the second recitative and air, "L'Avenir," one of the two cantatas included in the *Manuscript*, she notes that "[r]epeated phrases, something Campra [the composer] usually avoided in his own settings of poetry, abound here."[17] Other characteristics of French vocal technique of this period, as described by Andrew Justice, are striking for their similarities to the music of the African Americans:

— ... [t]hroat articulation and *agréments* for ornamented second verses. ... proper execution of syllabic quantity, and inflection of words to communicate meaning and underlying passion.
— ... another approach involved the lengthening of consonants to the point of influencing the length of subsequent vowels and, hence, rhythmic relationships.
— Ornamentation, including vibrato, was to be executed with a high degree of *délicatesse*, so as to perceive the finest nuances of textual articulation....
— Perhaps the one central distinguishing feature of French Baroque performance practice is the concept of *notes inégales*, or the custom of performing certain rhythmic divisions in alternately long and short values, even if they are written as equal. Originating as a method of invigorating passages or diminutions, inequality became a fairly standard expressive feature of French musical language well

into the late eighteenth century.... In modern practice, the aural result is often a kind of swing feel in passages notated as even ... the overall pulse of the music is unchanged when employing inequality.[18]

Of particular interest are the similarities between these French Baroque practices and the characteristics of Black American folk music—and later, jazz. Fertile ground for creolization, these similar practices potentially acted as dynamic points of contact where musical interchanges could spontaneously happen. Points of contact where singers could easily— at times somehow unconsciously—sing their own set of idiomatic embellishments, or rhythmic variations where the melody was already meant to be ornamented, slowly altering it over time and generations. A process that seems to have happened with the Creole's adaptation of the *cantiques*.

THE *CANTIQUES*

In 1955, Elizabeth Brandon completed a PhD in French at Université Laval in Quebec City with a dissertation titled "Moeurs [sic] et langue de la paroisse Vermillon en Louisiane." Brandon collected a body of folk songs and tales, which she used to make a thorough linguistic analysis of Louisiana French. It includes eight religious songs provided by two Black singers (*chanteurs nègres*), except for the last one, in which a group (a family?) heartily joined in. According to her research, these songs were no longer sung, but her informants had sung them in church some forty years earlier. Quoting Saxon's *Gumbo Ya-Ya*, she wrote briefly and not entirely convincingly about these songs having been influenced by Negro spirituals, adding that they were sung in a "plaintive tone and in a minor mode" with, she should have added, a little vibrato and slurred notes.[19] She also suggested that they were made of fragments of old French *cantiques* repeated ad infinitum, an idea supported by further analysis.

In a short two-page article published in the *International Folk Music Journal* in 1962, Oster argued that "[t]he Negro French cantique [sic] "—thirty-two of which he had recorded in 1957—"corresponds roughly to the Protestant Negro spiritual," without saying that one had been influenced by the other.[20] Described as "*cantiques nègres*," they are found among the 320 songs he collected during his field trips in southwest Louisiana in the late 1950s. They were sung by nine informants—six men, two women, and an unidentified group. Nicholas Augustin Panique stands out as the main contributor, providing twenty of the thirty-five *cantiques*. Oster also recorded three *cantiques* during a 1963 interview with one of his 1957 informants, Gilbert Martin, but only one was new.

Unfortunately, neither Oster nor Brandon mentioned the evangelical and educational work done by religious women since the early eighteenth century, in which music played such an important role and from which we can infer that Africans and Afro-Creoles were singing religious music in French long before they would have heard and learned Negro spirituals. Indeed, Oster observed that the *cantiques* are in a language "that approximates to standard French, though with deviations. Many of the songs were originally taught to Negroes by Catholic priests.... The texts have generally been condensed, usually preserving and intensifying the most dramatic elements of a white hymn."[21]

Tombeau, Tombeau Marie-Madeleine

Following his textual analysis of "Tombeau, Tombeau Marie-Madeleine" as sung by Gilbert Martin, which he compared with a nineteenth-century version collected in France by folklorist Achille Millien ("Madeleine au Tombeau"), Oster concluded that "[c]haracteristically" only the "most dramatic" lines of the song had been retained and "telescoped into fewer words ... repeated several times [in a way that] embodied subtle and complex rhythmic phrasing, in a style which is African in origin." Nevertheless, the shape and guiding tones of both melodies are very similar. (See appendix 3.)[22] Worth noticing is Martin's self-accompaniment with foot tapping, which we can hear only faintly but which clearly establishes the rhythmical drive to his simple rendition of the melody, adding only a few slurs. In the 1963 interview with Martin, Oster asked about the performance practices in the church where Martin seems to have been a cantor. "I'd be the leader and they'd answer ... or sometimes we sing everything all together." (The whole congregation or a group of singers?) Hand clapping or shouting were heard only "once in a while," because the congregation was normally "very quiet" during the performance.[23] Nonetheless, this body percussion is reminiscent of the distinctive practice of foot stomping and hand clapping of the religious-rooted Juré songs—the "unaccompanied black French and English Creole shouts and ring dances"—from southwest Louisiana that have been identified as one of the precursors of zydeco.[24]

Nicholas Augustin Panique's version is rather interesting, for it cleverly merges two (maybe three) *cantiques*, "Tombeau, Tombeau, Marie-Madeleine" and "Je M'en Vais Finir Mes Jours Avec la Madeleine," also sung by Martin.[25] Millien himself included two different versions of the melody and four variants of the lyrics (of Madeleine au Tombeau). The comments from composer and violinist Jean-Grégoire Pénavaire, who notated the melodies (for Millien), are striking for their resemblance to the observations often made about the challenge of writing African American melodies. He mentioned the difficulty of fitting them in a regular meter, and of the harder task of notating the subtleties of interpretations such as "color, timbre, and ornaments (*la manière*) of some old rural singers (*vieux chanteurs campagnards*)," which he described as a "mix of small notes, *grupetti* more or less quick, portamento (*ports de voix*) with *crescendo* or *diminuendo*, tremolos (*sons tremblés*), long fermatas etc."[26] In his own way, Panique could also be described as an "old rural singer," and his renditions also make use of various accents, vibratos, diminuendo, and rhythmic variations.

Dans un Jardin Solitaire

"Dans un Jardin Solitaire"[27] properly illustrates both Brandon's and Oster's arguments. It is an adaptation of the *cantique* "Au Sang qu'un Dieu Va Répandre," whose text, composed by Sulpician François Salignac de La Mothe-Fénelon (1651–1715), was fitted to a popular eighteenth-century melody, like the spiritual parodies discussed above. The melody, "Que ne Suis-Je la Fougère," was published in 1811 in *La Clé du Caveau*, a collection of hundreds of *airs* designed for general use. (See appendix 4.)[28]

Performed by Panique, it is truly a lament sung in the Aeolian mode, as the seventh tone is not raised as in the original melody, which he also ornamented with expressive voice inflections and vibratos, and is modified with the insertions of a few 2/4 bars in the 3/4 meter and syncopated accentuation. The overall structure is organized but flexible, as opposed to the strict AABA melodic organization of the original. Nonetheless, Panique's interpretation remains strikingly similar to "Que ne Suis-Je la Fougère"/"Au Sang qu'un Dieu Va Répandre." The second of the two recordings starts with, and is punctuated by, Panique's proud recitation of one of the "*prières de Dieu*" (God's prayers) in Latin. This may be what Oster described as "excerpts from the mass [sic] in folk form," for it might hint at one of the ways *cantiques* were performed in church, the priest reciting the prayer and the congregation singing in response.[29]

Fénelon's hymn was very long, and the text collected by Oster had been considerably shortened; it is also more repetitive, and a refrain and new title have been introduced using the only verse retained from the original, *Dans un jardin solitaire*. The rest of the lyrics refer to themes developed by Fénelon: God's (Jesus's) suffering in the garden (of Gethsemane), Judas's betrayal, the

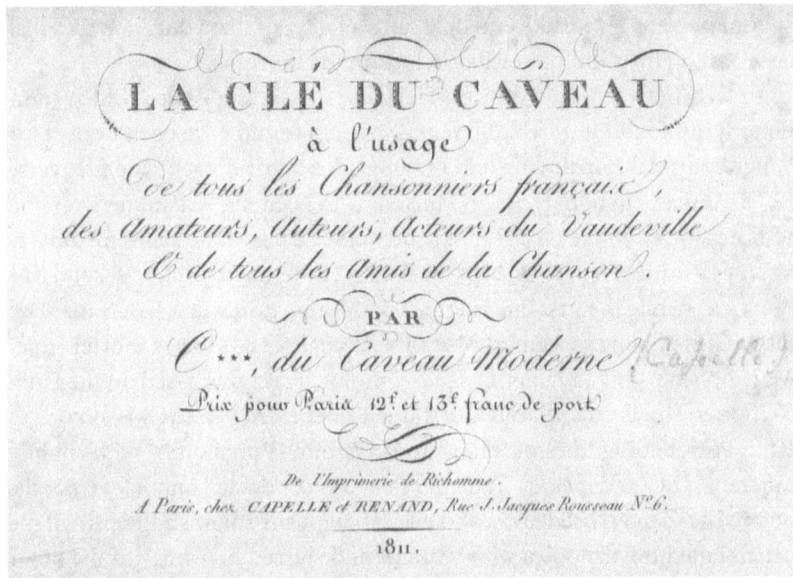

3.2. Cover page of *La Clé du Caveau* (Paris: Capelle et Renard, 1811).

judgment, and the Crucifixion, except for the most curious lines, "*Au berceau, j'ai perdu ma mère / mon père*" (In the cradle, I lost my mother / my father), which belonged either to another *cantique* or to a local version, for they fit the melody perfectly. Despite its length, Fénelon's "Au Sang qu'un Dieu Va Répandre," seems to have been a popular *cantique*, for it appears in various *Recueils* in France and in Quebec and could have come to New Orleans with any of the early missionary priests or Ursuline nuns. A textual analysis of four of Oster's *cantiques* related to Marie-Madeleine was conducted by André Prévos, who demonstrated their relationship with *cantiques* found in France, although he mentioned Nicholas Spitzer's assessment that "priests who were in charge of Black churches in Louisiana were mostly from Canada, the North [of the US], or Ireland," of which Canada stands as the most plausible for sending French-speaking priests.[30]

Marie-Madeleine, Laisse-Moi Passer

Practically all the *cantiques* of the Oster collection were recorded by men (only four were sung by women), which reflects the tradition of the male-dominated Catholic Church to allow only men as cantors and choir members. However, Alice Zeno, who went to church at St. Augustine, also remembered having sung *cantiques* both at church—though not during the service—and at home, where, for instance, people sang "plenty" of them during wakes that lasted all night, until four or five o'clock in the morning.[31]

Indeed, her version of "Marie-Madeleine, Laisse-Moi Passer," which combines lyrics found in three different *cantiques*, would have been perfect for a nightlong wake of singing and praying. (See appendix 5.)[32] The first verse (A) is similar—in both lyrics and melody—to Nicholas A. Panique's version of the same *cantique* (A). Her second verse (B) uses the same melody as Panique's third verse (C), except for the first note, and the same second line of lyrics—while the first line is found in "Marie, Je Souviens Ti"/"Enfant de Jésus-Christ," sung by Gilbert Martin. Although Zeno's line is shorter (than Martin's) and sung in major instead of minor, it remains based on the I and V chords. Finally, the repeated first line of her third verse (C) is similar to Panique's opening lines of "Dans un Brigatoire (Purgatoire)" with slightly different lyrics and melody. The interview was conducted only a few months before Ms. Zeno passed away, and even though she sounds a little tired, she ornamented the melodies with vibratos and slurred notes, as did the other singers. All four *cantiques* were recorded over a relatively short period of time: Zeno in 1960, Panique in 1958, and Martin in 1963. More than twenty years later, in 1976, Nicholas Spitzer recorded yet another version of "Marie-Madeleine, Laissez-Moi Passer" sung by Creole singer Inez Catalon, who used material found in both Zeno's and Panique's versions. Born ca. 1913–18, Catalon lived all her life in Kaplan, Louisiana, where she learned many songs in French from her mother. Catalon's lyrics of verse A are the same as Zeno's and Panique's, but set to a different melody. The lyrics of her verse B—also the same as Zeno's , but different than Panique's—are sung on a melody whose first half ("Je suis l'enfant de Jésus-Christ") is the same as Panique's beginning of his verse B and C ("Là-bas, là-haut, dessus ces montagnes" and "Tout en écrit, tout en compris").[33]

Grand Dieu du Ciel/Paradis l'Aura

Found in Brandon's collection, "Grand Dieu du Ciel/Paradis l'Aura," also performed by a woman, Célestine Morton, is notable for the simplicity and flexibility of its formal organization. The lyrics consist of only two verses (1 and 2), each set on a specific melodic line (A and B). However, while verse 1 is sung only over line A, verse 2 is sung on both melodic lines—with slight variations in the words, notes, or rhythmic cells. (See appendix 6.) Morton's rendition is clearly divided into two sections marked by a modulation, which appears to be voluntary, in which the order of the verses is variable, going from 1-2-2-2 to 2-2-1-2. Finally, the rhythmical drive is sustained by the inclusion of a bar in 3/4 at the end of line B and syncopated figures. The second verse also appears, in yet another variation, as the third and final verse of Gilbert Martin's "La Vierge Marie/Paradis l'Aura," which itself might have been formed by the assemblage of verses from diverse provenance, for each of the three sections has a distinct lyrical and melodic content.[34]

Another version—or at least a fragment—of "Grand Dieu du Ciel" was recorded as late as 1976 by Mary Louise Wilson, whose PhD dissertation argued for the preservation of Louisiana-French folk music as a state cultural heritage. It was sung by Mrs. Irma Landry from Lake Charles in southwest Louisiana, who "vaguely remembered" the lyrics, although she recalled her grandmother singing the lines for the children to repeat after her. She also remembered that "many times one 'side' of the house would answer the other side or at other times a single singer would be repeated by the whole group engaged in singing."[35]

Due to their small numbers and the time when they were recorded, the *cantiques* that survived provide only a glimpse of what they might have sounded like when regularly sung by whole communities of Afro-French Catholics. Oster, who not only heard and analyzed the *cantiques* but also saw them performed, nicely summed up his observations:

> The melodies are for the most part modal and regular in structure, and are performed in a style that shows traces of African or West Indian influence.... The style of performance is sometimes marked by syncopation, and almost always by the singer's ability to make a song a unified whole, instead of (as in much white singing) a series of verses connected in logic but not in rhythmic flow. Thus, the fluid movement of the tune to fit the words, the driving and musically sensitive sweep from verse to verse, the dynamic changes, and even the breathing, make the performance an organic growing thing.[36]

I agree with Oster. In fact, I would describe the *cantiques* themselves as "organic growing thing[s]" for their potential to be merged and adapted as the Creoles crafted their own interpretations of these Catholic songs.

Chapter 4

EUROPEAN MUSIC AND DANCES

The many balls, concerts, operas, and plays that punctuated New Orleans's entertainment season provided plenty of opportunities for the free and enslaved People of Color to be in contact with European music. As mentioned before, the Creoles viewed the appreciation of French culture as a form of refinement, so they enjoyed it not only as spectators but also as musicians and composers and, while in the military, serving as both valiant soldiers and musicians.

BALLS AND DANCE MUSIC

Balls were a significant part of the social life and the most popular entertainment for all classes before and after the Civil War, providing work for many musicians. In her memoir, Laura Locoul Gore (1861–1963), the last owner of the (White) Creole plantation named after her, recounted her first ball as a debutante in 1882 and how it marked the beginning of the season. "The rest of the winter was a round of countless balls, dinners and luncheons until Carnival [and Mardi Gras] came and ended it for a while."[1]

The popularity of Carnival and balls is not surprising, considering that from the early days of the colony, the *jours gras* were already celebrated in quite an elaborate fashion. Marc-Antoine Caillot, a clerk with the Company of the Indies, described the three days (and nights) he spent dancing and partying at the end of February 1730. On Sunday before Mardi Gras (*dimanche gras*), he and some friends "spent not only an evening but the whole night too, singing and dancing." The following day, Lundi Gras, he and ten friends put on costumes to form a party of maskers (*partie de masque*). "Some were in red clothing, as Amazons, others in clothes trimmed with braid, others as women. As for myself, I was dressed as a shepherdess in white. . . . I had my husband, who was the Marquis de Carnival."[2]

Accompanied by a violin and an oboe, they made their way up to a wedding party at Bayou St. John, where the ball lasted till four in the morning.

As the revelers were accompanied by a postilion, and eight enslaved men carrying flambeaux to light their way, these early celebrations surely allowed the enslaved to hear, if not actually see, European music and dances. On Mardi Gras, Caillot, his friends, and the musicians went back to the bayou to continue the party. They brought with them four dozen bottles of wine, and when they arrived,

> our instruments and the others got everything going again. . . . Monsieur de Périer, who had heard some talk about our previous night's masquerade, came and paid us the honor of tasting the wine, danced two minuets, and then left. I danced a *passepied* with Mademoiselle Carrière. . . . We left around five thirty in the morning, lamenting the end of the Carnival season [*les jours gras*].[3]

In 1854, historian Charles Gayarré wrote about the Marquis de Vaudreuil, governor from 1742 to 1753, being "fondly remembered [and that] long after he had departed, old people were fond of talking of the exquisitely refined manners, the magnificent balls, . . . and many other unparalleled things they had seen in the days of the *Great Marquis*." By then, there was even a "well known dancing master of New Orleans, named Baby," whose presence indicates the seriousness with which dancing was taken toward the end of the French regime.[4]

As historian Henry A. Kmen has noted, "[i]t is difficult to pinpoint the exact time when the public ballrooms began," but the first ballroom (*Salle de Bal*) opened on Condé Street (now Chartres Street) on October 4, 1792. By the beginning of the nineteenth century, concerts and plays were generally followed by evening balls often held in the same location, the same musicians most likely performing for both events. The Théâtre d'Orléans, rebuilt in 1819, had both a main hall for plays, operas, and concerts and a dance hall.[5] John Baron also tells about a "Créole comedy in two acts, with songs" performed in 1808, in which the author "played the role of Joseph, a negre [*sic*] cultivateur, and between acts there was a musical intermède by the orchestra." The piece was presented at the Théâtre de la Gaîté, which was "possibl[y] . . . a theater especially for Creoles of color."[6]

Balls, masked or not, were held practically every day of the week, and on Sundays, "[t]he French people generally came to the place of worship, arrayed in their ball-dresses [*sic*], and went directly from worship to the ball."[7] There were various kinds of private, semiprivate (on subscription), and public (admission-charging) balls, for Whites or African Americans, that would theoretically not authorize racially mixed participation with the exception of the Quadroon balls open only to Quadroon women and White men.[8] Enslaved people were generally forbidden to attend balls unless they had a permit from their masters. However, "[b]y 1781 under Spanish rule, the attorney general warned the City Commission of problems arising from 'a great number of free negroes and slaves who, with the pretext of Carnival season, mask and mix in bands passing through the streets looking for the dance-halls.'"[9]

Indeed, masked balls allowed for the participation of people from different social classes and races—masks, and clothing, especially for women, being the means by which this could happen. White women did go to Quadroon balls, and enslaved people attended "colored balls" (as they were then called) without permits. So-called "tricolor balls" were also held; in 1855, the Globe Ballroom, where "mixed dances had until then taken place," was closed by the police.[10]

Not surprisingly, "Negro musicians ... supplied much of the music at the quadroon balls.... And [they] also played for many white balls as well, from private parties to subscription dances." Described interchangeably by Kmen and some of his sources as "negro" or "colored," many of these musicians were most likely Creoles. Indeed, Cable specified that musicians playing at the Quadroon balls were "free male quadroon[s]."[11] Moreover, Baron noted that among the refugees from Saint-Domingue were "many African slaves ... well trained in European instruments [and] some white or mulatto plantation owners ... arriving ... without wealth and position, became professional musicians." As dance promoters aimed at offering the latest music in provenance from the North (of the United States) or from Europe to remain competitive, new pieces were "immediately purchased and played." To keep up with the novelty and variety of the many dances—the minuets, waltzes, cotillions, polkas, mazurkas, schottisches, and the much-loved quadrille—musicians surely needed a high level of musical literacy and proficiency.[12]

Dance music was also played at home, arranged for the piano. Through her analysis of the *Maxwell Sheet Music Collection*, most likely assembled between the end of the 1840s until the 1890s, Mathilde Zagala has identified a significant number of European popular dances that included waltzes, polkas, schottisches, lancers, quadrilles, galops, and mazurkas, as well as marches and military music (discussed below.) This particular collection seems to have belonged mostly to young women of the high society, both Francophone and Anglophone; but as she rightfully points out, "this collection gives a broad overview of the music played in New Orleans's parlors during the second half of the nineteenth century."[13] European dances remained in vogue until the beginning of the twentieth century, with the quadrille ever present and popular. Alice Zeno (born in 1864) recalled the dances of her youth where there were polkas, schottisches, mazurkas, quadrilles, and waltzes. "Because, before the quadrille time, you know—they'd give about two, three quadrilles a night—but before the quadrille come, they play a waltz, you'd have to waltz all around the hall."[14] By then, a lot of musicians, including early jazz musicians, played in dance bands, as they were in high demand around the city.

CLASSICAL MUSIC AND COMPOSERS

According to Baron, the quantity and quality of performances in the nineteenth century, which started to feature "world-class stars" as guest performers, as well as the arrival of many musicians from Europe and Havana, transformed New Orleans into a musical metropolis like no other in the United States at the time. But the audience had to sit in segregated sections. The French Opera House, a cultural and musical landmark of New Orleans that opened in 1859, had its fourth tier of seats reserved for "negroes" until 1874–75, when its administration yielded to the pressure of the White League to exclude African Americans altogether. In 1807, an advertisement for the Nouveau Theatre specified that "Free persons of color who desire to attend are advised that the gallery, in which they usually come . . . no slaves can be admitted there. There is a special place for domestics."[15]

Nonetheless, James M. Trotter discussed a concert given on October 14, 1877, as an example of concerts "frequently given in New Orleans," where the ensemble was formed by twenty instrumentalists, "all colored men," who played a varied program of operatic overtures and other classical pieces in front of an enthusiastic mixed audience. This initiative had been preceded by the *Société Philharmonique*, founded by Creoles of Color in the late 1830s, which eventually comprised more than a hundred musicians before the Civil War. The *Société* organized concerts and performances by local and invited artists—which sometimes provided opportunities for Black and White musicians to play together—and hired teachers to offer free lessons to talented students.[16]

Prominent Black and Creole composers such as Edmond Dédé (1827–1903), Lucien Lambert (1828 or 1829–1896), Louis Moreau Gottschalk (a White Creole, 1829–1869), Samuel Snaër (ca. 1832–ca. 1880), Sidney Lambert (ca. 1838–ca. 1900), and Basile Barès (1845–1902), among others, also contributed to the emergence of this rich music scene. Basile Barès stands out, for not only was he born into slavery—he belonged to a piano and music store owner—but one of his compositions, "Grande Polka des Chasseurs a Pied de la Louisiane," was published in New Orleans in 1860 while he was still enslaved. Generally speaking, Barès's music stays close to the Western musical tradition. However, the artful and elegant "Los Campanillas" (no date) is worth noticing for the habanera rhythm used in the left hand, a feature that had already appeared in the work of Louis Moreau Gottschalk.[17]

Gottschalk, arguably the most important American pianist and composer of the nineteenth century, was born in New Orleans in 1829 in a White Creole family—his mother was of French ancestry, refugee from Saint-Domingue, and his father, born in London, was a German Jew who had come to New Orleans in the early 1820s. Showing musical ability at a young age, he started to take lessons with St. Louis Cathedral's organist and choirmaster at age five. He traveled to Paris at age twelve to further his musical education, and in 1845, gave a successful recital, after which his talent was praised by the famous composer Frédéric Chopin. He made his formal professional debut in 1849, in a concert that included some of his Creole compositions that were to be part of the *Louisiana Quartet* (ca. 1846–1851): "Bamboula: Danse des Nègres," which opens with a few bars of "Quan Patate La Cuite"; "La Savane," based on "Pauv' Piti Mam'zelle Zizi" (also called "Lolotte, pov' piti Lolotte"); "Le Bananier: Chanson Nègre," based on the march "En Avant Grenadiers" (more below); and finally "Le Mancenillier," whose themes were borrowed from three different songs, "Chanson de Lizette," "Ou Som Somroucou," and "Ma mourri"/"Tant sirop est doux." Since Gottschalk's maternal grandmother and her enslaved nurse had been refugees from Saint-Domingue, the family seems to have had an intimate knowledge and appreciation of Creole songs—which young Moreau may have seen performed, if the family was among those enjoying strolling along Congo Square during the Sunday gatherings. In 1902, his sister Clara Gottschalk Peterson published a short compilation of Creole songs, specifying that she notated the melodies from memory and that they "ha[d] served to rock whole generations of Southern children," as Ms. Arguedas also recalled. (See chapter 1.)[18]

As noted by Zagala, Gottschalk's "The Banjo," published in 1855, contains four elements now considered characteristic of ragtime and jazz: the "oom-pah" pattern with the left hand alternating between a bass note, or octave, on the beat, and a chord on the offbeat of a 2/4 bar, a polyrhythmic formula of three over four, the tresillo, and the accentuation of the last offbeat of a group of two bars, motifs that are all "particularly rare in the published music of this time. Moreover: they are all simultaneous. Furthermore, this passage appears four times during the piece. The four bars containing them are immediately repeated, then the group of eight bars thus created is heard again at the return of the theme, just as in ragtime."[19] Zagala hypothesizes that "The

Banjo," would be Gottschalk's adaptation for the piano of the clawhammer technique of banjo-playing in which the fingers hit the strings downward with the back of the nails on the beat, but for the thumb marking the offbeat on the short drone (fifth) string.[20]

Still today, Gottschalk remains a well-respected figure. In an interview conducted by Nicholas Spitzer in 1998, Allen Toussaint (1938–2015), pianist, singer, songwriter, arranger, and record producer—as well as "beloved Creole gentleman . . . hometown hero and giant on the American music scene"—said this about Gottschalk:

> I *love* Gottschalk and, hum, the origin of his pieces of course. His interest in, in what the slaves were doing out in those houses late at night was really interesting, and he captured some of those things like in his piece "Banjo." . . . I think I love what he loved. . . . He was in love with that music and he brought it across, not only the basic theme of the songs, but his articulation of how it should go, and it's all documented. I just think he was, he is one of the finest servants to [*sic*] music has ever had.[21]

In his analysis of the *Louisiana Quartet*, Frederick Starr refers to the "artistic metamorphosis," an expression used by another Gottschalk scholar, to characterize the composer's adaptation and transformation of these Creole melodies. I like this expression. I think it well describes Gottschalk's reshaping of the songs as a deliberate and well-thought-out process located at the end of a creolization continuum stretching between a somehow involuntary and spontaneous creation at one end (see the section about the Ursuline Manuscript in chapter 3), and a crafted adaptation at the other end.

The *Louisiana Quartet*, along with other pieces such as "Réponds-moi (Dí que sí) (1859)," "Ojos Criollos (Les Yeux Créoles): Danse Cubaine" (1859) (with its left-hand accompaniment based on the habanera rhythmic cell), and "Pasquinade" (1869) (which features a syncopated rhythm supporting fast melodic lines), are now generally recognized as early precursors of ragtime—and by extension, early jazz—decades before the publication of Scott Joplin's "Maple Leaf Rag" (1899) or Jelly Roll Morton's use of Caribbean and Afro-Latin rhythms, which he described as the "Spanish tinge." (See chapter 5.)[22] Music historian Jack Stewart has proposed an "unbroken line" of pianist-composer-arrangers making the link between Louis Moreau Gottschalk and Jelly Roll Morton. Among many "competent and innovative pianists" (now largely unknown) were Laurent Dubuclet (1866–1909), "part of a wealthy Creole-of-color cultural elite" (also "one of the three early saxophonists in New

Orleans"); Henri Wehrmann (1870–1956), whose French mother and German father had immigrated in New Orleans in 1849, and were now "a part of Creole life in the Vieux Carré"; Paul Sarebresole (1875–1911), second-generation immigrant from France on his father's side and Irish on his mother's side; and the Verges brothers, Al (Alphonse, 1874–1924) and Joe (Joseph, 1882–1964), second-generation French immigrants. They all composed works (marches, rags, or songs) that included some form of polyrhythms, syncopations, or the three-over-four rhythmic unit.[23]

MILITARY MUSIC

As early as the 1720s, the center of New Orleans was occupied by the *Place d'Armes* (the parade ground, now Jackson Square), which was used for military exercises and official ceremonies, and by 1727, two musicians were identified among the city's residents: fife player Charles Doré and drummer Jean-Philippe Laprerie.[24] Although we don't know more about these musicians, the instruments they played were featured in the 1734 procession in honor of the Ursulines' relocation to their newly built convent:

> At five o'clock in the evening, we rang our two bells as a signal. Immediately, according to the order of Monsieur de Bienville, the Governor of Louisiana, the troops, both Swiss and French, began to march and drew up in order on both sides of our former house.... the procession began to march . . . The troops, drawn up on both sides of the street, marched in perfect order, single file, . . . The drums and fifes accompanied the songs and made agreeable harmony.[25]

During the transfer of power to Spain in 1769, (Spanish) Governor Alejandro O'Reilly "attended by his staff . . . crossed the Square of the church [most likely the *Place d'Armes* in front of St. Louis Cathedral], marching to the music of hundreds of instruments." According to Baron, Spanish military music was "impressive," citing as an example a collection of such music that was "set for two clarinets, two fifes and drums, or voice and piano, or male chorus, or four-voice choir."[26] While we can surmise that African Americans were part of the crowd present at these processions, we don't know much about the musicians themselves (although there were a large number of drummers and fifers in the city) and even less whether some were of African descent, even if some of them served in the military (see the section about the Free People of Color in chapter 1).

The War of 1812 and the Civil War

Hundreds of Free Men of Color fought in the Battle of New Orleans (December 1814 to January 1815), divided into two battalions. The first was composed mostly of volunteers coming from New Orleans and its surrounding area, and the second was composed mostly of men previously from Saint-Domingue. The First Battalion also had a small band of eight or nine musicians to provide music on and off the battlefield, drums and fife being the instruments needed for battlefield operations. The names of the musicians serving the company are evocative of their Creole ancestry: senior musicians were Louis Hazeur, Barthelemi Campanell, and Etienne Larrieu, and the bandsmen were Elie Beroche, Celestin Bizot, Louis Chariot, Michel Debergue, Raymond Gaillard, Emelian Larrieu, Emile Tremé, and Felix Tremé. Having reviewed the availability of various instruments, as well as military custom, Charles E. Kinzer suggests that the band was composed of pairs of oboes, clarinets, French horns, and bassoons (or four clarinets and no oboes) and that it performed for parades and ceremonial duties but also for the "officers' meals, parties, or dances," during which some musicians might have switched to string instruments, "converting the parade band into an orchestra."[27]

"En Avant Grenadiers," a battle cry sung by the battalions of Free Men of Color, is said to have come from Saint-Domingue, where it was composed during the revolution against France. Although Maud Cuney Hare doesn't cite her source, this assertion is plausible, for the lyrics are in Creole, and almost all the Free Men of Color in the Second Battalion were originally from Saint-Domingue. According to Mary Ellison, "En Avant Grenadiers" was also sung during the Civil War by the Native Guards, who later became the *Corps d'Afrique*. She provides only the English lyrics, but many officers and soldiers, such as Major Francis E. Dumas and Captains André Cailloux and Caesar Carpentier Antoine, were French-speaking Creoles of Color.[28] Few commemorative songs have also been preserved. In "Creole Slave Songs," Cable presents what looks like the last verse of a narrative song about the battle of Chalmette (during the Battle of New Orleans), from the point of view of an enslaved man who chose to go back to the plantation rather than being killed:

The singer ends thus:

Fizi z'Anglé yé fé bim! bim!	The English muskets went bim! bim!
Carabin Kaintock yé fé zim! zim!	Kentucky rifles went zim! zim!
Mo di' moin, sauvé to la peau!	I said to myself, save your skin!
Mo zété corps au bord do l'eau;	I scampered along the water's edge;

Quand mo rivé li té fé clair.	When I got back it was day-break [*sic*].
Madam' li prend' ein coup d'colère;	Mistress flew into a passion;
Li fé donn' moin ein quat' piquié,	She had me whipped at the "four stakes,"
Passequé mo pas sivi mouchié;	Because I didn't stay with master;
Mais moin, mo vo mié quat' piquié,	But the "four stakes" for me is better than
Passé ein coup d'fizi z'Anglé!	A musket shot from an Englishman.[29]

This is followed by a song related to Admiral David G. Farragut's 1862 victory that led to New Orleans's occupation under General Benjamin F. Butler. Unfortunately, he included only the refrain of this "long and silly" story, adding neither the title nor his source.

An-hé!	An-hey!
Qui ça qui rivé?	Who arrived?
C'est Farraguitt et p'i Botclair,	It's Farragut, and then Butler,
Qui rivé.	Who arrived.[30]

After the Civil War, brass bands composed predominantly of Creoles "who were generally musically literate, and otherwise fluent in Eurocentric methods" grew in number and visibility. From the 1870s, Kelly's Band, the St. Bernard Brass Band, the Excelsior Brass Band (active from 1879 to 1931), and the Onward Brass Band (ca. 1886 to 1930)—and many others that soon followed—played an active part in the quality and diversity of the New Orleans music scene, performing for parades, dances, concerts, and other social functions. As noted above, military music and marches were also played at home, arranged for the piano.[31]

Part II

Early Jazz

Chapter 5

EARLY JAZZ CREOLE MUSICIANS

Given all the music that was made in antebellum New Orleans and surrounding areas in which Creoles of Color took an active part, they could hardly have failed to have a significant role in the development of jazz. Music was part of the social life of communities in urban and rural areas alike. There were plenty of employment opportunities for musicians who were hired for dances, parades, weddings and funerals, lawn parties, fish fries, political rallies, sports events, and so on. According to Louis Armstrong's biographer, Thomas Brothers:

> The Creoles who dominated the music profession during Armstrong's youth were not the land-holding, well-educated artists and intellectuals ... of the early nineteenth century. Most of the Creoles Armstrong knew had only a fifth-grade education. They may best be described as belonging to an artisan class. Many worked in trades that had been associated with the *gens de couleur libres*. . . . Isidore Barbarin was a plasterer, Alphonse Picou and Manuel Perez were tinsmiths. Perez, George Fihle, and Barney Bigard rolled cigars. . . . Music fit right in with this artisan-class position.[1]

Having inherited a long tradition of music-making, Creole musicians were known for their discipline and skill. They had often been classically trained in solfège, sight-reading, theory, and instrumental technique, so that they played/read written arrangements from a score—stock arrangements—whereas most of the uptown Black musicians played a more improvised style of music, usually by ear, with head arrangements learned by ear and/or played by memory. This distinction is obviously a simplification of a more complex reality, as some Creoles played by ear and/or improvised, and some Blacks learned to read music.[2] Creole Albert Nicholas learned to read from fellow Creole Barney Bigard in exchange for teaching him how to "fake" (improvise) on the clarinet; Louis Armstrong learned to read music while working with Fate Marable on a riverboat up the Mississippi River;

and Baby Dodds, a drummer from uptown, learned to read as a child.³ The meeting of the two groups of musicians—the Creoles from downtown and the Blacks from uptown, both bringing their own musical cultures—was an important triggering factor in the birth of jazz. On the ground, this musical encounter was the result of a slow process in which social class, age, and musical taste played a role, more than the rise of segregation and Jim Crow laws (which would have forcefully pushed the two groups toward each other) as has been argued for a long time. For instance, Baby Dodds once told the story of having a Creole friend even if, when

> someone moved in [uptown] who did talk it [Creole], your mother kept you away from those people. . . . Anytime we'd be caught playing with any Creole children, "Come in here!" That's the way it was. . . . But in spite of that, I did have a little Creole friend. . . . When we got old enough, we used to go to Francs Amis Hall, but I couldn't get in until he would talk those fellows on the door in Creole.⁴

On the other hand, Natty Dominique remembered that "[Louis] 'Papa' Tio [1862–1922] is the old man . . . never liked jazz at all . . . He'd hear jazz and he'd run in your house. 'Under the bed, let me get under the bed, Listen out there. Those fools, just messing up good music.'" And as Louis R. Tio (Papa's nephew) recalled, "he used to call them the old Creole way *routiniers* [meaning they played without music], . . . he used to say all that time, bunch of *routiniers* see, they don't know what they're doing!"⁵ Nonetheless, as Kinzer noted, "although he was never considered a 'jazz clarinetist,' Louis Tio did eventually become reconciled to the prevalence of the style. As early as 1910, he joined the dance band of pianist Manuel Manetta (1889–1969), which performed syncopated music at nightclubs." As time went on, some younger musicians were attracted by the improvisational music and blues of the uptown Black musicians, most notably Sidney Bechet (1897–1959), who never learned to read music.⁶

By the time it was established, early jazz was characterized by an ensemble composed of a front line of horns—cornet (or trumpet), clarinet, and trombone—creating a polyphonic texture used for collective playing and improvisation supported by a rhythm section—banjo, guitar or sometimes piano, bass, and drums, maintaining a regular and syncopated beat in 4/4 time. (More in chapter 6 in the section "The Revival Recordings of Creole Songs.")

Although there was some tension—the Creoles were still holding on to their middle-class status, musical literacy, and instrumental technique as a way to assert their difference—Black and Creole musicians eventually formed a close-knit community, playing together in various groups. For instance, in New Orleans, Louis Armstrong was once part of Kid Ory's Creole Jazz Band, and in Chicago, Kid Ory took part in Armstrong's Hot Five recording sessions of 1927.

Among the numerous Creole musicians active in New Orleans at the beginning of the twentieth century—some of whom would take part in the revival of the 1940s discussed below—were the Tios, a family of clarinetists and music teachers; Jelly Roll Morton, pianist, composer, arranger, and bandleader considered to be the first jazz composer; Edouard/Edward "Kid" Ory, trombonist, bandleader, and composer; singer Lizzie Miles, one of the first touring and recording blues/jazz singers; and clarinetist and saxophonist Sidney Bechet, who greatly contributed to the development of jazz saxophone and the diffusion of jazz in Europe and the (then) USSR. It is worth noting that they all spoke French, at least in their youth, even though at the time, French culture and the use of the French language—banned as an official language in the 1868 Constitution—were declining in Louisiana. (See chapter 1, note 47.)[7]

The slow disappearance of French culture started as segregation was on the rise in the decades that followed the post–Civil War Reconstruction period, which lasted until 1877. Slowly but surely, the Creoles' cultural identity was forcibly redefined as Black American in a world where White supremacists were fighting hard, and succeeding, to disenfranchise Black people—an intercultural phenomenon that affected all strata of the population, for better or for worse. The loss of their language, middle-class status, and privileges prompted the Creoles of Color to maintain high standards of respectability and education that gave the word *Creole* an aura of sophistication. This could explain why, by the early jazz age, the word *Creole* had become a free-floating signifier rather than the marker of a cultural identity, as sophistication and education were certainly attributes that musicians, whether Creole or not, would have wanted to project to make it in the music business.[8]

However, the use of *Creole* as a free-floating signifier and the common description of Kid Ory's Creole Jazz Band as the first African American/Black band to record jazz—which is not quite exact (see below)—have created confusion around the Creoles as a distinct cultural community, even if some of the musicians enumerated above are well known. Therefore, a book about the Creoles' contribution to early jazz would be incomplete without a short review of their respective careers and contributions.[9]

THE TIO FAMILY

The Tios are a particularly interesting family that produced four generations of influential clarinetists and teachers. Their history goes back to the War of 1812, through the Civil War and the famous dance bands of the late nineteenth century, to the birth of jazz, with their influence also being felt to some extent on the Duke Ellington Orchestra.[10] Their long involvement in the music business—and so the wide variety of the music they played—combined with a strong practice of home music-making that included many members of the family, offers a tangible example of creolization as a creative process, happening slowly, on a day-to-day basis, year after year. For instance, Louis R. Tio (born ca. 1895) specified that his great-aunt (Antoinette Tio) played guitar, one of his aunts played guitar, and two of his sisters played both piano and guitar. Louis also remembered playing popular numbers at home with his brother Lorenzo Jr. (discussed below) on clarinet, his sister on piano, and himself on guitar. This was a "house of music all the time."[11]

The Tios were of French Canadian, French, Spanish, and African ancestry and were among the first families of Free People of Color of Louisiana. François Marie Joseph Hazeur (1709–1758) was born in Quebec and served in the colonial troops on the Gulf Coast during the 1730s and 1740s before retiring and marrying in *Louisiane*. Marcos Tio (1755–1823) was born in Catalonia and arrived in Spanish New Orleans "sometime before 1787."[12] Both families became well established in the colony as soldiers, businessmen, or planters.

According to Kinzer, the first professional musician of the family was Louis Hazeur (ca. 1792–1860, grandson of François Marie Joseph Hazeur), who enrolled in the First Battalion of Free Men of Color of Louisiana during the War of 1812 (see chapter 4), where he became one of the three senior musicians in the small regiment band. Hazeur became the father-in-law of his nephew Thomas Tio (1828–ca. 1881) when his daughter Marguerite Athenaïs Hazeur (1830–1903) married her cousin (Thomas), the son of Louis's sister Mathilde Hazeur (d. 1877). Thomas was a clarinetist and saxophonist, as well as a cigar maker, and probably played for musicales, concerts, dance orchestras, theaters, and marching bands. Kinzer adds that the impetus for a musical education most likely came from the Hazeur side of the family:

> his mother [Mathilde Hazeur] and aunt, Antoinette Hazeur Doublet may have had some musical training as well. . . . There is no evidence of any prior musical activity on the paternal sides of either of these families. Some amount of musical training was probably a family tradition on the Hazeur plantation, and whether [Mathilde and

Antoinette Hazeur] were well versed or not, each must have encouraged, if not initiated, the musical training of their children.[13]

Two of Thomas's sons, Louis "Papa" (1862–1922) and Lorenzo Sr. (1867–1908), became professional musicians. They both were born in Mexico, where the family lived from 1860 to 1877.[14] Following the Creole tradition, they received a formal music education and moved on to quite similar careers as musicians, arrangers, and music teachers. They both became renowned clarinetists, but Louis also played the bassoon and the oboe, and Lorenzo also played the saxophone and the bassoon. They played for minstrel shows, dance bands, and influential brass bands. Both were members of the Excelsior Brass Band, and Louis also joined the Onward Brass Band and, on a few occasions, the John Robichaux Orchestra. Lorenzo's early death in 1908 prevented him from getting much involved in the birth of jazz, but as mentioned

5.1. Lorenzo Tio Sr., Photograph dated 1894, Hogan Jazz Archive Photography Collection, PH004098. Tulane University Special Collections, Tulane University, New Orleans, LA.

above, Louis did adapt his style to the new syncopated music when playing with Manuel Manetta's dance band, from 1910 to 1913, that included ragtime arrangements in its repertoire.[15] Although never considered a jazz clarinetist, he taught future jazz players such as Achille and George Baquet, Barney Bigard, and Albert Nicholas.

A talented musician—his brother Louis said he could play all the reed instruments—Lorenzo Tio Jr. (1893–1933) followed in the footsteps of his father and uncle, eventually becoming "the leading clarinetist on the New Orleans music scene." He started his professional career after his father's death in 1908, playing with the Excelsior Brass Band, the John Robichaux Orchestra—in which he played clarinet and saxophone and "encountered squarely the popular musical styles of ragtime, blues, and their hybrid, jazz"—the Tuxedo Brass Band, and the Onward Brass Band, whose admirers included Sidney Bechet and Louis Armstrong. In the early 1910s, Lorenzo Jr. worked with the Eagle Band. Led by Willie Geary "Bunk" Johnson, the band was mostly composed of Buddy Bolden's former sidemen, nonreading uptown musicians who played improvised "hot" and "ratty" syncopated music. Playing with this group provided Lorenzo Jr. with the proper environment in which to sharpen his improvisational skills.[16]

From 1919 until the band broke up in 1928, Tio played both clarinet and tenor saxophone with violinist Armand Piron's orchestra. "By the mid-1920s, the Piron Orchestra had become the preeminent dance band in New Orleans," while gaining the respect of musicians as a "'cultured' band with abundant capacity to 'jazz it up.'" Their success and reputation led to a series of recordings for the Victor, Columbia, and OKeh labels in New York City in 1923–24, with two additional sides recorded in New Orleans in 1925.

> In general, each of the fifteen recordings . . . constitutes a dance number in the prevailing popular style, containing ragtime and jazz elements . . . In terms of syncopated rhythm, polyphonic texture, and multi-strain form, these numbers are similar to the music recorded by other early jazz groups associated with New Orleans, notably the Original Dixieland Jazz Band (first recorded in 1917) and Joe "King" Oliver's Creole Band (first recorded in 1923). However, perhaps owing to the longtime role of the ensemble as provider of music for social functions of the conservative white upper class, the recordings of the Piron Orchestra include somewhat less improvisation than those of the leading jazz bands of the day. . . . Lorenzo Tio, Jr., seems to have been the only member of the Piron Orchestra to improvise solos on a routine basis.[17]

Along with other Creole musicians such as Freddie Keppard (1890–1933), and Peter Bocage (1887–1967), Tio could read music and improvise. As such, he belonged to the generation that started to bridge the gap between the European-oriented Creole musical tradition that valued fluid instrumental technique, tone quality (clear sound and short vibrato), and music-reading skills with the new syncopated and improvised music. Like his late father and his uncle "Papa" Louis, with whom he sometimes exchanged students, Lorenzo Jr. played a significant role in the transmission of the Creole musical values that influenced a number of young jazz musicians, such as Sidney Bechet (although Bechet always refused to learn music notation), Barney Bigard, Omer Simeon, Albert Nicholas, and Jimmie Noone, to name but a few. Actually, "John Steiner has delineated a stylistic school of clarinet performance emanating from the Tios, and extending via either instruction or imitation through the work of pupils," to which Kinzer adds that Lorenzo Tio Jr.'s "leading role in the transmission of traditional concepts and ideals within a context of the newly popular jazz style itself marks Tio as an influential figure in the development of music in and beyond New Orleans."[18]

Despite his success as a music teacher in New Orleans, Tio moved to New York around 1930, where he concentrated his efforts mostly on performing but also on arranging and composing to supplement his income. At this time, his former student Barney Bigard was a member of the Duke Ellington Orchestra, with whom he is listed as composer of "Mood Indigo." However, in his autobiography, Bigard quietly tells the true story:

> My old teacher, Lorenzo Tio had come to New York and he had a little slip of paper with some tunes and parts of tunes he had written. There was one I liked, and I asked him if I could borrow it. He was trying to interest me in recording one or two maybe. Anyway, I took it home and kept fooling around with it.... I changed some of it around ... and got something together that mostly was my own but partly Tio's.[19]

FERDINAND JOSEPH LAMOTHE/JELLY ROLL MORTON (1885 OR 1890–1941)

Ferdinand Joseph Lamothe (or La Menthe), aka Jelly Roll Morton, is rightfully well known as a talented pianist, arranger, bandleader, and as the first jazz composer.[20] On the 1938 recordings conducted by Alan Lomax for the Library of Congress, he comes out as a fine analyst and theorist of his own music while discussing and demonstrating the various music to which he was exposed as a young Creole in New Orleans—opera and classical music, Mardi Gras Indians songs, Creole and Spanish popular tunes, ragtime, the blues, dance music, and marches.[21] He was also familiar with Black American musical traditions, for not only had he lived both downtown and uptown, but he also recalled going to Lincoln Park or Jackson Hall to hear Buddy Bolden play.[22] Interestingly, if the Tios stand at one end of the continuum of a process happening over decades and generations, Morton exemplifies creolization as experienced over the few decades of the life of a single individual.

In his research notes, Lomax, who places Morton's birth in 1885, wrote that Morton spoke French when he was young. Accordingly, speaking about his maternal grandparents, Morton explained that neither of them spoke "American or English" and claimed that his family had been in New Orleans since long before the Louisiana Purchase, having come directly from France. He didn't say much about his father or mother, who died when he was a teenager, except that his mother had "also married one of the French settlers in New Orleans."[23] However, according to Lawrence Gushee, who placed the birth of Morton in 1890, "it is important to point out that Morton is linked not just to the prewar society of the *gens libres de couleur* [sic] but more specifically to Haiti." Gushee adds that Morton knew and lived with a great-grandmother who would have been "a most influential link to antebellum culture of New Orleans's free colored French-speaking population."[24] Not surprisingly then, Morton recalled that there was "always . . . some kind of a musical instruments [sic] in the house, including guitar, drums, piano, trombone . . . everybody always played for their pleasure. . . . We always had ample time . . . to rehearse our lessons, which was given to anyone that was desirous in accepting lessons."[25]

It is as a composer and arranger that Morton made his most original contribution to jazz. His compositional devices included breaks—that eventually evolved into full solos—riffs, and the "Spanish tinge" that mainly describes Caribbean and Afro-Latin rhythms such as the tresillo and the habanera (see chapter 2), which he used as early as 1902 in his "New Orleans Blues." Morton composed and/or recorded close to twenty songs with a "discernible Spanish tinge," which he himself described as an essential element of jazz.[26] Charles H. Garrett argues that the tinge is found in more than just rhythms. It can also describe the performance of Latin American songs, such as "La Paloma" or "Tia Juana (Tee Wanna)," and the iconography of sheet music as on the cover art of "The 'Jelly Roll' Blues" (1915), where the design itself hinted that the music would "contain a mixture of African American and Latin musical elements."[27]

Looking back on his early days, [Warren "Baby"] Dodds identified what he felt was a distinctive Creole approach to the blues: "In the downtown district where the Creole lived, they played the blues with a Spanish accent. We fellows that lived Uptown [*sic*], we didn't play the Creole numbers like the Frenchmen downtown did—such as *Eh La Bas*. And just as we changed the Spanish accent of the Creole songs, we played the blues different from them. They lived in the French part of town and we lived uptown in the Garden district. Our ideas for the blues were different from theirs. They had the French and Spanish style, blended together." Dodds's position as an uptown outsider is of particular significance here, for he later notes that an interest in Spanish rhythms eventually spread from the Creole district throughout New Orleans.²⁸

Gunther Schuller has suggested that Morton's 1915 arrangement of his "Jelly Roll Blues," in which the tresillo rhythmic cell (see chapter 2) appears in the left-hand accompaniment of the last twelve-bar chorus—after a four-bar intro—was "probably . . . one of the first, if not the first, jazz orchestration ever published."²⁹

5.2. "The 'Jelly Roll' Blues" sheet music, cover art by Starmer (Chicago: Will Rossiter, 1915).

5.3. Last twelve-bar chorus of "The 'Jelly Roll' Blues" (Chicago: Will Rossiter, 1915).

Morton recalled that among the first blues he ever heard was the one played and sung by Mamie Desdunes, whom he heard as a child when visiting his godmother in the Garden District—a neighborhood located in the uptown Anglo-American section of the city. Years later, Morton was playing "Mamie's Blues" which, according to Bruce Raeburn, he "reconstructed from memory after hearing Mamie Desdoumes [sic], an Afro-French pianist, playing the blues with a habanera rhythm. . . . This may have been a singular epiphany for Morton, but it is important to note that this practice was already commonplace in New Orleans when he first heard it."[30] On a larger scale, Morton's "Spanish-tinged" compositions stand as forerunners for Juan Tizol's contribution to the Duke Ellington Orchestra, which he (Tizol) joined in 1929, and the 1950s development of Latin jazz prompted by Dizzy Gillespie's collaboration with various Cuban percussionists, beginning with Chano Pozo in 1949.

As for many other musicians, the economic crisis brought tough times for Morton, who eventually moved to Washington, DC, where he had been offered a residency in a bar. This is where Alan Lomax heard him before interviewing him for the Library of Congress in 1938, giving Morton the opportunity of a last contribution to the music he loved, as a jazz historian. Morton died in Los Angeles in 1941, sadly rather isolated. But I agree with James Lincoln Collier: the "new men" surely listened carefully to Morton and His Red Hot Peppers, because "it seems quite clear . . . that [they] showed Ellington, Henderson, Moten, Basie, Goodman, and the rest a way that jazz could go."[31]

EDOUARD/EDWARD "KID" ORY (1886–1973)

Despite his influential work as trombonist, bandleader, and composer, Edouard/Edward "Kid" Ory has often been overlooked, being generally mentioned for his 1922 recordings and as a sideman for Joe "King" Oliver, Louis Armstrong, and Jelly Roll Morton.[32]

Ory was born in 1886 on the Woodland Plantation, some thirty-one miles (fifty kilometers) northwest of New Orleans. His father was of French and German ancestry—Ory's paternal grandparents were sugar cane planters and slaveowners—and his mother was of Spanish, African, and Native American descent. They were Catholics, and they all spoke French, Ory's first language. Indeed, Ory remembered his mother singing to him in French when he was a child, and neither his father nor his father's cousins spoke English; according to John McCusker, Ory self-identified as a Creole.[33] Nevertheless, since he had one grandparent of African heritage, the one-drop rule made him legally Black. (See chapter 1.)

Ory began his musical career on the plantation, where he formed and led his first band before moving to New Orleans in 1910. Musically speaking, he belonged more to the uptown Anglo-American musicians who played "hot" improvised music by ear than to the musically literate downtown French Creoles. Before moving, Ory and his band had made several trips to the city to hear and learn from the popular bands of the day, such as (Black) Buddy Bolden's and (Creole) John Robichaux's bands. McCusker suggests that Ory, influenced by Robichaux, "smoothed out the rough edges" of Bolden's hot style, thereby contributing to the creative melding of the two styles. Bassist Wellman Braud later recalled that Ory and his band "[took] New Orleans by storm," quickly gaining a popularity that enabled him to cross over the color line and get hired by Creole, Black, and White patrons.[34]

Among his qualities as bandleader, Ory had the ability to discover talented musicians and give them the opportunity to play and develop musically. In 1917, Ory hired cornetist Joe Oliver (later to become "King" Oliver), allowing him to polish his style and talent as a soloist and bandleader before leaving for Chicago the following year. After Oliver's departure, Ory replaced him with a young, unknown cornet player named Louis Armstrong, which enabled the young cornetist to develop as a professional musician. In his autobiography, Armstrong spoke about his debut with Ory:

> What a thrill that was! To think I was considered up to taking Joe Oliver's place in the best band in town! . . . Kid Ory was so nice and kind, and he had so much patience, that first night with them was a pleasure instead of a drag. . . . After that first gig with the Kid I was in. I began to get real popular with the dance fans as well as the musicians. All the musicians came to hear us and they'd hire me to play in their bands on the nights I wasn't engaged by Kid Ory.[35]

During the same time, Ory took part in the development of—and eventually became associated with—the tailgate trombone style, a defining element of early jazz. In this style of playing, the trombone supports the melody by playing countermelodies, generally in the lower register, while providing a "rhythmic upper bass part" occasionally ornamented with glissando or "smear" obtained by extending or retrieving the slide of the trombone while holding a note.[36]

In 1919, Ory and his Creole Jazz Band moved to Los Angeles. During May and June 1922, the band, nicknamed the Sunshine Orchestra, recorded four sides as backup for two singers and two instrumentals, "Ory's Creole Trombone" and "Society Blues."[37] The record appeared with two labels, one covering the other, after the Spikes Brothers, musicians, songwriters, owners of a music store in Los Angeles and producers of the recordings, pasted their Sunshine label over the Nordskog label (founded and owned by Arne A. Nordskog) who owned the studio where the session took place—making it difficult to determine whether the recordings were made in 1921, as previously accepted, or 1922. Of course, there could have been some delay between the recording sessions and the release of the record, considering the time involved in sending the masters to be pressed in New Jersey (Nordskog didn't have pressing equipment) and the label dispute. In any case, it seems that 1922 is more and more accepted and it is under that date that the recordings have been entered in the National Recording Registry of the Library of Congress in 2005. As David Sager points out in his essay accompanying the designation, these recordings were "commonly referred to as the first jazz record by African Americans. Actually it is not [but they are] the first recordings of black/Creole New Orleans jazz, though, due to their loose feel and hot nature, many think of these as the first recognizable jazz performances on record."[38]

The recordings provide a good example of the early jazz style, although the numerous trombone breaks in "Ory's Creole Trombone," which he composed, gave him a more predominant role than usual in the polyphonic setting of this early style (more in chapter 6 in the section "The Revival Recordings of Creole Songs"):

> The trombone is shifted back and forth from lead to countermelody. Its first strain is a "smear" strain and in its third strain are some "breaks" where the soloist [Ory] performs some simple but demanding pyrotechnics. In his various recordings of the piece, Kid Ory added so much of his own wit and charm that it could never be considered a "set piece" to be written down and played the same way each time.[39]

Here, the word *Creole* in the song title can act both as the trendy, market-oriented free-floating signifier discussed above and as a marker of Ory's cultural identity, regardless of the fact that the band was, and still is, often described as a Black or African American band—once again creating confusion and somehow erasing the Creole sociocultural identity.

From 1925 to 1927, Ory lived in Chicago, where he took part in Louis Armstrong's Hot Five seminal recordings that included two of Ory's compositions: "Muskrat Rumble" (now a jazz standard) and "Ory's Creole Trombone." He also recorded with King Oliver's Jazz Band, also called King Oliver and

His Dixie Syncopators, and with Jelly Roll Morton's Red Hot Peppers. In all of these important sessions, we can hear Ory's innovative playing, even though the role of the trombone was to support the main theme or soloist: "I wanted to put some harmony and legato and you know, other stuff in it, mix it up. And [Jelly Roll] told me, 'Don't worry about your music; I can't write your music.'"[40]

In 1928, Ory went back to California, but as for many others, the 1929 economic crash put an end to his musical career, and by the 1930s, he was working as a janitor. A decade later, Ory was slowly working his way back into the music business, as researchers and fans developed an interest in jazz's formative years. In 1944, filmmaker and radio host Orson Welles, a New Orleans jazz fan, asked Marili Morden of the Jazz Man Record Shop (and early manager of T-Bone Walker) to gather a band for his show. She called Ory, and Welles hired him for his radio show, opening the door for Ory to become a major figure of the early jazz revival of the 1940s.[41] Ory retired to Hawaii in 1966 and died in Honolulu in 1973, two years after a last appearance at the Jazz and Heritage Festival in New Orleans.

ELIZABETH MARIE (MARY) LANDREAUX/LIZZIE MILES (1895–1963)

Elizabeth Marie (Mary) Landreaux, known as Lizzie Miles, was a blues and early jazz singer born on Bourbon Street (in the section now named Pauger Street, in the Seventh Ward) in 1895. In *Hot Jazz*, David Griffiths included a summary of letters from Lizzie Miles, with whom he corresponded over several years. According to this compilation, both her parents read and spoke French; they also spoke Creole French, which she described as "broken French." Her paternal grandmother was "an [American] Indian and she spoke French," and her maternal grandmother was from "San Dominique" (Saint-Domingue?). Miles was exposed to music and started to sing at an early age, for she wrote to Griffiths: "I don't guess there's no one who can tell you how that ragtime 'raddy' [sic] music started, because I started singing ragtime when I was five and my mother used to be always singing and there was ragtime then."[42]

Miles's mother sang in public only in her later years, "in old folks concerts and singing old Creole songs." She apparently knew many songs that Miles surely heard plenty of times in her youth but never learned. Nonetheless Miles later said that "Make Me a Pallet [on the Floor]" was "the first song [she] learned from [her] mother when [she] was little."[43] She also recounted to Griffiths that as a child, she sang with her neighbors: Sidney Bechet played a "little nickel tin flute," and "Wilhelmina Barth would play piano."[44]

Young Elizabeth started to perform in her catechism school under the guidance of Ms. Atkins, who "used to teach us how to sing and dance and she'd give little concerts on Sundays for the neighborhood." In the absence of more information, it is hard to know what kind of songs were featured in these concerts, but we can safely surmise that chanting during the actual catechism lessons included Catholic hymns and maybe even some *cantiques*. In any case, Ms. Atkins's little concerts grew in popularity:

> [E]verybody start [sic] doing it in pretty [much] every ward, every now and then you hear of a concert, usually on Sundays and on holidays . . . and then they'd pay us, give us 50¢, 75¢. Well, it went up to a $1.50–$2.00 . . . as we start getting bigger and bigger, we start getting bigger pay. Then, I start getting offers from the halls then, Francs Amis Hall, L'Équité Hall, Artisan Hall, Hope's Hall [sic], Globe's Hall [sic], Tokyo, finally the Dixie Park, the Lincoln Park, then the Pythian Temple, then the Pythian Theater.
>
> . . . Usually, it would be what they called a Concert and Ball, meaning the concert would start at about 8h–8h30 and last until about 10h30–11h o'clock . . . in order to make money, so they could charge . . . 50¢–75¢, they had to have a band, that's when I start working with King Oliver, and Ory, and all those different musicians, you know, Picou, and Manuel Perez, and all, Bunk Johnson and all of that, it's in those times that I sang with those fellows. They'd hired them, you know, they'd play for the concert, then after, they'd played for them to dance, and the dance would last maybe till 3h–4h o'clock in the morning.[45]

She was in her early teens when she played with them, for around 1910, at the age of fifteen, she joined her sister, coon shouter Edna Benbow (later Edna Hicks), and brother-in-law who had a touring show together, which led her to work with various other bands on the southern vaudeville circuit. A few years later, she was touring the country with the J. C. Miles Band and Minstrels as they performed in "colored show[s]" then commonly featured by circuses in the United States. According to Lynn Abbott and Doug Seroff, these sideshows played an "important role in the commercial ascendency of blues and jazz."[46] Indeed, the band regularly reported to the *Freeman*, a newspaper for professional troupers based in Indianapolis, J. C. Miles's hometown. The correspondents sometimes commented about the band's repertoire. While touring in Virginia, North Carolina, Maryland, and Pennsylvania in

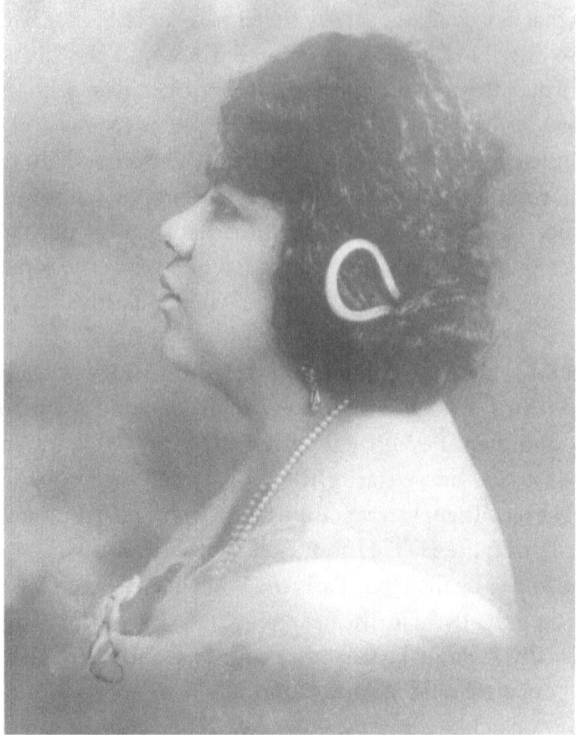

5.4. Lizzie Miles. Hogan Jazz Archive Photography Collection, PH002762. Tulane University Special Collections, Tulane University, New Orleans, LA.

1914, J. C. Miles recounted that the band played "principally the latest rags and popular airs" and that the "Blues . . . goes bigger here than it does in Bam." Then again, in a 1915 unsigned report from New Hampshire and Vermont, the author indicated, "we have drifted almost entirely from the standard marches and have gone into the popular ragtime stuff which seems to be more desired by the public of this region." In May 1916, the band performed for the inmates of the Indiana State Prison, and "[t]he acts that went the biggest with the prisoners . . . and when Mrs. Miles sang the 'Hesitating Blues,' the riot commenced." The band was severely hit by the 1918 Spanish flu pandemic: almost all the musicians got sick, and J. C. Miles died on October 9. Miles also got the flu, and although she recovered, the doctors recommended that she stop singing for at least a year because her lungs had been affected by double pneumonia.[47]

After a break of a "year and a half, almost two years"—which would put her back to work in the summer of 1920—she got her first cabaret job in Bucktown (now a neighborhood of New Orleans, on the south shore of Lake

Pontchartrain) playing with various musicians such as Kid Rena, Manuel Manetta, and Amos White. Realizing that she could make good money singing in cabarets, she went up to Chicago where, the day after her arrival, she was hired by King Oliver—then playing at the Dreamland—whose band included Louis Armstrong (cornet), Lil Hardin (piano), Baby Dodds (on drums, although Miles wasn't sure she recalled well), and Eddie Garland (bass).[48] From November 1920 until May 1921, Joe "King" Oliver's band was indeed playing at the Dreamland; however, Armstrong was not in the band yet. Oliver played at the Dreamland—and sometimes simultaneously in other venues—on and off from his arrival in Chicago in 1919, first with Lawrence Duhé's band, of which he became the leader in October of the same year. The personnel were not stable yet, but judging by the musicians that Miles recalled, it seems that she would have joined somewhere between the end of 1920 or the beginning of 1921—the estimated time when Ed Garland joined the band—and May 1921. By then the band probably included James Palao (violin), Johnny Dodds (clarinet), Lil Hardin (piano), Ed Garland (bass), and Minor Hall (drums), all listed as having accompanied Oliver to San Francisco on May 21, 1921, where the Pergola Dancing Pavilion was waiting for them.[49] So Armstrong could not have been in the band when she joined; but Armstrong has been so much associated with the band after his arrival in August 1922 that Miles could easily have been confused.

Following a few other engagements in and around Chicago, with fellow New Orleanian Freddie Keppard and pianist Glover Compton, among others, Miles made her recording debut in February 1922 for OKeh in New York.[50] She also sang in various nightclubs, most notably at The Capital on Lenox Avenue in Harlem, where she stayed about three years, until she left for Paris, probably in the second half of 1924. She stayed in France for a year or so, working at Chez Mitchell, a cabaret that she said was named for, and managed by, drummer and bandleader Louis Mitchell. "They called me La Rose Noire, The Black Rose . . . I didn't have no trouble getting along in French, because I learned Creole French from my mother." Back in New York, she played in various cabarets and resumed her recording career.[51] Between 1922 and 1930, Miles recorded some fifty-eight titles, often with unidentified musicians of the studios' house bands but also with renowned musicians such as King Oliver and Jelly Roll Morton.[52]

With these recordings, Miles joined the ranks of the classic female blues singers who became popular following the success of Mamie Smith (1883–1946), whose 1920 recording of "Crazy Blues" sold millions of copies. Backed by early jazz musicians, their repertoire, usually about lost or unrequited love and unhappy love affairs, came from various sources—from vaudeville and show tunes to popular songs and the blues, all of which Miles had been singing since her teenage years, making her one of the pioneers of blues and jazz singing.[53] The two sides with Morton (1929) stand out as piano and voice duet masterpieces. On "I Hate a Man Like You," Morton's refined piano accompaniment alternates between nice runs and fills in the right hand, chordal passages, and short solo bass lines in the left hand, whereas Miles carries a woman's hatred for her man in a controlled, somber voice, adding only a light expressive vibrato and swing. "Don't Tell Me Nothin,'Bout My Man" is more upbeat. The two musicians still complement each other well, although each of their renditions could stand by itself. It starts with a little "mise-en-scène" in the form of a dialogue (possibly inspired by their vaudeville years) that sets up Miles's vocals, somehow brighter, colored with her light vibrato, slight pitch inflections, and expressive phrasing over Morton's ragtime-like accompaniment.[54]

In 1938, Miles went back to New Orleans to take care of her sick mother, apparently hoping to continue singing professionally. Indeed, in 1939, after a hiatus of nine years, she did a final session, recording eight more songs in Chicago, where according to Griffiths she stayed until 1942.[55] Miles made a successful comeback during the 1950s, recording new LPs, performing regularly in New Orleans, appearing with Bob Scobey in Las Vegas and San Francisco, and at the first Monterey Jazz Festivals in 1958 and 1959. That same year, she went into retirement and died peacefully in New Orleans in 1963.

Three of her last LPs, which she considered the best she had ever made, recorded by Emory Cook for his *Sounds of Our Times* series, are now part of the Smithsonian Folkways Recordings.[56] They should not be seen as a mere revival of the early New Orleans jazz style but rather as Lizzie Miles's original style, which she still performed wholeheartedly. Most of the songs are in the piano-voice format at which she excelled. She used her powerful but flexible voice as an instrument that she controlled skillfully. It had retained its bluesy color, to which she sometimes added a growling raspy tone, still using her light, expressive vibrato, inflections, and phrasing, with good diction and control, even in fast passages. Her performances—some bilingual—are lyrical, at times intimate, but also swinging and joyful, with some scat improvisation.[57]

SIDNEY BECHET (1897–1959)

Sidney Bechet's life has been well documented, and his career as one of the first great soloists on both clarinet and soprano saxophone is already acknowledged in jazz history. For the purpose of this book, it's worth remembering that Bechet was born in New Orleans, the youngest child of a musical French-speaking Creole family, and that his father and four brothers were all tradesmen by day and musicians by night. At either six or eight years of age, he received his first clarinet; though mostly self-taught, he irregularly took lessons with prominent Creoles such as George Baquet, Alphonse Picou, Louis and Lorenzo Tio Jr., and finally with Johnny St. Cyr when he (Bechet) was around thirteen years old. It was also around this time that he began playing with his brothers' Silver Bells Brass Band and soon was playing with many others, including the popular John Robichaux Orchestra.[58]

Regardless of his Creole musical upbringing, Bechet always refused to learn musical notation, and definitely preferred the blues and the "ratty" rough sound of the rag music of the uptown Black musicians. Louis "Big Eye" Nelson (born Delisle [Deslisle or DeLille] 1880 or 1885–1949) with whom Bechet also took a few lessons, became Bechet's "stylistic model." Along with Nelson and cornetist Freddie Keppard (1890–1933), Bechet belonged to the group that Thomas Brothers calls the "Creole Rebels," for they willingly chose to learn and play with the uptown hot bands.[59] Around 1913, Bechet replaced Lorenzo Tio Jr. in Bunk Johnson's Eagle Band. As Bechet put it, this was "a real gutbucket band—a low-down band which really played the blues, and those slow tempos."[60] Even if Leonard Bechet, Sidney's older brother, didn't seem to think much of the uptown Blacks, whom he described as the "rough element . . . naturally always rough, ignorant," he also thought that Sidney got to be good because "you have to play real hard when you play for Negroes."[61]

Nonetheless, Bechet retained some of his early musical training with regard to tonal quality, articulation—to which he added some effects coming from the "ratty" sound of the real gutbucket bands—form, and phrasing, making him one of the best instrumentalists of his generation. Two of his students, jazz critic Richard Hadlock and Bob Wilber, who studied with him in the 1940s, recalled some of their lessons:

> "I'm going to give you one note today," he [Bechet] once told me [Hadlock]. "See how many ways you can play that note—growl it, smear it, flat it, sharp it, do anything you want to it. That's how you express your feelings in this music. It's like talking.
>
> "Always try to complete your phrases and your ideas . . . There are lots of otherwise good musicians who sound terrible because they start a new idea without finishing the last one."

Bob Wilber has described another facet of Bechet:

> One thing he was very interested in was the concept of interpreting a song. You start out with an exposition of the melody in which you want to bring out the beauty of it. And then you start your variations, but at first they are closely related to the melody. Then, as you go on to another chorus, you get further away—you do something a little less based on the melody but more on the harmony. Sidney was much more harmonically oriented than most of the players of his generation . . . Then at the end, you would come back to the melody and there would be some kind of coda which would bring the thing to a conclusion . . . The idea of the form was very important to him.[62]

However, Bechet's musical artistry was developed long before his students provided these precious insights on his teaching, and conception of pitch alteration, song interpretation and melodic variation. In June 1919, Bechet traveled to England with William Marion Cook's Southern Syncopated Orchestra. An avid spectator of their performances at the Royal Philharmonic Hall, Swiss conductor Ernest Ansermet (1883–1969) published a now-famous article about the orchestra in the October 10, 1919, issue of the *Revue Romande*. In the last paragraph, Ansermet paid tribute to Bechet,

> an extraordinary clarinet virtuoso who is, so it seems, the first of his race to have composed perfectly formed blues on the clarinet. I've heard two of them which he had elaborated at great length. . . . Extremely different, they are equally admirable for their richness of invention, force of accent, and daring in novelty and the unexpected. . . . artist of genius.[63]

Four years later, on June 30, 1923, Bechet made his first recordings with Clarence Williams' Blue Five, playing the soprano saxophone on "Wild Cat Blues" and "Kansas City Man Blues." Barney Bigard (1906–1980) later recalled, "I heard Sidney Bechet's records while I was in New Orleans and I used to copy him note for note." "Everybody had that record. That was all you could hear."[64] Clarence Williams, who had previously hired Bechet both in New Orleans and for his touring shows, was aware of his friend's talent and made sure to put him in the forefront, having him (instead of the cornetist) play the melody and all the breaks, allowing Bechet to develop his melodic ideas, through their reoccurrences.[65] Moreover, Bechet's 1923–24 recordings established him as a skilled and creative improviser, paving the way for the emergence of the jazz soloist, at a time when collective playing was still the norm.[66] During these two years, Bechet recorded thirty-eight pieces, among which nine feature him on solos ranging from eight to thirty-two bars, six on the soprano sax, two on the clarinet, and one the bass sarrusophone—actually, considering the range of the solo, Bechet was most likely playing a contrabass sarrusophone in E♭.[67] Generally speaking, his solos remain close to the melody, or to his well-built countermelody, but with creative variations and ornamentations—mostly vibratos, glissandi, fast repeated notes (or short motives), dramatic changes of register, bend notes, and little growls. His melodic ideas are also expressed through an effortless flowing rhythm against the steady four beats in a bar marked by the piano and the banjo throughout the usual three minutes of these early recordings.

Five of these solos were played while accompanying various blues singers, the first of which is a moody eight-bar sax solo on "Lady Luck Blues" by Mamie Smith accompanied by The Harlem Trio.[68] The well-executed thirty-two-bar sarrusophone solo on "Mandy, Make Up Your Mind" sung by Eva Taylor is impressive for the unusual instrument and the low range of the solo with Armstrong's countermelody on the cornet (unfortunately, too much in the background on the recording).[69] The clarinet solos are found on "Achin' Hearted Blues," a fast upbeat piece (despite its name) that allowed him to display his virtuosity, and on "Off and On Blues," sung by Sippie Wallace with Bechet nicely answering her vocals, and playing a solo alternating between the high and low registers of his instrument.[70] These recordings establish Bechet as one of the first great jazz saxophonists, and the first and uncontested master of the soprano for decades, eventually giving some instruction to Johnny Hodges (1907–1970), with whom he also played in 1925, before Hodges joined the Duke Ellington Orchestra in 1928.

As he had done a few years earlier when performing with Cook's Southern Syncopated Orchestra in England, Bechet continued to play a significant role in the international diffusion of jazz, as part of the crew of *La Revue Nègre* that debuted at the Théâtre des Champs-Élysées in Paris in the fall of 1925. The show was a success and eventually traveled to Brussels and Berlin, before coming to an end after a year. Bechet then joined trombonist Frank Withers, who was organizing a band that toured in the USSR during the first few months of 1926. The band—who played in concert-like settings for audiences largely new to jazz—was very well-received, especially Bechet, dubbed "the Talking Saxophone," whose picture appeared on large posters advertising his coming performances. Back in Europe, Bechet played various gigs (mainly in France and Germany), including as musical director for a reincarnation of *La Revue Nègre* (later renamed *Black People* and *Black Flowers*), which toured extensively in Greece, Turkey, Sweden, Spain, Egypt, Hungary, Czechoslovakia, Italy, and Germany.[71]

More than twenty years later, the early jazz revival proved beneficial to Bechet, as French jazz promoter and critic Charles Delaunay invited him to appear in a music festival in Paris in 1949. During the festival, he played with French clarinetist Claude Luter and his band, sitting in many times at the Vieux-Colombier. Trumpeter Pierre Merlin later remembered:

> I think we mostly played numbers from our repertoire, but Bechet made them into something quite different. . . . I think only one of our band spoke English fluently, so it was obvious that Sidney would speak in French, but because of his accent this made things difficult. I suppose he was out of practice, but it wasn't only accent, it was his vocabulary as well.

Bechet relocated permanently in France in 1950, enjoying a successful career performing and recording as one of the key figures of the revival movement in France until his death in 1959.[72]

Chapter 6

THE EARLY JAZZ REVIVAL AND THE CREOLE SONGS

The first articles or books about jazz criticism and history, which appeared in both Europe and the United States during the 1930s, were the work of "hot" jazz collectors seeking to document the music they loved.[1] Although it had been previously suggested, *Jazzmen*, published in October 1939 after much research and many interviews, clearly established New Orleans as the birthplace of jazz, consequently attracting jazz aficionados to the city. Unfortunately, changes in demographics, the growing popularity of radio, and the appearance of jukeboxes in public venues contributed to the sharp decline in employment for jazz musicians. In 1942, when Sterling Brown, an African American professor, poet, and jazz lover traveled to New Orleans, he was disappointed to find none of the jazz musicians or venues that he had expected to easily encounter. Brown later wrote about his disappointing trip:

> There were a few good jazz combinations in town, I learned, but most of them were playing in white places where I could have gone only at the cost of problems.... In spite of the resurrection of more persistent researchers, however, I think that there still is truth in what I sensed in 1942: that in New Orleans the feeling for jazz was nostalgic, commemorative, quite different from the force that sustained young Louis Armstrong, Sidney Bechet, Jimmy Noone, and Johnny Dodds. Bunk Johnson had to go to the coast for a real hearing.[2]

Similarly, William "Bill" Russell wrote to a friend in October 1942: "There isn't any good jazz, strictly speaking. Just the smell of it. But I like that and talking to Bunk [Johnson]."[3] Nonetheless, this new scholarship in the history of jazz led to a revival of the New Orleans jazz style. In the late 1930s, Russell, while researching and collecting material for *Jazzmen*, "discovered" sixty-year-old trumpeter Bunk Johnson (1879–1949) in New Iberia, 130 miles (215 kilometers) west of New Orleans. By then, Johnson did not even own an instrument, but Russell helped him get new teeth and a trumpet, and made arrangements to record him. The session took place in New Orleans on June 11, 1942, and the results were issued on the Jazz Man label.[4] This was just the first of many sessions Russell conducted with musicians in various locations, including New Orleans, and in 1944, he founded the American Music label to market the product of his efforts.[5]

At the same time Marili Morden, second owner of the Jazz Man Record Shop established in 1939 in Hollywood, and her husband, Nesuhi Ertegun, founded the Crescent Records label to record Kid Ory, who had become popular again after his appearances with his All Star Jazz Group on the *Orson Welles Almanac* radio show.[6] A first session took place in Los Angeles in August 1944, followed by three others in August, September, and November 1945, and the records were distributed at the Jazz Man Record Shop.[7] The Crescent label was short-lived; it was folded into the Jazz Man label after Ertegun (with Morden?) bought it back from David Stuart in early 1947. Morden had been the owner of Crescent Records but Cary Ginell doesn't specify if she also became one of the owners of the Jazz Man label. In February 1945, Kid Ory also recorded for the independent Exner label before moving to the major labels—Decca, Columbia, and Verve.[8]

Impressed by Baby Dodds's drum solos, Harriet Janis and Rudi Blesh founded Circle Records in 1946 for the purpose of recording him. The label was active from 1946 to 1952 and also produced hundreds of recordings with early jazz players—such as Lizzie Miles and the *Jazz a la Creole* [sic] session. In 1947, Circle issued an abridged version of the Jelly Roll Morton Library of Congress recordings, rendering them accessible and popular, mostly among collectors.[9] Indeed, since the mid-1930s, the demand from "hot" jazz collectors had prompted the creation of new labels dedicated to reissuing early recordings, with proper information designed to please them, while Victor, Decca, and Columbia were also capitalizing on the old masters they had acquired from pioneering labels in the late 1920s and during the time of the Great Depression. A few years after the rediscovery of Bunk Johnson and the publication of *Jazzmen*, revivalist movements involving older and younger musicians were flourishing in New York City and on the West Coast.[10]

THE CREOLE SONGS

The evidence shows that Creole songs were popular and became part of the repertoire of early jazz musicians (more below), even though none appeared on the recordings of the late 1910s and 1920s, probably because producers saw no commercial value in them. However, Creole songs were surely performed (at least) in Francophone families for many years, as home music-making and singing was a very popular activity during the nineteenth and early twentieth centuries. Indeed, as Mathilde Zagala noted, "more than a third" of the scores of the *Maxwell Sheet Music Collection*, most likely assembled between the end of the 1840s until the 1890s (see chapter 4), were for voice and piano. They included songs of various origins—Irish, English, French, Spanish, Mexican, Cuban—and from the United States ("popular songs, comic songs, [E]thiopian songs, and minstrel songs"). A repertoire as cosmopolitan as the New Orleans area's population.[11]

Accordingly, it is interesting that, when notated, almost all the songs presented in both of Cable's 1886 articles, "The Dance in Place Congo" and "Creole Slave Songs," appeared with a piano accompaniment, somehow catering to the music lovers among his audience.[12] In 1902 Clara Gottschalk Peterson (ca. 1842–1910) published *Creole Songs from New Orleans in the Negro Dialect*, a collection of twelve songs she described as "melodies of the Louisiana negroes, which quaintly merry or full of a very tender pathos have served to rock whole generations of Southern children, are historical documents of some interest to the student and lover of music," and for which the "accompaniements [*sic*] have purposely been written in the simplest possible style so as not to detract from the naive and quaint character of the songs themselves."[13]

The other collections published in the first decades of the twentieth century—Emilie Le Jeune, "Creole Folk Songs" (1919), in which she provided only the lyrics, but her arrangements of two songs appeared in Cable "Creole Slave Songs"; Maud Cuney Hare (African American pianist and music scholar), *Six Creole Folk-Songs* (1921) for "Medium Voice and Piano Accompaniment"; and Mina Monroe, *Bayou Ballads: Twelve Folk-Songs From Louisiana* (1921), also arranged for voice and piano with the hope to "render them both suitable and attractive for concert singers"—present old plantation songs rebranded as bayou ballads or Creole songs, while being arranged and performed in the Eurocentric music tradition.[14] A trend reflective of what Lawrence W. Levine refers to as the sacralization of culture "that saw the very word 'culture' becoming synonymous with the Eurocentric products of the symphonic hall, the opera house, the museum and the library. . . . Thus by the early decades of this [twentieth] century the changes that had either begun or gained velocity in the last third of the nineteenth century were in place."[15] But not everybody agreed with such piano arrangements, including Jeanne Wogan Arguedas, who found that the collection assembled by Mina Monroe, her cousin who also grew up on the Labranche plantation, was wrong:

6.1. Sheet music cover with a mammy holding a White baby and a blackface "happy Negro" in the upper corners, with a Carnival scene and a romanticized harvest of corn in the lower corners. One can only guess, but the center image might be Nickerson, wearing a tignon like her great-grandmother used to wear. Camille Nickerson, *Five Creole Songs* (Boston: Boston Music Company, 1942).

> . . . all of those songs, we sang together . . . I think the words are correct, so the songs, but I think the accompaniment is wrong . . . the Negroes did not have any piano when they sang the songs. They kept time by clapping hands or beating the ground with their foot, or they had a drum called the Bamboula drum, but the accompaniment is too many notes and too many, . . . I should say, how to express, it's not correct.[16]

Nonetheless, numerous references about "mammies" singing to their White protégés, as well as Ms. Arguedas and Ms. Monroe singing plantation songs together as children, exemplify the way the songs became part of

The Creole Songs 97

6.2. Camille Nickerson in her "Louisiana Lady" dress. Scurlock Studio Records, Archives Center, National Museum of American History, Smithsonian Institution.

childhood memories crossing over the color line. Camille Nickerson (1887 or 1888–1982), herself a Creole, was the daughter of William Nickerson (1865–1928), who toured with the Georgia Minstrels along with Louis Tio and played viola in the Tio and Doublet String Band around 1890. Camille herself played in Louis "Papa" Tio's large ensemble.[17] In her 1932 thesis, she shared a childhood memory:

> My first introduction to this Creole music . . . came about on the occasion when as a very small child, I beheld my father playing an accompaniment in double-stops on his violin to a most attractive, jolly little tune—one "Suzanne, Belle Femme." My father also sang the tune as he played its accompaniment. But the sole performer in this interesting picture was my great grandmother who, with a brightly colored tignon, or head-handkerchief, tied neatly around her head, made graceful play with a madras handkerchief, which she held by its

corners, while she danced gaily up and down and all around, unable to resist the strains of "Suzanne."[18]

In 1942, she published *Five Creole Songs Harmonized and Arranged by Camille Nickerson* while in the middle of her performing career, during which she became known as "The Louisiana Lady" as she toured the United States and visited England and France, performing lecture-recitals of Creole songs in "Creole costume" (an antebellum crinoline dress), arguably taking part in the romanticization of the Old South.[19]

THE CREOLE SONGS AND EARLY JAZZ

Coming from a different but contemporaneous historical interest, and thanks to the dedication of passionate scholars, the New Orleans jazz revival of the 1940s and 1950s was largely prompted by the desire to document the origins of jazz. Collectors, producers (now seeing a demand), and Creole musicians alike seem to have thought it important to finally record what they remembered of this uniquely Louisianan repertoire. Their dynamic and creative approach to Creole songs (and to the *cantiques*) closely linked to the social life and music of their community also reveals their resilience and the development of a fluid cultural identity—albeit with various degrees of acceptance—as both African Americans and Afro-French Creoles at the time when jazz was emerging. A time when they had been disenfranchised as second-class citizens (especially following the defeat in the *Plessy* decision), and the French language (and by extension their culture) had been banned twice by the Louisiana Constitutions of 1868 and 1921. (See chapter 1, and notes 47 and 55 therein.)

They must have been painfully aware of this lower-class status imposed on them, as they fought to maintain some dignity among their losses. The career of the pioneering Original Creole Band—in which Jimmy Palao, George Baquet, and later Louis "Big Eye" Nelson were Creoles (also Freddie Keppard, but according to Gushee, he "can't be identified as 'Creole'")—reflects the challenges the band had to face. First formed as a dance orchestra around 1908, the band toured the vaudeville circuit between 1914 and 1918, where they performed dressed like field hands in a stereotyped plantation act, distorting the Creoles' history and identity. But as Gushee importantly observes, "one doubts that they could have succeeded in any other way than by embracing the plantation formula."[20] After seeing the band, Jimmy Palao's wife Armontine "was distressed by the fact that they were dressed like field

6.3. The Original Creole Orchestra (Band). Back row: Edward Vincent (trombone), Freddie Keppard (cornet), George Baquet (clarinet), Bill Johnson (bass). Front row: Dink Johnson (drums), James Palao (violin), Norwood Williams (guitar). "Photograph taken in Los Angeles, summer of 1914." Reproduced with permission of Oxford Publishing Limited through PSL Clear. Gushee, *Pioneers of Jazz*, ii; Gushee and Carr, "How the Creole Band Came to Be," 84 (quote).

hands, overalls, straw hats, and red bandannas. As good as they were, she said, they shouldn't have had to dress that way."[21]

Despite the musical literacy and technical ability of the musicians, popular dance music, ragtime, and jazz were despised as low class, especially as per the new Eurocentric definition of "culture." That comes across in Jelly Roll Morton's exclamation about one of the strains of "Tiger Rag" as "[t]he mazooka time!" in reference to the European mazurka, from which it would have been derived.[22] Yet, in the midst of the changing dictates of cultural appreciation, the Creole songs made their way both to the concert hall and to the dance hall. Indeed, Morton's performance and recollection of the Creole song "C'était N'aut' Can-Can, Payez Donc" clearly indicates that Creole songs were performed in the formative years of jazz:

> This one . . . was one of the early tunes in New Orleans. It's from French origin. And I'm telling you, when they start to playing this thing in the dance hall they would really whoop it up. . . . [t]his was

6.4. Ad from *Indianapolis Sunday Star*, December 2, 1917. The picture also appears in Gushee, *Pioneers of Jazz*, 97.

around about *nineteen-five, nineteen-six*. All the bands—the little bands that was around—played it . . . it happened to be a favorite so far as the tune goes. But there seemed to be some vulgar meaning to it that I have never understood. I know what all the rest mean, but the can-can—I can't understand the can-can business. [Laughs.] But I'll tell you, everybody got hot and they threw their hats away when they get to start playing this thing.[23]

However, as mentioned above, before jazz musicians started to include Creole songs in their professional repertoire, they doubtless played and sang them with relatives and friends. In 1949, while working on his biography of Morton, Alan Lomax met with Creole guitarist and banjoist Johnny St. Cyr (1890–1966). As they were discussing the Golden Rule Band, "the *first* real *hot* band . . . back around nineteen hundred," St. Cyr explained that the band was what they "called a dance orchestra. Seven piece band," which mostly played ragtime pieces and "popular numbers," and that the "Creole tunes [came] up in the later years. . . . we had lots of Creole tunes during that time but the bands never bothered with them."

Lomax: What do you mean? Who played those Creole tunes then?
St. Cyr: Ah, people used to just sing 'em. They'd always get a bunch of Creoles—Creoles are noted for good times, you know. On Sundays,

they'd have what we call a *cowan* in Creole, turtle dinners, you see. It was famous around Creole section [*sic*]. Until today they's quite a few of 'em still has those *cowan* dinners. And, uh, they have their wine and their beer there, and—wasn't as many musicians then as they have now. And those babies get out there and they'd get happy. And they'd get to get to [*sic*] singing and clapping. [claps] People would be dancing and that's it! [Laughs.]

Wanting to demonstrate his point, or getting carried away by reminiscence, St. Cyr went on to play and sing his own version of two verses of the popular song "Eh La Bas."

> **Lomax:** Now you said you couldn't sing!
> **St. Cyr:** No, no I can't, I can't. [Laughs.] I don't consider that no singing.[24]

In the same round of 1949 interviews, Lomax met with clarinetist Alphonse Picou (1878 or 1879–1961). Although the story of his debut as a professional musician when he was sixteen years old, which would have been around 1894, contradicts St. Cyr's assessment that the Creole songs came later, the two can be reconciled if we take notice of what Morton said. That is that "All the bands—the *little* bands that was around—played it" (my emphasis), in which case bands like the Golden Rule Band would not fall under the category of a "small band." In any case, Picou recalled his first rehearsal:

One day Bouboul Augustat, the trombone player, heard me practicing at the house and ask me if I want to come to one of his rehearsals. I say, "You got any music?"

"You don't need no music," say Bouboul.

"That's impossible. What I'm gonna play? Just sit there and hold my instrument?" I ask.

"Don't worry. You'll know." That's what Bouboul tell *me*.

So I went. They were playing some good jazz that I didn't know nothing about . . .

Femme en dans lit	Woman in bed
'N homme en bas lit	Man under bed
Moi pas l'aimez ça	I don't like that
Moi pas l'aimez ça	I don't like that
Ai, ai, ai	Ai, ai, ai
Moi pas l'aimez ça	I don't like that

Well, I had a good brains [sic] at that time and I caught on quick. When Bouboul heard me filling in, he say [sic] "See, you know how to play without music." So I played with Bouboul's string band then. We had guitar, bass, trumpet, clarinet, and a songster.[25]

Nine years later, in an interview conducted in 1958, Picou repeated the story of this first rehearsal without mentioning any songs, but still explaining how he had to improvise his part and even a solo. This time he called the leader Bouboul Fortunette and the band was the Independence/Independent Band, "the first band that I [Picou] played in." As Vic Hobson rightfully observes, "if this event did take place when Picou was sixteen, [this means] that the downtown Independent Band would have been playing improvised music at a time when Bolden was only just beginning to take lessons on cornet from Manuel Hall, circa 1896."[26]

Speaking about playing with other New Orleans clarinetists, Picou remembered the last time he played with Lorenzo Tio at a party in Los Angeles. "They gave a party for me.... I'm telling you, we had a time, that night. That's the time they made me sing 'Eh La Bas.'"[27] This prompted questions about Creole songs. Picou clearly remembered playing them on dance jobs and during Carnival, explaining that "Mo Pas l'Aimé Ça" was a Mardi Gras song. He did not remember many other songs, apart from "Les Oignons," when asked about it. But he spoke very fondly about Ulysse Picou, his (mostly unknown) brother, a singer-songwriter and guitarist who had died four years earlier. According to Alphonse Picou, Ulysse wrote Creole songs such as "Qui Veut Qu'y Volé Ma Bouteille?" (Who Stole My Bottle?) and "Qui Veut Qui Dit Toi Que Mo T'Apé Lé Là-Bas?" (Who Told You I Was Going Over There?). "He was a great tenor... and a great composer and a great singer with French ... French and Creole, [unclear] he composed."[28] During the 1949 interview, Picou was joined by Ulysse, then sixty-six years old, and Paul Dominguez on guitar for a performance of one of Ulysse's compositions called "La Misère" (Misery). This impromptu performance opens a small window into intimate music playing as it might have taken place in the privacy of people's homes. All the elements of New Orleans jazz are present: the guitar standing as the rhythm section playing four in a bar, and the clarinet ornamenting the melody performed by the singer.[29]

Creole songs were clearly a part of having a good time in general—at *cowans*, at parties, and at Carnival. In a 1959 interview, Paul Barbarin (1899–1969) and Theresa Wilson (Barbarin's sister) described Carnival as it was in "those days"—which, from their point of view, was better than in 1959—when "colored people" were masking, singing, and dancing, with some men cross-dressing as women and dancing with other men. They were asked what people would sing during Carnival time:

> **Wilson:** They would sing all kind of French songs. Creole songs, and all.
> **Barbarin:** Oh yes, all Creole songs.
> **Allen:** Do you know any of them?
> **Barbarin:** Just a few words, I mean, you used to say most of them. Then say, "Ai Ai Ai Mo' Pas Lemmé Ça, Mo' Pas Lemmé Ça, Mo' Pas Lemmé Ça." . . .
> **Wilson:** We'd sing all kind of Creole songs. We'd put all kind of words in them—well, they know how to talk that kind of stuff, you know, and they—
> **Barbarin:** Yeah.
> **Wilson:** They all—they'd make a real song out of it. They'd rhyme it up.[30]

According to Kim Marie Vaz, the Million Dollar Baby Dolls, who started the Mardi Gras tradition of costuming as Baby Dolls in the 1910s (see chapter 5, note 42),

> paraded in their neighborhoods, singing bawdy lyrics to vaudeville show tunes and Creole songs, playing tambourines and cowbells, chanting, and dancing. . . . Through performing gender "buffoonery," they created a safe space for cross-dressing men [who] also masked in the short satin dresses with bonnets and bloomers and paraded with women.[31]

Leonard Bechet, Sidney Bechet's older brother, also recalled that musicians "had a variety of pieces . . . that they make up themselves." Finally, Danny Barker later spoke about "Long Head Bob" who had "a string group . . . They played a lot of Creoles songs, . . . They would sing original things . . . Would invent lyrics as they went along."[32]

Those excerpts, taken from many interviews, all indicate that Creoles had a practice of singing and improvising music and/or lyrics—at least when it came to Creole songs—during informal events such as parties and *cowan* dinners or during Carnival. This practice was compatible with the improvisational approach and head arrangements of the Black uptown musicians that Creoles are usually said to have incorporated during the formative years of jazz. It also allowed for Creole songs to be adapted and composed in the early jazz style: such compatibilities were, and still are, fertile ground for creolization.[33]

THE REVIVAL RECORDINGS OF CREOLE SONGS

"Eh La Bas" stands out as the song most often recorded by jazz musicians. Kid Ory recorded it in 1946, twenty-four years after his landmark recording of "Ory's Creole Trombone" (see chapter 5.)[34] Despite the title, "Ory's Creole Trombone" is not a Creole song per se. Its multiple trombone breaks—almost all two bars long but for a few longer ones—give Ory a more predominant role than the usual lower countermelody assigned to his instrument—hence the title—but it is in keeping with the popular genre of slide trombone specialties of the time.[35] However, it does exemplify the early New Orleans jazz style characterized by a front line of three horns with the cornet (or trumpet) playing the melody, the clarinet playing an ornamented countermelody in a high register, and the trombone playing a melodic and rhythmic bass line, therefore creating a polyphonic texture used for collective playing and improvisation. The horns were supported by a rhythm section made up of a banjo, guitar or piano, a bass (or sousaphone [tuba] in marching bands), and drums, maintaining a regular but swinging beat in 2/4, although with a strong feel of 4/4—or, as mentioned before, carrying the Caribbean rhythms, such as the tresillo and the habanera, also used by Creole musicians (the "Spanish tinge").[36]

Ory revisited his old composition in 1945 with his Creole Jazz Band.[37] Although slower, this later version shares a similar instrumentation and arrangement with the 1920s versions, from which we can infer that Ory's musical approach was similar during the 1920s and 1940s—keeping in mind that live performances are not subject to the constraints of studio recordings, and that long instrumental solos were not common in the 1920s.[38]

Eh La Bas

Nonetheless, Ory's recordings of "Ory's Creole Trombone" suggests that his 1946 and 1947 recordings of "Eh La Bas," the latter live from the Green Room in San Francisco (similar arrangement and instruments, but with a piano) reflect the way he would have played it in the early years of jazz—although Ory and his band might have use more of the "Spanish tinge" rhythms during his years in New Orleans in the 1910s.[39] The piece begins with four instrumental choruses of eight bars each, with slight melodic variations (BBBB) moving smoothly to two verses, also eight bars long, and back to two choruses (AABB), all played in the New Orleans jazz style.[40]

BBBB	**AABB**	**ABB**
Collective playing	Collective playing	Ory on vocals / 1st verse
		Chorus in call & response
32 bars	32 bars	24 bars

BB	**ABB**	**BBBB**
Clarinet solo	Ory on vocals / 2nd verse	Collective playing
	Chorus in call & response	
16 bars	24 bars	32 bars

6.5. Arrangement of "Eh La Bas"—Kid Ory (1946).

Only then does Ory come in to sing his first verse, followed by two choruses, sung in call and response between him and other musicians, while the clarinet continues to play a countermelody (ABB). The clarinet takes over for a sixteen-bar solo (BB), after which Ory comes back with his second verse, and two more choruses (ABB). The piece ends as it started with thirty-two bars of collective playing on the chorus, with more variations on the melody on the first two (BBBB).[41]

Ory's 1960 Verve recording of the same song is also built around the "irregular" organization of the thirty-two-bar form, using the same kind of sectional grouping as in 1946. The piece begins with thirty-two bars of collective playing, on both the chorus and the verse (BBAA). Then Ory and the band come in to sing two call-and-response choruses (BB) followed by his first verse and two more choruses (ABB).

BBAA	**BB | ABB**	**BBAB**	**BB | ABB**
Collective playing	Ory on vocals - 1st verse	Clarinet solo	Ory on vocals - 2nd verse
	Chorus in call & response		Chorus in call & response
32 bars	24 bars | 16 bars	32 bars	24 bars | 16 bars

BBBB	**BBB**	**BBAA**	**BBB**
Trumpet solo	Piano	Collective playing	Collective playing
			4-bar drum solo in last 8
32 bars	24 bars	32 bars	24 bars

6.6. Arrangement of "Eh La Bas"—Kid Ory (1960).

After a thirty-two-bar clarinet solo (BBAB), Ory and the band come back for a few choruses and his second verse arranged as before (BB/ABB), this time moving to a thirty-two-bar trumpet solo (BBBB) and an unusual twenty-four-bar piano solo (BBB). The band comes back for a full form of thirty-two bars (BBAA), followed by three last choruses (BBB), all in collective playing, apart from the four-bar drum solo on the last eight.[42]

In 1956, Lizzie Miles recorded "Eh La Bas" with Bob Scobey and his Frisco Band, then one of the key figures of the West Coast revival.[43] Not surprisingly, the band stayed close to the traditional collective playing, but the arrangement offers some originality: it starts with an eight-bar military-style drum solo, followed by the chorus sung by the band without the response to the call, backed by the rhythm section (B).

INTRO	B	AB
Drum military style	Rhythm section	Horns come in
	Musicians singing	Collective playing
	Only the call, no response	
8 bars	8 bars	16 bars

ABAB | ABAB	A	BB
Miles on vocals	Horns	Trumpet & Miles
Chorus in call & response	Collective playing	Call & response
32 bars | 32 bars	8 bars	16 bars

6.7. Arrangement of "Eh La Bas"—Lizzie Miles (1956).

Then the horns come in with Scobey leading on trumpet for an instrumental verse and chorus (AB), and only then does Miles come in, accompanied only by the rhythm section. She sings four verses, each followed by the chorus sung in call and response between Miles and the band, with the trombone filling in with some typical smears (ABAB/ABAB). She starts with the standard first verse and then, as is the pattern for this song, continues with three verses of her choice. The horns come back for an instrumental verse (A), with Miles joining them to end the piece with two choruses in call and response between trumpet and voice, cleverly varying her lyrical responses in the last eight (BB).

In the liner notes of Billie and Dede Pierce, *Gulf Coast Blues*, Richard Allen explained that "the central idea of the song is that the singer eats good food and drinks plenty of wine at his cousin's house and the hospitality costs him nothing."[44]

Eh La Bas/Hey Over There
Kid Ory Lyrics (1946 and 1960) **Translation**[45]

Mon cher cousin, mon chère cousine,   My dear cousin [male],
       my dear cousin [female],

J'ai l'aimé la cuisine,   I like [your] cuisine [cookin'],
J'ai mangé plein, j'ai bois du vin,   I ate plenty, I drank wine,
Ça pas coûté à rien.   It cost me nothin'.

Eh la bas (Eh la bas),   *Eh la bas (Eh la bas),*
Eh la bas (Eh la bas),   *Eh la bas (Eh la bas),*
Eh la bas (Eh la bas),   *Eh la bas (Eh la bas),*
Mon cher la bas (Mon cher la bas). (2x)   *My dear la bas (My dear la bas). (2x)*

Et j'ai tué cochon, j'ai tué lapin,   And I killed a pig, I killed a rabbit,
Et j'ai mangé plein,   And I ate plenty,
J'ai fait gombo, mo mangé trop,   I made gumbo, I ate too much,
Et ça fait moi malade.   And it made me sick.

Chorus   Chorus

Lizzie Miles Lyrics (1956)   Translation

Mon chère cousine, mon cher cousin,   My dear cousin [female],
       my dear cousin [male],

Mo l'aimé tout la cuisine,   I like all [your] cuisine [cookin'],
Mo mangé plein, mo boire du vin,   I ate plenty, I drank wine,
Ça va coûter à rien.   Gonna cost me nothin'.

Eh la bas (Eh la bas),   *Eh la bas (Eh la bas),*
Eh la bas (Eh la bas),   *Eh la bas (Eh la bas),*
Eh la bas chère (Eh la bas chère),   *Eh la bas dear (Eh la bas dear),*
Eh la bas (Eh la bas).   *Eh la bas (Eh la bas).*

Mo allée au la halle,   I went to the market,
Pour acheter saucisson cochon,   To buy pork saucisson [a large sausage],
Non, là tu n'as pas saucisson cochon,   No, now you don't have pork saucisson,
Mais donne-moi saucisson piment.   But give me pepper saucisson.

Chorus   Chorus

Mo allée au la glacière,	I went to the icebox,
Pour get court-bouillon,	To get court-bouillon,
Avec court-bouillon tes food pas bon,	With court-bouillon, your food is not good,
Mais donne moins dérangement	But it gives less trouble [stomach upset].
Chorus	Chorus
Tu connais Madame Joséphine?	Do you know Ms. Josephine?
A vient aller vivre dessus la rue Dauphine,	She just moved on Dauphine Street,
Madame Mongo, dessus la rue Congo,	Ms. Mongo, on Congo Street,
Tombée, cassée son grand zozo.	Fell, broke her big bone.
Chorus	Chorus

According to Sybil Kein, "'Eh La Bas' . . . is based on 'Vous Conné Tit la Maison Denis' [and] was sung by Creole men dressed as women and playing small guitars on Mardi Gras as late as the 1940s."[46] The link between the two songs is clearly established by the 1877 version of a song, "Denise Lacage," the first and last verse of which are "Mo cher cousine" etc. followed by the long story (sixteen verses) of a man hoping to marry her.[47] The structure of the song made it simple to modify its lyrics to tell different stories. For instance, Philomène Butler—who appears to have been a servant on the Labranche Plantation—interviewed by French ethnologist Julien Tiersot during his 1905–1906 trip in North America, sang this short verse presented under the generic title of "Coonjai." I have not seen it anywhere else, but it is interesting for its AABA bluesy form, and for the lyrics sung from the perspective of a servant cook—although somehow demeaning.

> Mo cher cousin, Mo chèr' cousine, Mo l'aimé la cuisine
> Mo cher cousin, Mo chèr' cousine, Mo l'aimé la cuisine
> Depi milat' dans la cuisin', Ya pas des os pou chien
> Mo cher cousin, Mo chèr' cousine, Mo l'aimé la cuisine[48]

Lyle Saxon wrote that "'Mo Ché [sic] Cousin, Mo Ché Cousin' was one of the most popular of all the Creole songs. It is said that more than one hundred verses were written to the same tune, all dealing with cooking and mulattoes striving to pass for Whites," like the second verse found in *Gumbo Ya-Ya*:

Mo ché cousin, mo ché cousin,	My dear cousin, my dear cousin,
Mo laimin la kisine,	I love to do the cooking,
Mo manzé bien, mo boi di vin,	I eat well, I drink wine,
Ca pas couté moin a rien.	It does not cost me a thing.
Tou to milatresses layé,	All you mulattresses there
Apé passé pou blanc,	Are passing for white,
Avec to blancs layés	With your white men
Yé allé dans l'Opera Français	You go to the French Opera
Mais yé fout yé déyer.	But they throw you out.[49]

This second verse was most likely inspired by the real case of Anastasie Desarzant, nicknamed "Toucoutou," who attempted to pass for White (*Passé Blanc*) but was defeated in the Louisiana Supreme Court in December 1859.[50] Her story became the subject of a very satirical song (discussed below) composed by Joseph Beaumont (1820–1872). I have not found other versions of "Eh La Bas" alluding to people trying to pass for White; the closest would be the one sung by Danny Barker, whose opening verse refers to Toucoutou. He recorded it with Paul Barbarin (his uncle) in 1955, and was still performing it some thirty-five years later—using the same verses (minus one) and, most interestingly, the tresillo rhythm—with Louis Nelson and His Palm Court Jazz Band, of which a live recording from May 1, 1989, appeared on the 2015 CD *Danny Barker New Orleans Jazz Man and Raconteur*.[51]

Eh La Bas—Danny Barker (1989)

Toucoutou mon chère amie	Toucoutou, my dear friend
Mo cuit dans ton cuisine	I cooked in your kitchen
Mo mangé bien, mo boire du vin	I ate well, I drank good wine
Mo laissé vous tranquille	I left you alone
Eh la bas (Eh la bas),	*Eh la bas (Eh la bas),*
Eh la bas (Eh la bas),	*Eh la bas (Eh la bas),*
Eh la bas chérie (Eh la bas chérie),	*Eh la bas darling (Eh la bas darling),*
Comment ça va?	*How is it going?*
Mam'zelle Joséphine	Mam'zelle Josephine
Si la resté dans la rue Dauphine	Lives on Dauphine Street
La glissé aussi est tombée	She slipped, so [she] fell
Cassé son petit jambe fine	Broke her fine [thin] little leg

Chorus

Si vous cuire un poule pour moi
Cuit li dans un fricassé
Après metter la sauce tomate
Avec un gros gallon du vin

Chorus

Salee dame, salee dame
Salee dame, bonjour
Salee dame, salee dame
Salee dame, bonjour

Salee dame, salee dame
Salee dame, bonjour
Salee dame, laisser mo voir
Gros noir to to

Chorus

Chorus

If you cook a chicken for me
Cook it in a fricassee [stew]
Then put the tomato sauce
And a big gallon of wine

Chorus

Sullied woman, sullied woman
Sullied woman, hello
Sullied woman, sullied woman
Sullied woman, hello

Sullied woman, sullied woman
Sullied woman, hello
Sullied woman, let me see
Big black toe (or "backside")

Chorus[52]

This 1989 version is very laid back and displays Barker's talent as *raconteur* (storyteller) and the flexibility of the Creole songs.[53] The seven-bar intro played by the rhythm section smoothly moves to the tresillo rhythm over which Barker comes in for two choruses sung in call and response with the musicians (BB). Then comes an extended section of five verses—borrowing the chorus from "Salee Dame" as the fourth and fifth verse—alternating with the chorus (ABAB/ABAAB).[54]

Intro	BB	ABAB | ABAAB
Rhythm section	Barker on vocals	Borrowing from Salee Dame
	Chorus in call & response	Chorus in call & response
	Barker & musicians	
	Tresillo rhythm	
7 bars	16 bars	32 bars | 40 bars

C	D	BB | Tag
Spoken presentation	Spoken presentation	Barker on vocals
Calypso song	"African song"	Call & response
BBAB of "Mary Ann"	Verse chord progression AA	Voice and trumpet
8 bars | 33 bars	20 bars | 16 bars	16 bars | 4 bars

6.8. Arrangement of "Eh La Bas"—Danny Barker (1989).

"Now we're gonna go to the Caribbean Islands," he explains in an eight-bar spoken presentation before moving to the Calypso song "Mary Ann" or "Marianne." This song has a chord progression based on the I and V chords, similar to "Eh La Bas," allowing Barker to easily move to its chorus. He then continued with what seems to be his own lyrics for a verse to which he added an extra bar, before coming back with only the first eight bars of the chorus (BBAB of "Mary Ann" forming section C). This is immediately followed by a song from "Africa, the home of my ancestry," which he introduces for twenty bars, and sings over the verse chord progression of "Eh La Bas" (AA forming section D). This leads him back to two choruses in which the response is given by the trumpet (BB), and a tag of four bars.

The large variety of lyrics found in the many versions recorded by jazz musicians demonstrates the interesting way in which the flexibility of the lyrics contrasts with the stability of the short eight-bar chorus and chord progression of the verse. Although there are some exceptions, the chorus is usually sung in call and response—"Eh La Bas" being the call to which the response presents many variations, sometimes within the same version—followed by the first verse that is almost always the same as Ory's and Miles's (Mon cher cousin) but, once again, with a few exceptions—as in Barker's version. The number of subsequent verses varies, but they all seem to come from a pool allowing singers to create different versions of the song by using common verses, sometimes with variations, sung in the order of their choice—a practice reminiscent of the way the Calinda song "Michié Préval"/"Mesieur Mazureau" was performed, or the way the *cantiques* were adapted. It's worth noting again that drummer Warren "Baby" Dodds—quoted in chapter 5—said that the uptown "fellows . . . didn't play the Creole numbers like the Frenchmen downtown did—such as *Eh La Bas*, . . . we changed the Spanish accent of the Creole songs. . . . They had the French and Spanish style, blended together." This not only indicates different musical approaches, but also that uptown musicians played Creole songs.[55]

Toucoutou/Blanche Touquatoux

On March 21, 1945, Kid Ory recorded a version of Beaumont's song under the title "Blanche Touquatoux" for Decca Records, with Cecile Tregre Ory (his sister-in-law) joining him on vocals, strong testimony that the songs really were being sung by the whole Creole community. Contrary to Beaumont's song written in the common verse-chorus form, Ory's version is strophic, made of the repetition of a four-bar introduction and three eight-bar verses in which the lyrics are sung over the same melody (Intro/AAA).

Lyrics of Toucoutou, by Joseph Beaumont

Toucoutou[56]	**Toucoutou**[57]
Si vous té gagné vous procé	If you win your lawsuit
Oh, nègue cé maléré.	Indeed, O Negress, this is bad;
Mové dolo qui dans focé	Bad for those who force it
Cé pas pou méprisé.	And the harm cannot be disregarded.
Refrain:	Refrain:
Ah! Toucoutou, ye conin vous,	Ah, Toucoutou, we know you!
Vous cé tin Morico.	You are a little Mooress.
Na pa savon qui tacé blanc	Who does not know you?/There is no soap strong enough
Pou blanchi vous lapo.	No soap will make you white./To whiten your dark skin.
Au Théâtre même quand va prend loge,	At the theater, if you go there/In the theater, when you take a box
Comme tout blanc comme y fot,	Like all white people should/Like all the nice white folks,
Ye va fé vous prend Jacdéloge,	They will treat you like Jacdeloge,
Na pas pacé tantôt.	Who did not pass so well as white, did he?
Refrain: Ah Toucoutou ...	Refrain: Ah Toucoutou ...
Quand blancs loyés va donin bal	When these white lawyers give a dance
Vous pli capab aller,	Will you be able to go?/You will never be able to go
Comment va fé, vayante diabal	Will you, O beautiful devil,/What will you do, you pretty devil,
Vous qui laimez danser?	You who love to dance so!/You who like to dance?
Refrain: Ah Toucoutou ...	Refrain: Ah Toucoutou ...
Mo pré fini mo ti chanson	I have finished my little song
Pasqui manvi dormi;	Because I want to sleep;
Mé mo pensé que la leson	But I think the lesson will serve,
Longtemps di va servi.	For a long time to keep you meek.
Refrain: Ah Toucoutou ...	Refrain: Ah Toucoutou

Blanche Touquatoux, Kid Ory and Cecile Ory (1945)[58]

Kid Ory	Ah Blanche, La misère (spoken)	Eh Blanche, It's misery (spoken)
	Ma palé la Cou(r) Suprême	I'm gonna speak to the Supreme Court
	Quandé chargé la laitue	When they'll charge us the lettuce*
	Société, fini pour nous	Society is finished for us
	Pour nous cacher ton cas passe	To hide from us, your case of passing
Cecile Ory	Commandant mon tendre frère,	Commander, my dear brother
	Ton conseil, il est affreux,	Your advice is terrible
	J'aime mieux vendre la terre,	I'd rather sell the land
	De enfoncer mes deux yeux	Rather than push my eyes in
	Une Blanche! Ah es-tu fou?	A White Woman! Are you crazy?
	Mon nom n'est pas Toucoutou	My name is not Toucoutou
	Une Blanche! Ah es-tu fou?	A White Woman! Are you crazy?
	Mon nom n'est pas Toucoutou	My name is not Toucoutou

* "Laitue/lettuce" is slang for money, so he could be referring to being charged a fine.

Musically speaking, this version exemplifies the "Spanish accent of the Creole songs" that Dodds was referring to (the "Spanish Tinge"), as the first two forms are performed with the tresillo rhythm—the first one in the early jazz style of collective playing (Intro/AAA), and the second with vocals and clarinet playing a countermelody (Intro/AAA).[59]

INTRO	AAA	INTRO TO VOCAL SECTION	AAA
Rhythm section	Collective playing	Spoken opening line	Kid Ory – 1st verse
		Rhythm section	Cecile Ory – 2nd & 3rd
Tresillo rhythm	Tresillo rhythm	Tresillo rhythm	Tresillo rhythm
4 bars	24 bars	4 bars	24 bars

AAA	AA	AA
Collective playing	Clarinet solo	Trumpet solo
	Tb countermelody	Cl & tb accompaniment
Swinging 4/4	Swinging 4/4	Swinging 4/4
24 bars	16 bars	16 bars

6.9. Arrangement of "Blanche Touquatoux"—Kid and Cecile Ory (1945)

The vocal section is immediately followed (the intro is not repeated) by a whole form of collective playing (AAA), and a change of rhythm from the tresillo to a swinging 4/4. The form is then shortened to sixteen bars for a clarinet solo with the trombone playing a lower countermelody (AA), and a trumpet solo with the clarinet and the trombone providing their usual accompaniment (AA). The rhythmical change from tresillo to the swinging 4/4, also illustrates what Ernest Borneman perceived as a "tangent" in jazz:

> [D]uring the very years which, in recording history, appear to be the most fruitful ones—the years when the New Orleans jazzmen migrated to Chicago and were recorded there for the first time. It must have been during these very years that jazz lost its "Spanish tinge" and reduced itself to a series of improvisations in straight 2/4 and 4/4 time on Tin Pan Alley tunes. What got lost at that time was the essence of jazz: the African and Creole themes of the formative years, and the Creole manner of rhythmic accentuation.[60]

On one of his 1960 Verve sessions, Ory recorded a solo version of "Blanche Touquatoux" that incorporated elements coming from later jazz developments, such as an eight-bar intro arguably based on the I-vi-ii-V progression of the "Rhythm changes," and what would be best described as a walking bass line in 2/4, while the guitar and the bass carry a strong feel of 4/4.[61]

INTRO	AA | AA	AA | AA
Spoken line	Vocal verses	Tpt melody | Tb melody
Rhythm section	Rhythm section	Clarinet countermelody
I-vi-ii-V		
8 bars	16 bars | 16 bars	16 bars | 16 bars

AA	AA	TAG
Piano solo	Collective playing	
16 bars	16 bars	2 bars

6.10. Arrangement of "Blanche Touquatoux"—Kid Ory (1960)

This time the form is based on two repetitions of the verse. After the eight-bar intro with Ory's speaking the opening line, he continues with four vocal verses (the form repeated twice (AA/AA). They are followed by two forms of collective playing, with the trumpet and trombone taking the melody one after the other, supported by the clarinet playing a countermelody (AA/AA). After a bouncy piano solo (AA), the piece closes with a recap of the melody played by the three horns in typical New Orleans style (AA) before a short contrasting tag of two bars. The lyrics of both Ory's version are substantially different from those given by Rodolphe Desdunes and reproduced by Saxon, according to whom there were dozens of versions of "Toucoutou."[62] As Desdunes explained, Beaumont composed a few songs as the trial proceeded, of which he provided a few examples (two lines of which were sung verbatim by Cecile Ory as the third verse of the song). Ory's lyrics are also shorter—better fit to be jazzed up—but considering that Beaumont wrote many verses, and that both are clearly a satire of the "Toucoutou Affair," we can identify them as variants of the same song.

Blanche Touquatoux, Kid Ory (1960)[63]

Ah Blanche, La misère (spoken)	Eh Blanche, It's misery (spoken)
Ma palé la Cou(r) Suprême	I'm gonna speak to the Supreme Court
Quandé chargé la laitue	When they'll charge us the lettuce*
Société, fini pour nous	Society is finished for us
Pour nous cacher ton cas passe	To hide from us your case of passing
Commandant mo tendé frère,	Commander, hear me brother
Ton conseil, ça li tôt faire	Your advice, that's soon to do [to be done]
(A)pré les Vieux kolié m'ont mis	After the Elders, [the] collar [they] put [on] me**
Pour nous cacher ton cas passe	To hide from us, your case of passing
Ma palé la Cou(r) Suprême	I'm gonna speak to the Supreme Court
Quandé chargé la laitue	When they'll charge us the lettuce*
Société, fini pour nous	Society is finished for us
Pour nous cacher ton cas passe	To hide from us your case of passing
Commandant mo tendé frère,	Commander, hear me brother
Ton conseil, ça, li tôt faire	Your advice, that's soon to do [to be done]
J'ai connais ça li, li fé	I knew that it [this], he/she did
Pour nous cacher ton cas passe	To hide from us your case of passing

*As above, "Laitue/lettuce" is slang for money.
** To "Mettre le collier/Put the collar" is to be arrested.

During the same session, Ory also recorded "C'est L'autre Can-Can (aka Creole Song)," in a longer version of the same song that Jelly Roll Morton sung for Lomax, and "Creole Bobo," which also appeared on his 1946 Columbia album. This last song, a Creole version of the well-known song "Ah! vous dirai-je maman" ("Twinkle, Twinkle, Little Star"), might have "naturally" led to the series of traditional French children songs that followed.[64] "[S]omeone at Verve [had taken] notice of Ory's success in France" and wanted to release an album of French songs, but they remained unreleased for years because "[w]hat the French really wanted . . . was traditional jazz, not FRERE JACQUES." Nonetheless, the songs are well performed, mixing good early New Orleans jazz style with solid vocals and instrumental solos.[65] Although this choice of songs might have been a faux pas, I suggest that Ory was drawn to record them as a tribute to his French heritage, as he most likely heard and sang them as a child; as mentioned in chapter 5, he remembered his mother singing to him in French—not such a foolish idea considering the interest in French Creole songs from Louisiana prompted by the revival.

Les Ognons

Finally, "Les Oignons" (often spelled "Les Ognons"), a rather creative song, was inspired by the street cries of an onion vendor and a *marchande de calas* (see chapter 2). In the November 14, 1958 interview, Alice Zeno laughed while remembering "Les Oignons," which both she and George Lewis (her son) knew as a little ring-around song. Although she spoke more than she sang, her enunciation suggests that she was hearing the melody of the song as she was reciting the lyrics: "Les Oignons sont à bon marché / Celles-ci, celles-çà / Ma commère tourné le dos" (see translation below).[66] In the liner notes for the 2000 CD reissue of the original Circle album, *Jazz A' La Creole* [sic], Rudi Blesh remembered an unexpected reception:

> The *Jazz A La Creole* [sic] session sticks in my memory for a peculiar aftermath. We set up the date for the Creole Serenaders to wax some traditional cooking A 'La Creole [sic], with Nick [Albert Nicholas], Pops [Foster], Danny Barker, and the Harlem stride giant, James P. Johnson. Nick and Danny did the Creole singing. There was much Creole laughter after the vocals one of them in particular. Within weeks we had a mysterious best selling single in Montreal and Quebec. Later on we found that our little Circle, dedicated to "pure" jazz, ha[d] innocently waxed a "party" record in patois we didn't dig. But they did dig it in Canada where the local French and the New Orleans Creole are strongly similar—both being Early French.[67]

I suspect that the mysterious hit was "Les Ognons," as its call-and-response refrain *"Belles calas tout chauds!"* can be a double entendre with sexual connotations.

Les Ognons, Albert Nicholas (1947)

Les Ognons, les ognons,	Onions, onions
Les Ognons tout de bon marché	Onions going cheap
C'est li ci, c'est li ça,	These ones, those ones,
Ma commère tourné le dos.	*Ma commère* turns her back.
Poules couchées? / Oui Madame!	Chicken asleep? / Yes Madam!
Vous pas mentez? / Non Madame!	You're not lying? / No Madam!
Belles calas tout chauds,	Nice calas all warm,
Belles calas tout chauds,	Nice calas all warm,
Belles calas, belles calas,	Nice calas, nice calas,
Belles calas tout chauds.	Nice calas all warm.[68]

The presence of James P. Johnson, with his superb piano playing, and the sophistication of the arrangement are reminiscent of Jelly Roll Morton's recordings with his Red Hot Peppers or with Lizzie Miles. After a four-bar intro on the piano, Albert Nicholas sings the eight-bar verse about the cheap onions (twice) supported by Danny Barker four-in-a-bar chordal playing on guitar and Pops Foster walking bass, while the piano discreetly harmonizes with, and ornaments the melody, with some punctuating chords on the left hand (AA).

INTRO	AA	INTRO TO B / INTERLUDE	BB
Piano	"Les Ognons"	Call & response	"Belles calas"
	Nicholas on vocals	Nicholas & Barker on vocals	Nicholas on vocals
4 bars	16 bars	4 bars	16 bars

BB	INTERLUDE	BB | BB	INTERLUDE
Clarinet solo	Call and response	Clarinet solo	Call & response
	Clarinet & voice		Clarinet & voice
16 bars	4 bars	32 bars	4 bars

B	BB
Clarinet solo	Nicholas on vocals
8 bars	16 bars

6.11. Arrangement of "Les Ognons"—Albert Nicholas (1947)

This section actually serves as a prelude for the rest of the performance which is based on a street cry, "Belles calas tout chauds!" introduced by a four-bar intro—acting as an interlude—in call and response between Nicholas and Barker. After his vocal rendition of the "Belles calas" eight-bar verse (BB), Nicholas picks up his clarinet for a sixteen-bar solo, close to the melody (BB), followed by the four-bar interlude between the clarinet and Barker singing the response. Then Nicholas takes the lead again for four choruses, during which he nicely develops his improvisation around the melody, backed by Johnson, who uses his right hand more and more like the clarinet of a traditional horn section by providing a countermelody in the high register of the piano (BB/BB). Finally, the four-bar interlude between the clarinet and voice leads to a last eight on the clarinet (B), after which Nicholas finishes by singing two more verses (BB), slightly varying the last eight with the insertion of two other calls—"Croissants Madame"/"Chevrettes Madame" (this last one being similar to Louisa's cry described by Ms. Arguedas in chapter 2). Recorded in 1949 as an instrumental, Sidney Bechet's version of "Les Oignons"—based only on the "Oignons theme"—accompanied by the Claude Luter Orchestra became a huge hit in France, where Bechet was at the forefront of the revival movement.[69]

In the original liner notes of the 1947 Circle Record *Jazz a la Creole* [sic], Harriet Janis wrote:

> [s]o natural and casual is the creation of these [Creole] songs, so adaptable to many occasions and purposes, that they almost seem to originate spontaneously. The Creole troubadour invents songs ... Such playful mockery, and teasing and spoofing in general are favorite themes. Known as "signifying songs" they resemble in intent the "songs of derision" in Africa.[70]

Unfortunately, she didn't say to whom the songs were known as "signifying songs." In other words, did the musicians of the band or the Creoles themselves use this expression, or did she perform research of her own and made the link with the signifying songs herself? After quoting "Sali Dame" and citing the Circle record, Marshall W. Stearns added that "the New Orleans Creoles call it a 'signifying song,'" but, then again this could be him extrapolating on Janis's notes. In any case, he also added that "[i]n West Africa, these numbers are called songs of allusion and the people at whom they are directed actually pay the singers to stop singing and go away."[71]

On the other hand, in the *The Myth of the Negro Past* (1941), Melville J. Herskovits noted that "many other instances of the principle of indirection

... might be given from" West Africa, the West Indies, and "the United States, such as the oblique references in the 'songs of allusion.'" For, as he explained, "the situation of the Negro in the New World, past and present, has been such as to force discretion upon him as a survival technique."[72] Such a technique was used by the enslaved to exchange information without the knowledge of their masters. In a late 1930s interview, Wash Wilson, born and enslaved in Louisiana before being bought and moved to Texas with seven other families, recalled:

> When de n----rs go round singin' "Steal Away to Jesus," dat mean dere gwine be a 'ligious meetin' dat night. Dat de *sig'fication* of a meetin'. De masters 'fore and after freedom didn't like dem 'ligious meetin's, so us natcherly slips off at night, down in de bottoms or somewheres. Sometimes us sing and pray all night.[73]

Whether or not there is a link with the Creole songs, the concept of signifying has now come to encompass a wide variety of practices that include (among many others) satire, parody, and double meaning.[74] However, songs like "Michié Préval" and "Mesieur Mazureau" (see chapter 2) or "Toucoutou" clearly demonstrate that, long before the development of jazz, the Creole community had a well-established practice of writing and singing satirical songs, also characterized by their lyrical flexibility and improvisational and storytelling nature.

Since the 1867 publication of *Slave Songs of the United States*, discussed in chapter 2, some eighty to a hundred Creole songs have been collected by various musicians and scholars who all observed and described African- and Caribbean-derived elements—complex syncopated rhythms, vocal and melodic inflections, formal flexibility, and improvisation—as important, but difficult to notate, characteristics of the songs.[75]

The revival recordings of Creole songs were generally made in a joyous and festive mood, and often include some call and response certainly appropriate for *cowan* dinners, dances, fish fries, lawn parties, Mardi Gras, and so on, with the exception of Ulysse Picou's song, which offers a glimpse into a calmer and more intimate context of music-making. Apart from Lizzie Miles's, the vocal renditions are slightly ornamented with only a short ending vibrato or some light growl used once in a while, depending on the singer, often an instrumentalist of the band. Finally, the adaptation, spontaneous composition, improvisation of lyrics, and formal flexibility stand out as striking features of the Creole songs, as the recordings, the oral history, and the literature all clearly demonstrate. Judging by the number of Creole songs that were collected at a time when the French Creole culture was either declining or had almost disappeared, it is safe to assume that early jazz musicians had access to a large repertoire, and sometimes composed/improvised some new songs. As Nickerson wanted us to know, "there was a time when the songs were plentiful and popular."[76]

Mentioned only briefly, if at all, in jazz histories,[77] the Creole songs form an original repertoire—a micromusic—that belongs both to the Black American folk music that gave birth to jazz, and to Franco-American folk music, reflecting not only the multicultural and creolized nature of jazz, but also the cultural heritage of the Creoles of Louisiana as Creole songs are still being played and recorded to this day.[78]

EPILOGUE

In 2016, as I was getting ready to read, listen, transcribe, and analyze the recordings, interviews, articles, and books I had gathered so far, Danny Barker's autobiography, *A Life in Jazz*, was reissued by The Historic New Orleans Collection. Through his mother Rose Barbarin, Barker was born in this influential family of Creole early jazz musicians. Radio host Gwen Thompkins, who wrote the introduction, jumped on the occasion to record a show—"Remembering Danny Barker"—for her weekly program *Music Inside Out* in front of a live audience. Being in New Orleans, I obviously had to go.

    The evening was lovely: nice wine, good food, informative presentation, interesting interviews, and great music. I was delighted. After Thompkins's show, as the Shannon Powell Traditional Jazz Band got on stage to conclude the evening, I was just having a good time, no more in research mode, no note-taking. So, I have to admit that I don't recall any of the pieces they played, except for one. How could I forget? That moment toward the end of the evening, when the band began to play "La Vie en Rose"—the song that put me on the path of this research so many years ago.[1]

Appendices

Appendix 1

MORE ABOUT CREOLIZATION AND CREOLE IDENTITY

As mentioned in chapter 1, creolization is both a concept and the model of a historical and sociological process that aims to describe and explain the many facets of contact, exchange, and cross-fertilization between cultures—especially in colonial and postcolonial societies—that leads to the creation of new languages and new cultural products or practices. Working on the meaning of the concept of *Creole* as a signifier for both culture and identity, Jean-Luc Bonniol has used the model offered by the "old French colonies" to identify the basic components of creolizing situations (*situations créolisantes*):

—Heteronomy of a colonial project characterized by the predominance of a plantation economy controlled from afar, and designed to meet the needs of a metropolis;
—Disappearance, in the case of the Caribbean, or absence (in the Indian Ocean) of an indigenous population, so that all people came from somewhere else (*viennent d'ailleurs*). Besides the European colonizers, the flow of newcomers predominantly comes from the forced immigration of Africans as a result of the demand for enslaved workers for the plantations;
—Hierarchical ideology based on the diversity of physical appearances of the newcomers, where "race" is used to justify the social organization (the color prejudice).[1]

As a model of analysis, these three basic components rightfully describe colonial Louisiana as a creolizing location—which the state continued to be, before and after the Civil War.[2]

To better understand the concept of creolization, it is useful to review its development in the social sciences. As with many others, Bonniol noted that the concept of creolization, first introduced by linguists to explain the process that leads to the formation of new languages, was later expanded to social and cultural studies.[3]

In 1938, anthropologist Melville J. Herskovits (1895–1963) published *Acculturation: The Study of Culture Contact*, in which he informs his readers:

> Intensive study of contact between peoples is a relatively recent development in the anthropological repertory, and is to be attributed to a constantly increasing interest in the dynamics of human life.... In the United States, though the past decade or two have seen the word *acculturation* pass into the ethnological vocabulary, it has only been toward the latter part of this period that specific field studies of the results of cultural contact have been made.[4]

After reviewing the various current theories/definitions of acculturation and assimilation, Herskovits and two of his colleagues proposed the following definition: "Acculturation comprehends those phenomena which result when groups of individuals having different cultures come into continuous first-hand contact, with subsequent changes in the original cultural patterns of either or both groups."[5]

Three years later, in *The Myth of the Negro Past*, in which he argued against the myth that African Americans had retained none of their ancestral culture, Herskovits described the process of acculturation and reinterpretation with which Africans held on to their traditions with regard to religion (renaming of old deities), social organization (adapting patterns of cooperative insurance for the sick, and "of mutual self-help in matters pertaining to death"), and culture ("reworking of song and dance in accordance with the demands of the new setting"), in a social environment dominated by European beliefs, terminology, and conventions. "This principle of disregard for outer [European] form while retaining inner values, characteristic of Africans everywhere, is thus revealed as the most important single factor making for an understanding of the acculturative situation. That ... reveals intellectual sophistication rather than naïveté...."[6] As might be expected, similar processes of adaptation occurred in other colonies of the Caribbean. In 1940, Cuban anthropologist Fernando Ortiz (1881–1969), coined the term *transculturation* "to express the highly varied phenomena that have come about in Cuba as a result of the extremely complex transmutations of culture that have taken place here." By doing so, Ortiz was aiming to describe the many cultural contacts that took place in, and forged, the nation of Cuba, which included the processes of deculturation (losing one's culture) and acculturation (acquiring—or being imposed—a new one) that lead to the creation of new cultural phenomena by various social groups engaged in the reconstruction of their identity. He suggested calling the end result neoculturation.⁷ Both Herskovits's and Ortiz's concepts of reinterpretation and neoculturation underline the defining characteristic of creolization, that something new is created through the cross-fertilization of various cultures, as people adapt to a new environment.

While he was reflecting about the problematics of cultural diversity and cultural difference, this dynamic and creative aspect of creolization was nicely articulated by Homi Bhabha's suggestion of hybridity as a "third space":

> [A]ll forms of culture are continually in a process of hybridity. But for me the importance of hybridity is not to be able to trace two original moments from which the third emerges, rather hybridity to me is the "third space" which enables other positions to emerge.... The process of cultural hybridity gives rise to something different, something new and unrecognisable, a new area of negotiation of meaning and representation.⁸

Similarly, Paul Gilroy's work on the Black Atlantic points to the potentialities and challenges of cultural contacts. Building on the idea of "double-consciousness" proposed by W. E. B. Du Bois (1868–1963) in *The Souls of Black Folk*, Gilroy writes that "[s]triving to be both European and [B]lack requires some specific forms of double consciousness" and rejects the notion of "ethnic absolutism":⁹

> However, where racist, nationalist, or ethnically absolutist discourses orchestrate political relationships so that these identities appear to be mutually exclusive, occupying the space between them or trying to demonstrate their continuity has been viewed as a provocative and even oppositional act or political insubordination.... Regardless of their affiliation to the right, left, or center, groups have fallen back on the idea of cultural nationalism, on the overintegrated conceptions of culture which present immutable, ethnic differences as an absolute break in the histories and experiences of "black" and "white" people. Against this choice stands another, more difficult option: the theorisation of creolisation, métissage, mestizaje, and hybridity.... All of them ["post-slave, black cultural forms"] are configured by their compound and multiple origins in the mix of African and other cultural forms sometimes referred to as creolisation.¹⁰

Both Louisiana and the Caribbean were once contact zones where colonization and slavery, the Louisiana Purchase, the Haitian Revolution, and the

Civil War successively led to either intentional or forced migrations, and the need to (re)adjust to different situations, making them locations propitious for creolization. There were challenges related to cultural identity for all the communities involved, but maybe more for the dominated groups such as the enslaved Africans and, eventually, the *Gens de Couleur Libres*.

IDENTITY POLITICS AND *CRÉOLITÉ*

"Neither Europeans, nor Africans, nor Asians, we proclaim ourselves Creoles."[11] When they wrote these words as the opening statement of their manifesto *In Praise of Creoleness*, Jean Bernabé, Patrick Chamoiseau, and Raphaël Confiant had been preceded by a few generations of Black and Creole intellectuals who had been working to share and promote their culture. In the 1920s Martinican Paulette Nardal and her sisters held an influential salon in Paris, where Antilleans, Africans, and African Americans met regularly. Nardal was also the cofounder, general secretary of, and contributor to *La Revue du Monde Noir* (1930–32), which, along with the salon, paved the way to the work of Aimé Césaire, also from Martinique; Léopold Senghor from Senegal (and later its president); and Léon-Gontran Damas, from French Guiana.[12] The three of them are usually credited for founding the Négritude movement that put forward a "theory of the distinctiveness of African personality and culture [developed] in Paris in the period immediately before and after the Second World War"[13] The Négritude movement is not without similarity with the Harlem Renaissance—from late 1910s to late 1930s—to which its founders were exposed (for instance at the Nardal salon), and by which they were influenced.

However, long before the Harlem Renaissance and the emergence of Négritude and *Créolité*, the *Gens de Couleur Libres* claimed their cultural identity as French Creoles and not Anglo-African Americans. Even if, at a time when African ancestry was disparaged as second-class citizenship, they put the emphasis on their French and Spanish ancestry, the emergence and affirmation of *Créolité* in the 1970s retrospectively validates their claim of forming a distinct people, whose history was briefly chronicled by Rodolphe Desdunes in *Nos hommes et notre histoire* published in 1911.

Appendix 2

CHANSON DU VIÉ BOSCUGO/MICHIÉ PRÉVAL (DANSEZ CALINDA)

In the first column, the incomplete chorus is reproduced as it appears both in *Textes anciens en créole louisianais* and in Coleman's 1885 *Historical Sketch Book*. The translation in the second column comes from Krehbiel (*Afro-American Folksongs*, 151–53), apart from verses or words in italics that indicate translation or modifications made by the author (to remain close to the Creole text). In the second and third column, the numbers correspond to the order of the verses as they appear in Krehbiel or in Monroe (*Bayou Ballads*, 40–55). It's worth noticing that, in *Textes anciens*, the verses consistently rhyme mostly in AABB with a few exceptions in ABAB or AAAA.

From *Textes anciens en créole louisianais*	Translation from Krehbiel or by the author	From Mina Monroe's *Bayou Ballads*

1- Mouché Préval
  Li donné grand bal,
  Li fé nègue payé
  Pou sauté ainpé.
	1- Monsieur Préval
	  Gave a big ball,
	  He made the *negroes* pay
	  For their little hop.
		1- Michié Préval
		  Li donnain grand bal,
		  Li fé nég' payé
		  Pou sauté in pé.

Chorus:
  Dansé Calinda, etc. . . .
	Dance Calinda,
	  Boudoum, boudoum!
	  Dance Calinda,
	  Boudoum, boudoum!
		Dansez Calinda,
		  Boudjoum, boudjoum!
		  Dansez Calinda,
		  Boudjoum, boudjoum!

2- Li donné soupé
  Pou nègue régalé,
  So vié la misique
  Té baye la colique.
	4- He gave a supper
	  To regale the *negroes*,
	  His old music
	  Gave you the colic.
		9- Li donnain soupé
		  Pou nous régalé,
		  So vié la misique
		  Donnain nous la colique.

	2- *In the barn*
	  Was a grand gala,
	  I imagine the horses
	  Were very surprised.
		2- Dans l'équirie-là,
		  Ya-vé grand gala,
		  Mo cré chouals la-yié
		  Té bien étonnés.

3- Mouché Préval
    Té capitaine bal,
    So cocher Louis
    Té maite cérémoni.
	3- Monsieur Préval
	    Was Captain of the ball,
	    His coachman, Louis
	    Was Master of Ceremonies.
		3- Michié Préval
		    Li té capitaine bal,
		    So coché Louis
		    Té mait' cérémonie.

4- Ala ain bourrique
    Tendé la misique,
    Li vini valsé
    Com quand li cabré.
	5- *Then the old Jackass*
	    Heard the music,
	    He came to waltz
	    As when he rears.	

	Monsieur Mazuro
	    In his big office,
	    Looks just like a frog
	    In a water tub.
		4- Michié Mazuro,
		    Dans so gros biro,
		    Li jist som crapaud,
		    Dans in baille d'olo.

5- Yavé des négresses
    Belle com yé maîtresse,
    Yé té volé bel bel
    Dans l'ormoir Mamzel.
	6- *There were negresses*
	    As pretty as their mistresses,
	    They had stolen fineries
	    From the armoire of Mamzel.
		5- Yé té gain négresses
		    Belles passé maîtresses,
		    Qui volé belles-belles
		    Dans l'armoir momzelles.

6- Blanc et pi noir
    Yé dansé bamboula,
    Vou pas jamais voir
    Ain pli grand gala.
	7- *Whites and Blacks*
	    They danced the bamboula,
	    You will never see
	    A grander gala.	

7- Ala gardien la geole,
    Li trouvé ca bin drole,
    Li dit "Mo aussi,
    Ma fé bal ici."
	11- *The jail keeper,*
	    He found it very droll,
	    He said: "I, too
	    Will give a ball here."
		7- Alà mait' géole
		    Li trouvé ça si drôle,
		    Li dit: "Moin aussi,
		    Mo fé bal ici."

8- Et pi le wacheman
    Yé tombé la dan,
    Yé fé branle-bas
    Dans lichiri là.
	And then the watchman
	    They walked in,
	    They made a big mess
	    In the barn.	

9- Yé mené yé tous
    Dans la calabous,
    Lendemain matin
    Yé fouetté yé bin.
	They brought them all
	    In the "calabous" [the jail]
	    The morning after
	    They whipped them well.	

	13- *They took Monsieur Préval*
	    And put him in jail,
	    Because he gave a ball
	    To steal our money.
		8- Yé prend Maît' Préval
		    Yé metté li prison,
		    Pasqué li donnain bal
		    Pour volé nous l'arzent.

Chanson du Vié Boscugo/Michié Préval (Dansez Calinda)

10- Yé té volé bel chaine,
    Yé té volé Romaine,[1]
    Yé té volé n'écrin,
    Et pi souyé fin.

They stole the nice chain,
    They stole the "Romaine,"
    They stole the case
    And the fine shoes.

11- Ain mari godiche
    Vini mandé postiche,
    Qui té servi so femme
    Pou fé la bel dame.

A gawky husband
    Asked for a hairpiece,
    That was used by his wife
    To look like a belle.

8- *Poor* Nancy Latiche
    Who had skinny legs,
    Stole the false calves
    Of Madame Mazuro.

10- Pauv' Nancy Labiche
    Qui gain jambe fizeau,
    Volé faux mollets
    À Madame Mazuro.

12- Comment sapajou,
    To pran mo kilotte,
    Non, mo maîte, mo di vous
    Mo jis pran vos botte.

9- "How now Sazou
    You stole my trousers,"
    "No master, *I told you*
    I took only your boots."

6- "Commen don, Zazou,
    To volé mo quilotte?"
    "Non, non, non, mo maît',
    Mo jist prend vos bottes!"

13- Piti maîtresse
    Li tapré crié,
    To voir négresse
    C'est mo robe to vole.

10- And a little Miss
    Cries out,
    "*I see you*, negress
    You stole my dress."

14- Chez Mouché Préval
    Dans la ri n'opital,
    Yé té nègue payé [2]
    Pou sauté ainpé.

12- At Monsieur Préval's
    In Hospital street,
    The *negroes* had to pay
    For their little hop.

15- Pove Mouché Préval
    Mo cré li bin mal,
    Ya pli encore bal
    Dans la ri n'opital.

14- Poor Monsieur Préval!
    I guess he feels pretty sick,
    He'll give no more balls
    In Hospital street

11- Pauv' Michié Préval
    Mo cré li bien malade,
    Li va pli donnain bal
    Dans la rue Hôpital.

16- Li payé cent piasse

    Li couri la chasse,

    Li dit: C'est fini,

    Ya pli bal sans permi.

15- He *paid* a hundred dollars,
    He found a hundred dollars
    He had to run for it, /
    To pay his fine,
    He said: "*It's over* /
    He said: "Well thank you,
    No more balls without a permit."

12- Li trouvé cent piast'

    Pou payé so l'amande,

    Li dit: "Bien merci,
    Pli bal sans permis!"

Michié Préval / Mesieur Mazureau (Dansez Calinda)

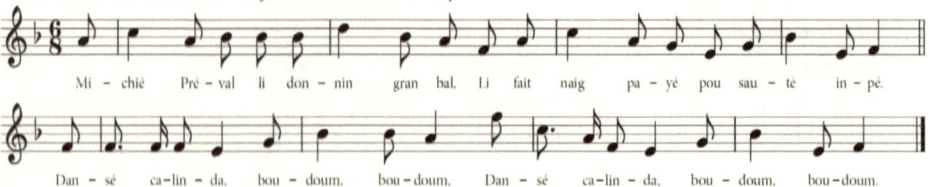

From Allen, Ware and Garrison, *Slave Songs of the United States*, (1867), p. 111

Mi-chié Pré-val li don-nin gran bal, Li fait naig pa-yé pou sau-té in-pé.

Dan-sé ca-lin-da, bou-doum, bou-doum, Dan-sé ca-lin-da, bou-doum, bou-doum.

Michié Préval li té capitaine bal,   Dans lequirie la yavé gran gala,   Yavé des négresse belle passé maitresse,
So cocher Louis té maite cérémonie   Mo cré choual layé té bien étonné.   Yé volé bébelle dans l'ormoire mamzelle.

From G. W. Cable, "The Dance in Place Congo" (1886), p. 528

Mi-chié Pre-val li don-né youn bal, Li fé naig payé trois pi-ass pou ren-tré.

Dan-cé Ca-lin-da, Bon-djoum! Bon-djoum! Dan-cé Ca-lin-da, Bon-djoum! Bon-djoum!

The low e in the 6th. might have been meant to be an f# as in the last bar

Dans l'equirie la 'y' avé grand gala,   Michié Preval li té capitaine bal,   Y avé des négresses belle passé maitresses,
Mo cré choual la yé t b'en étonné.   So cocher Louis, té maite cérémonie.   Qui volé bel-bel dans l'ormoire momselle.
Ala maite la geôle li trouvé si drôle,   Ouatchman la yé yé tombé la dans,
Li dit, 'moin aussi, mo fé bal ici.'   Yé fé gran' déga dans léquirie la.

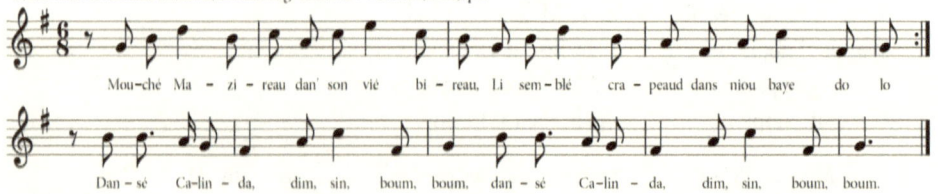

From Clara Gottschalk-Peterson, *Creole Songs from New Orleans* (1902), p.4

Mou-ché Ma-zi-reau dan' son vié bi-reau, Li sem-blé cra-peaud dans niou baye do lo

Dan-sé Ca-lin-da, dim, sin, boum, boum, dan-sé Ca-lin-da, dim, sin, boum, boum.

From H. E. Krehbiel, *Afro-American Folksongs* (1914), p. 152

Mi-chié Pré-val li don-nin gran' bal, Li fait nèg pa-yé pou' sau-ter in pé.

Dan-sé Ca-lin-da, bou-doum, bou-doum, Dan-sé Ca-lin-da, bou-doum, bou-doum.

Chanson du Vié Boscugo/Michié Préval (Dansez Calinda)

From Mina Monroe, *Bayou Ballads* (1921), pp. 40-53

Sung by Jeanne Arguedas (1939)
Library of Congress, LWO 4872 R 207-B, 21m17, Transcript p. 12. Transcription: Caroline Vézina.

Sung by Albertine Hilaire Alexis (1939)
Creole woman, born in 1865 in St. John the Baptist Parish, learned it as a child from her Godmother who was a White woman.
Library of Congress, LWO 4872 R 207-B, 43m30, transcript p. 19. Transcription: Caroline Vézina.

Sung by Caroline Durrieux in Baton Rouge (1957)
Archives de folklore et d'ethnologie, Université Laval, Fonds Harry Oster, Song 185, CD 1672, Track 41. Transcription: Caroline Vézina.

Appendix 3

CANTIQUE: TOMBEAU, TOMBEAU MARIE-MADELEINE

Tombeau, Tombeau Marie-Madeleine

Singer: Gilbert Martin
Fonds Harry Oster, CD 1672-45
Transcription: Caroline Vézina

Madeleine au Tombeau as collected by Achille Millien (version B)
Chants et Chansons in 1906

Tombeau, Tombeau Marie-Madeleine

Je M'en Vais Finir Mes Jours Avec la Madeleine

Tombeau, Tombeau Marie-Madeleine/Madeleine au Tombeau

The bold text indicates the lines from Achille Millien's version of the *cantique* that were adapted by Gilbert Martin and Nicholas A. Panique.

From Millien—Version B¹ quoted by Oster

Sur le tombeau la Madeleine
Ne faisait rien que pleurer.
Sur le tombeau la Madeleine
Ne faisait rien que pleurer.
Les anges vont la consoler,
Ne pleurez pas, la Madeleine:
Jésus-Christ est ressuscité,
Il est plus beau que le soleil.

C'est dans le Jardin des Olives,
Allez et vous le trouverez.
C'est dans le Jardin des Olives,
Allez et vous le trouverez.
—Beau jardinier, beau jardinier,
Que vous avez la face belle!
Vous avez les yeux de mon Dieu,
Et la couleur de mon Sauveur.

—Jardinier puisque tu m'appelles,
Tu me dis bien la vérité,
—Jardinier puisque tu m'appelles,
Tu me dis bien la vérité,
Car j'ai tout répandu mon sang
Pour tous les hommes sur la terre,
Car j'ai tout répandu mon sang
Pour racheter les pénitents.

La Madeleine se rapproche
De Jésus-Christ pour l'embrasser.
Jésus lui dit tout doucement:
—Retirez-vous, la Madeleine.
C'n'est point à vous à m'embrasser,
Mais c'est à vous à m'adorer.

From Gilbert Martin

Tombeau, tombeau, Marie-Madeleine,
Qu'avez-vous? J'entends pleurer.
Tombeau, tombeau, Marie-Madeleine,
Qu'avez-vous? J'entends pleurer.

Mon doux Jésus m'a dit
Tout doucement,
Retirez-vous, la Madeleine,
Ce n'est pas à vous de m'embrasser,
Mais oui, c'est à vous de m'adorer!

From Nicholas A. Panique

Tombeau, tombeau, la Vierge Madeleine,
Qu'avez-vous? J'entends pleurer.
Tombeau, tombeau la Vierge Madeleine,
Qu'avez-vous? J'entends pleurer.

Ah, nous pleurons le sort de not' Seigneur
Qui a donné son âme au paradis.

Je l'ai vous dit, tout doucement,
Retirez-vous avec la Madeleine.
Je vais finir mes jours avec la Madeleine,
Je vais finir mes jours avec mon trépas.

Oui j'ai trop tardé, Oui j'ai trop tardé,
Oui j'ai trop tardé avec la Madeleine.
Ce n'est à vous de m'embrasser,
Oui c'est à vous de m'adorer.

Here the bold text indicates the lines that appear in both cantiques. Both the lyrics and the melody of Nicholas A. Panique's second verse seem to come from another *cantique*.

Tombeau, Tombeau Marie-Madeleine **Nicholas A. Panique**	**Je M'en Vais Finir Mes Jours Avec la Madeleine** **Gilbert Martin**

Tombeau, tombeau, la Vierge Madeleine,   **Je m'en vais finir mes jours**
Qu'avez-vous? J'entends pleurer.   **Avec la Madeleine,**
Tombeau, tombeau la Vierge Madeleine,   **Je m'en vais finir mes jours,**
Qu'avez-vous? J'entends pleurer.   Seigneur, à mon salut. (2x)

Ah, nous pleurons le sort de not' Seigneur,   C'est la, c'est la Madeleine,
Qui a donné son âme au paradis.   **Je m'en vais finir mes jours** avec vous. (2x)

Je l'ai vous dit, tout doucement,   C'est là **j'ai trop tardé**
Retirez-vous avec la Madeleine.   Quand je suis un infidèle,
Je vais finir mes jours avec la Madeleine,   C'est là **j'ai trop tardé,**
Je vais finir mes jours avec mon trépas.   Seigneur, secourez-nous. (2x)

Oui j'ai trop tardé,   Paradis en nous, secourez-nous ah!
Oui j'ai trop tardé,   Paradis en nous, délivrez-nous. (2x)
Oui **j'ai trop tardé** avec la Madeleine.
Ce n'est à vous de m'embrasser,   Mais, à la Madeleine,
Oui c'est à vous de m'adorer.   **Je m'en vais finir mes jours** avec vous. (2x)

Appendix 4

CANTIQUE: DANS UN JARDIN SOLITAIRE

Dans un Jardin Solitaire

Singer : Nicholas Augustin Panique
Fonds Harry Oster., CD 1675-8
Transcription : Caroline Vézina

(Prière) Dans un jardin solitaire, Un seul Dieu qui souffre pour nous. Dans

un jardin solitaire, Un seul Dieu qui souffre pour nous. Le Ju-

da, ils l'ont pris, oui, Ils l'ont vendu aux Juifs, Un seul Dieu qui souffre pour nous. Au ber-

ceau, j'ai perdu ma mère, À la Cour et sous Pilate. Au ber-

ceau, j'ai perdu mon père, À la Cour et sous Pilate. (Prière)

DANS UN JARDIN SOLITAIRE

As sung by Nicholas A. Panique

Version 1	Version 2
Fonds Harry Oster	**Fonds Harry Oster**
1674, Track 35	**1675, Track 8**
	A bit slower than the previous version
	Inserted in between prayers in Latin

0m28 Prayer

Dans un jardin solitaire,
Un seul Dieu qui souffre pour nous.
Dans un jardin solitaire,
Un seul Dieu qui souffre pour nous.

— Version 1 —

Dans un jardin solitaire,
Un seul Dieu qui souffre pour nous.
Dans un jardin solitaire,
Un seul Dieu qui souffre pour nous.

Le Juda, ils l'ont pris, oui,
Ils l'ont vendu aux Juifs,
Un seul Dieu qui souffre pour nous.

Dans un jardin solitaire,
Un seul Dieu qui souffre pour nous.

Au berceau, j'ai perdu ma mère,
A la Cour et sous Pilate.
Au berceau, j'ai perdu mon père,
A la Cour et sous Pilate.

— Version 2 (continued) —

Le Juda, ils l'ont pris, oui,
Ils l'ont vendu aux Juifs,
Un seul Dieu qui souffre pour nous.

Au berceau, j'ai perdu ma mère,
A la Cour et sous Pilate.
Au berceau, j'ai perdu mon père,
A la Cour et sous Pilate.

1m31 Prayer

Dans un jardin solitaire,
Un seul Dieu qui souffre pour nous.
Dans un jardin solitaire,
Un seul Dieu qui souffre pour nous.

Le Juda, ils l'ont pris oui,
Ils l'ont crucécifié, [sic]
Un seul Dieu qui souffre pour nous.

2m 21 Prayer

Dans un jardin solitaire,
Un seul Dieu qui souffre pour nous.

Au berceau, j'ai perdu ma mère,
A la Cour et sous Pilate.
Au berceau, j'ai perdu mon père,
A la Cour et sous Pilate.

TEXT FROM FÉNELON—AU SANG QU'UN DIEU VA RÉPANDRE/LA PASSION DE NOTRE SEIGNEUR J. S.

From *Cantiques du Petit Séminaire de la Primatiale de Lyon, recueillis, harmonisés ou composés par l'abbé A. Stanislas Neyrat*, 72–73.

The bold text indicates the lines or themes found in the *cantique* "Dans un jardin solitaire" sung by Nicholas A. Panique (see page 146).

1. Au sang qu'un Dieu va répandre,
Ah! mêlez du moins vos pleurs,
Chrétiens, qui venez entendre
Le récit de ces douleurs.
Puisque c'est pour vos offenses
Que ce Dieu souffre aujourd'hui,
Animés par ses souffrances,
Vivez et mourez pour lui.

2. **Dans un jardin solitaire**
Il sent de rudes combats;
Il prie, il craint, il espère;
Son cœur veut et ne veut pas.
Tantôt la crainte est plus forte,
Et tantôt l'amour plus fort:
Mais enfin l'amour l'emporte,
Et lui fait choisir la mort.

3. **Judas,** que la fureur guide,
L'aborde d'un air soumis;
Il l'embrasse, et ce perfide
Le livre à ses ennemis.
Judas, un pécheur t'imite,
Quand il feint de l'apaiser:
Souvent sa bouche hypocrite
Le trahit par un baiser.

4. On l'abandonne à la rage
De cent tigres inhumains;
Sur son aimable visage
Les soldats portent leurs mains.

Vous deviez, Anges fidèles,
Témoins de ces attentats,
Ou le mettre sous vos ailes,
Ou frapper tous ces ingrats.

5. **Ils le traînent au grand-prêtre,**
Qui seconde leur fureur,
Et ne veut le reconnaître
Que pour un blasphémateur.
Quand il jugera la terre,
Ce Sauveur aura son tour;
Aux éclats de son tonnerre
Tu le connaîtras un jour.

6. Tandis qu'il se sacrifie,
Tout conspire à l'outrager:
Pierre lui-même l'oublie,
Et le traite d'étranger;
Mais Jésus perce son âme
D'un regard tendre et vainqueur,
Et met, d'un seul trait de flamme,
Le repentir dans son cœur.

7. **Chez Pilate on le compare**
Au dernier des scélérats;
Qu'entends-je? ô peuple barbare,
Tes cris sont pour Barabbas!
Quelle indigne préférence!
Le Juste est abandonné,
On condamne l'innocence,
Et le crime est pardonné.

8. On le dépouille, on l'attache,
Chacun arme son courroux;
Je vois cet Agneau sans tache,
Tombant presque sous les coups.
C'est à nous d'être victimes,
Arrêtez! cruels bourreaux!
C'est pour effacer vos crimes
Que son sang coule à grands flots.

9. Une couronne cruelle
Perce son auguste front;
A ce chef, à ce modèle,
Mondains, vous faites affront.
Il languit dans les supplices,
C'est un homme de douleurs:
Vous vivez dans les délices,
Vous vous couronnez de fleurs!

10. **Il marche, il monte au Calvaire
Chargé d'un infâme bois:**
De là, comme d'une chaire,
Il fait entendre sa voix:
Ciel! dérobe à la vengeance
Ceux qui m'osent outrager!
C'est ainsi, quand on l'offense,
Qu'un Chrétien doit se venger.

11. Une troupe mutinée
L'insulte et crie à l'envi:
Qu'il change sa destinée,
Et nous croirons tous en lui.
Il peut la changer sans peine,
Malgré vos nœuds et vos clous;
Mais le nœud qui seul l'enchaîne,
C'est l'amour qu'il a pour nous.

12. Ah! de ce lit de souffrance,
Seigneur, ne descendez pas;
Suspendez votre puissance,
Restez-y jusqu'au trépas;
Mais tenez votre promesse,
Attirez-nous après vous;
Pour prix de votre tendresse,
Puissions-nous y mourir tous!

13. Il expire, et la nature
Dans lui pleure son auteur:
Il n'est point de créature,
Qui ne marque sa douleur.
Un spectacle si terrible
Ne pourra-t-il me toucher?
Et serais-je moins sensible
Que n'est le plus dur rocher?

THEMES DEVELOPED IN FÉNELON'S TEXT FOUND IN THE LYRICS SUNG BY NICHOLAS A. PANIQUE

- **God (Jesus) suffering in the garden (of Gethsemane)**
  Que ce Dieu souffre aujourd'hui   Dans un jardin solitaire
  Dans un jardin solitaire   Un seul Dieu qui souffre pour nous

- **Followed by Judas's treason and the judgment by the High Priest and Pilate**
  Judas ... Le livre à ses ennemis   Le Juda, ... Ils l'ont vendu au Juifs
  Ils le traînent au grand-prêtre
  Chez Pilate on le compare   A la Cour et sous Pilate

- **Before being crucified**
  Il marche, il monte au Calvaire   Ils l'ont crucécifié [*sic*]
  Chargé d'un infâme bois

As mentioned in chapter 3, there are two intriguing lines in Panique's rendition, not related to the others, which belong either to another *cantique* or to a local version:

"Au berceau, j'ai perdu ma mère" and "Au berceau, j'ai perdu mon père"
In the cradle, I lost my mother   In the cradle, I lost my father

QUE NE SUIS-JE LA FOUGÈRE?

"Que ne suis-je la fougère," melody no. 490 in *La Clé du Caveau à l'usage de tous les Chansonniers français, des Amateurs, Auteurs, Acteurs de Vaudeville & tous les Amis de la Chanson* (1811), 215.

(40)

Que j'aime à voir les hirondelles. 487
Que j'aime à voir un corbillard (*voyez* air du pas redoublé).
Que je dois de reconnaissance. 655
Que le jour me dure. 488
Que le sultan Saladin. 489
Que l'on goûte ici de plaisirs (*voyez* ne v'là-t-il pas que j'aime).
Que n'avons-nous la verve heureuse (*voyez* j'aime ce mot de gentillesse).
Que ne suis-je la fougère, *ou* d'une amante abandonnée. 490
Que Pantin serait content. 491
Que ta porte, ô ma tendre amie, *ou* c'est à mon maître en l'art de plaire. 493
Quel désespoir! 494
Quel spectacle s'offre à mes yeux (*voyez* nous sommes précepteurs d'amour).
Qu'elle est, qu'elle est bien. 492
Quels accens, quels transports. 495
Qu'en voulez-vous dire? qu'en voulez-vous dire?. 496
Qui par fortune trouvera. 497
Qui trouve au bois belle endormie (*voyez* du serin qui te fait envie).
Qui veut entendre une chanson (*voyez* je suis un marchand épicier).
Qui veut savoir l'histoire entière. 498
Qu'il pleuve, qu'il vente, qu'il tonne (*voyez* à boire, à boire, à boire).
Qu'il tarde à ma tendresse. 499
Quinze ans, ma vielle et l'espérance, *ou* aux montagnes de la Savoie. . . 500
Quinze ans, Thémire, oh! le bel âge (*voyez* des simples jeux de son enfance).

CANTIQUE DE FÉNELON "PASSION DE N. S."

CANTIQUES
DU
PETIT SÉMINAIRE
DE LA PRIMATIALE
DE LYON,
RECUEILLIS, HARMONISÉS OU COMPOSÉS
PAR
L'abbé A. STANISLAS NEYRAT,
MAITRE DE CHAPELLE DE LA PRIMATIALE.

Ouvrage approuvé et recommandé
par Son Em. le Cardinal archevêque de Lyon, NN. SS. les archevêques
d'Alby, de Reims, et les évêques de Nancy, de Dijon,
de Strasbourg, de Grenoble, de Nîmes,
de St.-Brieuc et de Coutances ;
et apprécié avec éloges par M. Fétis, directeur du conservatoire
royal de Bruxelles
et M. Ch. Gounod, de l'Institut.

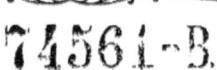

PARIS,
FÉLIX GIRARD, LIBRAIRE-ÉDITEUR,   CARTEREAU, ÉDITEUR DE MUSIQUE,
RUE CASSETTE, 30.   QUAI DE L'ÉCOLE, 10.

LYON,
PAUL CLOT, ÉDITEUR DE MUSIQUE,   FÉLIX GIRARD, LIBRAIRE-ÉDITEUR,
RUE DE L'IMPÉRATRICE, 1.   PLACE BELLECOUR, 30.

TOUS DROITS RÉSERVÉS.

Nº 36.
PASSION DE N. S.

Fénelon.
Mélodie rendue populaire par Fénelon.

Appendix 5

CANTIQUE: MARIE-MADELEINE, LAISSE-MOI PASSER

Marie-Madeleine, Laisse-Moi Passer

Singer: Alice Zeno
Interview January 25, 1960
Reel 1, 927_01, 15m28–16m20
Transcription: Caroline Vezina

Humming

Ma-rie - Ma-de-leine, lais-se - moi-pas-ser,   Lais-se-moi pas-ser   pour l'a - mour___ de Dieu,

Je suis___ en-fant de Jé - sus-Christ,   Lais-se-moi pas-ser   pour l'a - mour___ de Dieu.

Dans le pur-ga-toire,   y'a___ bien des âmes,   Dans le pur-ga-toire,   il y'a

(Spoken)

bien___ des âmes,   Lais - se - moi pas - ser   pour l'a - mour   de Dieu.

Ms. Zeno was 95 years old at the time of the interview. She sounded a little tired and her pitch was sometimes getting flat,

Marie-Madeleine, Laissez-Moi Passer

Singer : Nicholas Augustin Panique
Fonds Harry Oster, CD 1675-11
Transcription : Caroline Vézina

Ma-rie-Ma-de-leine, lais-sez - moi pas-ser, Lais-sez-moi pas-ser pour l'a - mour— de Dieu.

Là - bas,— là-haut, des - sus ces mon-tagnes, Nous— trou-ve-rez du nom de Jé-sus.

Tout en— é-crit, tout en com-pli, (pour) Lais-sez-moi pas-ser pour l'a - mour— de Dieu.
(ac - com-pli) 2nd time: du Ciel

The form is sung three times with the first phrase repeated twice in the first occurence
- First time : A A B C
- Second time : A B C
- Third time : A B C

Cantique: Marie-Madeleine, Laisse-Moi Passer

Marie, Je Souviens Ti / Enfant de Jésus-Christ

Dans un Brigatoire (Purgatoire)

Singer: Nicholas Augustin Panique
Fonds Harry Oster, CD 1674-34
Transcription: Caroline Vézina

The natural A grace note is almost a ghost note, but, although it varies, the singer seems to slide down voluntarily a little lower than Bb in his articulation of the glissando.

Marie-Madeleine, Laissez-Moi Passer

Singer : Inez Catalon
Nick Spitzer, *Zodico*, Side 1 : 6
Transcription : Caroline Vézina

The text in bold indicates the lyrics from Alice Zeno's *cantique* found in the other *cantiques*.

Marie-Madeleine, Laisse-Moi Passer
As sung by Alice Zeno

Marie-Madeleine, Laissez-Moi Passer
As sung by Nicholas A. Panique

A **Marie-Madeleine, laisse-moi passer,**
   Laisse-moi passer pour l'amour de Dieu.
B **Je suis l'enfant de Jésus-Christ,**
   Laisse-moi passer pour l'amour de Dieu.
C **Dans le purgatoire, y'a bien des âmes,**
   Dans le purgatoire, y'a bien des âmes,
   Laisse-moi passer pour l'amour de Dieu.

A Marie-Madeleine, laissez-moi passer,
   Laissez-moi passer pour l'amour de Dieu.
B Là-bas, là-haut, dessus ces montagnes,
   Nous trouverez du nom de Jésus.
C Tout en écrit, tout en compli,
   Laissez-moi passer pour l'amour de Dieu.

Marie, Je Souviens Ti/Enfant de Jésus-Christ
As sung by Gilbert Martin

Dans un Brigatoire (Purgatoire)
As sung by Nicholas A. Panique

Marie, je souviens ti,
Tu m'as fait manger par un chez vous. (2x)
L'enfant, je suis l'enfant, l'enfant de Jésus-Christ,
L'enfant, je suis l'enfant, c'est l'enfant du paradis.

Marie, je souviens ti,
Tu m'as fait manger par un chez vous. (2x)
L'enfant, je suis l'enfant, l'enfant de Jésus-Christ,
Mais Gabriel, je suis l'enfant, c'est l'enfant du paradis.

Me Domine Mysticum, Mysticum, Mysticum,
Me Domine.

Dans un brigatoire, pleins, pleins Chrétiens,
Dans un brigatoire, pleins, pleins Chrétiens,
J'ai dit pense à la mort, quand il faut mourir.

Si il faut mourir, si il faut rester,
Si il faut mourir, si il faut rester,
J'ai dit pense à la mort, quand il faut mourir.

J'ai fait mes adieux, Adieu famille,
J'ai fait mes adieux, Adieu parents,
J'ai dit pense à la mort, quand il faut mourir.

Marie-Madeleine, Laissez-moi Passer
As sung by Inez Catalon

Lyrics of verse A similar to Zeno's and Panique's, but set on a different melody. Verse B has the same lyrics as Zeno's, with the first line sung on the same melody as Panique's first line of verse B (Là-bas, là-haut, dessus ces montagnes) and C (Tout en écrit, tout en compli).

A Marie-Madeleine, Laissez-moi passer,
   Laissez-moi passer, c'est pour l'amour de Dieu.
B Je suis l'enfant de Jésus-Christ—
   Laissez-moi passer, c'est pour l'amour de Dieu.

Appendix 6

CANTIQUE: GRAND DIEU DU CIEL/ PARADIS L'AURA

Grand Dieu du Ciel / Paradis l'Aura

Singer : Célestine Morton
Fonds Elizabeth Brandon. CD 1173-24
Transcription : Caroline Vézina

- It is not clear if the modulation is intentional or not, although it sounds like it is.
- According to the analysis presented in chapter 3, capital letters stand for the melodic lines, and numbers stand for the verses.

Grand Dieu du Ciel/Paradis l'Aura
Célestine Morton—Melodic and Lyrical Analysis

Verse		Melodic Line
1	Grand Dieu du ciel, il y'aura du monde, Quel mérite avez-vous?	A
2	Tous c'qui servira la Vierge Marie, Paradis l'aura.	B
2	Tous c'qui servira la Vierge Marie, Paradis l'aura,	A
2	Tout ceuss' qui serviront la Vierge Marie, Paradis l'aura.	B
2	Tous c'qui servira la Vierge Marie, Paradis l'aura,	A
2	Tout ceuss' qui serviront la Vierge Marie, Paradis l'aura.	B
1	Grand Dieu du ciel, il y'aura du monde, Quel mérite avez-vous?	A
2	Tout ceuss' qui serviront la Vierge Marie, Paradis l'aura.	B

La Vierge Marie / Paradis l'Aura

Cantique: Grand Dieu Du Ciel/Paradis L'Aura

Grand Dieu du Ciel

Singer: Irma Landry
Mary Louise Wilson PhD Diss. p.46
Interview, February 26, 1976
Lake Charles, Louisiana

Grand Dieu du Ci - el, Il y'a du Mon - dé. Le Roi du Mon - dé.

Tout par - tout du Ciel, Le Roi du Mon - dé.

Grand Dieu du Ciel/Paradis l'Aura
La Vierge Marie/Paradis l'Aura

The text in bold indicates the lyrics from Célestine Morton's *cantique* found in Gilbert Martin's and Irma Landry's *cantiques*.

Grand Dieu du Ciel/Paradis l'Aura
Célestine Morton

Grand Dieu du ciel, il y'aura du monde,
Quel mérite avez-vous?
Tous c'qui servira la Vierge Marie,
Paradis l'aura.

Tous c'qui servira la Vierge Marie,
Paradis l'aura,
Tous ceuss' qui serviront la Vierge Marie,
Paradis l'aura.

Tous c'qui servira la Vierge Marie,
Paradis l'aura,
Tous ceuss' qui serviront la Vierge Marie,
Paradis l'aura.

Grand Dieu du ciel, il y'aura du monde,
Quel mérite avez-vous?
Tous ceuss' qui serviront la Vierge Marie,
Paradis l'aura.

Grand Dieu du Ciel/Paradis l'Aura
Célestine Morton

Grand Dieu du ciel, il y'aura du monde,
Quel mérite avez-vous?
Tous c'qui servira la Vierge Marie,
Paradis l'aura.

La Vierge Marie/Paradis l'Aura
Gilbert Martin

La Vierge Marie, jour et nuit, j'entends pleurer,
La Vierge Marie, jour et nuit, j'entends pleurer.
Mais Jésus la demande, de m'am'ner avec vous,
Mais Jésus la demande, de m'am'ner avec vous.

Et nous avons si tant de gens,
Et not' Seigneur, quoi faire en nous?
Et nous avons si tant de gens,
Et not' Seigneur quoi, faire en nous?

Celui qui servira la Vierge Marie,
Celui qui servira, paradis il aura.
Mais pauv'e il aura, l'aura, il aura,
Mais pauv'e il aura, paradis il aura.

Grand Dieu du Ciel
Irma Landry

Grand Dieu du ciel, il y'a du mondé [sic]
Le roi du mondé
Tout partout du ciel,
Le roi du mondé.

NOTES

INTRODUCTION

1. The word *Creole* has a long history and fluid meaning that is discussed in chapter 1. In this book it is used to designate the people of mixed descent of Louisiana unless indicated otherwise. The album *Jazz a la Creole* [sic] is discussed in chapter 6.

2. "La Vie en Rose" was created by Marianne Michel in 1946 and recorded by Édith Piaf in October of the same year. Although Piaf was surely involved in composing the music, Louiguy (Louis Guigliemi), Piaf's accompanist, is credited as the composer on the *Bulletin de Déclaration* dated November 4, 1945, although the song was probably written during 1944 and 1945. Piaf was registered as a lyricist but not yet as a composer at the Société des auteurs, compositeurs et éditeurs de musique (SACEM).

3. Allen, Ware, and Garrison, *Slave Songs of the United States*.

4. Ernest Borneman stands as an exception when, in 1959, he wrote that "While Anglo-Saxon music showed only harmonic similarities to African music, the music of the French, Spanish and Portuguese settlers also showed similarities in the handling of rhythm and timbre." Borneman, "Creole Echoes," Part 1, 14.

5. Even if jazz historians Rudi Blesh and Marshall Stearns have both written about the use of Afro-Spanish rhythms in some of the early rags and jazz pieces at the turn of the twentieth century. Moreover, in "Creole Echoes" (1959), Borneman argued for the importance in the development of jazz of "a mature and developed form of Afro-Latin music" that "flourished" in the mid-nineteenth century among "French and Spanish speaking Negroes and Creoles." However, Borneman's theory was strongly refuted by Gunther Schuller in 1968 for whom the "role [of Creole music], in the development of jazz is demonstrably a limited one." After Schuller's comment, Caribbean rhythms were generally mentioned only when speaking about Morton's "Spanish tinge" until Thomas Fiehrer's 1991 article, "From Quadrille to Stomp: The Creole Origins of Jazz" and Ted Gioia's *The History of Jazz* (1997), in which he noted that "[t]he Latin tinge was already a long-established fact of New Orleans music well before the arrival of jazz." Blesh, *Shining Trumpets* (1958 [1946]), 178, 350–51; Stearns (1956), *The Story of Jazz*, 73; Borneman "Creole Echoes," Part 1, 14; Schuller, *Early Jazz*, 59; Fiehrer, "From Quadrille to Stomp: The Creole Origins of Jazz"; Gioia, *The History of Jazz*, 6.

6. This quote comes from a section in which Giddins and DeVeaux are discussing "Congo Square, Creoles of Color and Uptown Negroes." In this context, "Creole music" refers to the music of the Creoles of New Orleans. The fact that some Creoles had Native American

ancestry is completely ignored, and that some also spoke Spanish is hardly ever mentioned. Giddins and DeVeaux, *Jazz*, 77–80, quote in text, 79.

7. I am borrowing the term *micromusic* from Mark Slobin, *Subcultural Sounds: Micromusics of the West*. See chapter 1, for more about micromusic.

8. Alice Zeno was interviewed three times on behalf of the Hogan Jazz Archive. The January 25, 1960, interview should not be confused with the ones conducted on November 14, 1958, and December 10, 1958, and used by Tom Bethell in *George Lewis—A Jazzman from New Orleans*. The 1960 interview, the first twenty minutes of which are in French in conversation with Harry Oster, was more focused on Ms. Zeno's life (although it had been discussed in 1958) and the songs, *cantiques*, and dances she remembered.

9. This description comes from the lists of songs found in the Fonds Harry Oster at the Archives de folklore et d'ethnologie at Université Laval in Quebec City. (See chapter 3.)

10. See Warren Baby Dodds's comment about "Creoles numbers" played by the "fellows that lived Uptown [sic]" in the section about Jelly Roll Morton in chapter 5.

11. Per the alternative spelling given in both the *New Oxford American Dictionary* and *Merriam-Webster's Unabridged Dictionary*, I have capitalized the words *Black* and *White* when referring to people or "races," as it is already done with nouns and adjectives referring to nationality, such as French Canadian. Similarly, I have chosen to capitalize the expressions *Free People of Color*, *Gens de Couleur Libres*, *Creoles of Color*, and *People of Color*, as they also designate groups of people based on their cultural identity. However, when used in quotations, I have retained the orthography used by the original author. I did the same for the word *Quadroon*. Finally, I use African American instead of "Colored" as was used before, apart from when it appears in quotes.

CHAPTER 1. CREOLE, CREOLIZATION, THE CREOLE STATE, AND THE CREOLES

1. Bonniol, "Situations créoles, entre culture et identité," 49–50; Hall, *Africans in Colonial Louisiana*, 157; Knörr, "Towards Conceptualizing Creolization and Creoleness," 2–3; Domínguez, *White by Definition*, 13–14.

2. "*C'est un nom que les Espagnols donnent à leurs enfants qui sont nez aux Indes.*" French spelling as in the original but for the old ſ replaced by the modern s. Antoine Furetière, *Dictionnaire universel*, Tome Premier, 1690 (translation by the author).

3. Tregle adds that both "Iberville and Bienville referred to *creole* as a matter of course in their communication with royal officials, and church functionaries regularly so described native parishioners." Domínguez, *White by Definition*, 95–97; Tregle, "Creoles and Americans," 137 (quote in text and in note).

4. In Diderot's *Encyclopédie*, the 1765 entry about *Negre* [sic] specified that those born in the American colonies are called *negres créols* [sic]. Still, in 1768, Bossu defined a *Créole* as being the child of a French father and French or European mother. Diderot and d'Alembert, "Negre" [sic] in *Encyclopédie ou Dictionnaire raisonné*; Bossu, *Nouveaux voyages*, 26.

5. Some scholars speak about the creolization of the world, such as Édouard Glissant in "Créolisation," Édouard Glissant, edouardglissant.fr (website); Ulf Hannerz, "The World in Creolisation"; and Jean Benoist, "La créolisation: locale ou mondiale?" For more information and various case studies about creolization, see Baron and Cara, *Creolization as Cultural*

Creativity; Stewart, *Creolization: History, Ethnography, Theory*; Gutiérrez Rodríguez and Tate, *Creolizing Europe: Legacies and Transformations*.

6. Usner, "The Facility Offered by the Country: The Creolization of Agriculture in the Lower Mississippi Valley," 35–62.

7. Cohen, "Creolization and Cultural Globalization," 382n3, 383.

8. Cohen, "Creolization and Cultural Globalization," 373.

9. Logsdon and Bell, "The Americanization of Black New Orleans 1850–1900," 244–45.

10. He also writes that by micromusics "[he] mean[s] the small units within big music cultures." I prefer his observation about "big systems," since musical endeavors are influenced by more than music itself. He also specifies that he has "rarely seen [the word *superculture*] used elsewhere, even though it seems a logical companion" to *subculture* and *interculture*. Slobin, *Subcultural Sounds: Micromusics*, xiii (quote in text, and second quote in note), 11 (first quote in note), 29 (third quote in note), 39, 42, 45, 50–57, 61–69.

11. Raeburn, "'That Ain't No Creole,'" 13 (quote); Domínguez, *White by Definition*, 126.

12. Raeburn, "'That Ain't No Creole,'" 8 (quote), 46, 52.

13. About Oliver, see Raeburn, "'That Ain't No Creole,'"14, 16, 22 (quote)–24, 29, 31. Discussing the deceptively simple question of why the (Original) Creole Band (active between 1914 and 1918, more in chapter 6) was called the Creole Band, Gushee suggests that "for many Americans around this time" (end of nineteenth century, beginning of twentieth century), "Creole" simply meant "light-skinned African-American," while it is also possible that "to say 'Creole Band' might be to say that this was not just a bunch of illiterate country blacks only a generation removed from slavery, but, rather, a group that comprised some 'real musicians.'" Gushee, *Pioneers of Jazz*, 59 (first quote in note), 293, 294–95 (quotes in note).

14. After the fall of Napoleon in 1814, France ceded Dominica and Saint Lucia to Great Britain. Today, Guadeloupe, Martinique, and French Guiana are the only remaining French territories in the Caribbean.

15. Usner, "From African Captivity to American Slavery," 26–27; Havard and Vidal, *Histoire de l'Amérique française*, 164; Hall, "The Formation of Afro-Creole Culture," 67, 70.

16. Johnson, "Colonial New Orleans," 34–35, 38; Hall, "The Formation of Afro-Creole Culture," 63–65; Havard and Vidal, *Histoire de l'Amérique française*, 87, 162–64, 169; Dollar, "Ethnicity and Jim Crow," 1–2.

17. Johnson, "Colonial New Orleans," 40 (quote); Zeno interview by Russell, Allen, and Oster (January 25, 1960), reel 1, 26m52–28m25, transcript by the author 10.

18. From 1699 to 1763, *La Louisiane* was ruled by French Canadian governors for approximately forty-one years, including twenty-nine years by Bienville in four different periods, and three years by French-born Antoine de Lamothe Cadillac who had already spent twenty years in New France before taking office. Johnson, "Colonial New Orleans," 12 (second quote)–13, 15–16 (fourth quote), 19 (first quote), 28 (third quote).

19. Eccles, *The Canadian Frontier, 1534–1760*, 1–12; Nash, *Red, White and Black*, 99–109; Hanger, "Origins of New Orleans's Free Creoles of Color," 1.

20. Brasseaux, "A New Acadia: The Acadian Migrations," 129–31; Hall, *Africans in Colonial Louisiana*, 277; "History/Historia" Los Isleños Heritage and Cultural Society (website); Conrad, "The History of New Iberia."

21. For a detailed account of the arrival of refugees to New Orleans, see Dessens, *From Saint-Domingue to New Orleans*, 22–31; Lachance, "The Foreign French," 103–5, 117.

22. Lachance, "The Foreign French," 104, 117–20.

23. Raeburn, "Stars of David and Sons of Sicily," 126; Boulard, "Blacks, Italians and the Making of New Orleans Jazz," 53–54. For the sake of precision, it should be noted that the history of Jews in Louisiana goes back to the early days of the colony.

24. *Le Code Noir, ou Édit du Roy*, 1724, articles II, V, VI, VII, XVIII, XX, XLIII.

25. Usner, "From African Captivity to American Slavery," 30, 31, 34 (quote); Havard and Vidal, *Histoire de l'Amérique française*, 325.

26. Both Nancy M. Miller Surrey and Gwendolyn Midlo Hall give this figure without provenance, but I think we can make an educated guess that they came from the Caribbean, as did the enslaved who arrived in 1709. Miller Surrey, *The Commerce of Louisiana*, 230–31 (quote); Hall, *Africans in Colonial Louisiana*, 57–58.

27. Hall, *Africans in Colonial Louisiana*, 34–35, 159 (quote); Hall, "The Formation of Afro-Creole Culture," 65–69; Havard and Vidal, *Histoire de l'Amérique française*, 165.

28. Ingersoll, "The Slave Trade and the Ethnic Diversity," 133–61, 134 and 137 (quotes).

29. Ingersoll, "The Slave Trade and the Ethnic Diversity," 156; Seck, *Bouki fait Gombo*, 53; Hall, *Africans in Colonial Louisiana*, 277–86.

30. Taylor, "The Foreign Slave Trade in Louisiana after 1808," 36–43.

31. Picone, "Anglophone Slaves in Francophone Louisiana," 404–32.

32. English-speaking enslaved also learned some French. Lachance, "The Foreign French," 117–19 (quote 117 and 119); Gore, *Memories of the Old Plantation Home*, 33.

33. Brothers, *Louis Armstrong's New Orleans*, 189.

34. *Le Code Noir, ou Édit du Roy*, Articles VI, X, L, LI, LII, LIII, LIV; Dumont de Montigny, *Mémoires Historiques sur la Louisiane*, Tome Second, 243; Usner, "From African Captivity to American Slavery," 46.

35. *Code Noir ou Loi municipale*, 1788; Ingersoll, "Free Blacks in a Slave Society," 180; Spear, *Race, Sex, and Social Order*, 109–10. Spear cites Gwendolyn M. Hall's *Database for the Study of Afro-Louisiana History and Genealogy, 1699-1860: Computerized Information from Manuscript Sources* as a source for this figure.

36. Hanger, *Bounded Lives, Bounded Places*, 1 (quote), 2; Hanger, "Origins of New Orleans's Free Creoles of Color," 1–2. As noted above, the *Code Noir* contained provisions to protect White supremacy and control social relations in colonial Louisiana. Yet, for various reasons linked to the challenge of establishing a new colony, the harsh conditions of frontier life, and the self-interest of slaveowners, the *Code* was loosely enforced, especially in New Orleans, where enslaved people lived rather freely, ignoring the legal barriers imposed on them. Native Americans, people of African descent, and Whites socialized together in various formal or informal situations, sometimes living together and having children, legally or illegally. Hall argues that during the Spanish regime, "poor whites, slaves and free people of African descent continued to socialize freely," despite the repression of the dominant planter class. Hall, *Africans in Colonial Louisiana*, 379. See also Dawdy, *Building the Devil's Empire*, 144–50, 185–88; Usner, "From African Captivity to American Slavery," 37–39.

37. "An Act to Regulate the Conditions and Forms of the Emancipation of Slaves," 427–29; *Civil Code of the State of Louisiana with the Statutory Amendments from 1825 to 1853, Inclusive*, Title VI, Chapter 3, 28–33.

38. In the nineteenth century, the word *Quadroon* was used to designate people with one-quarter African ancestry. Aslakson, "'Quadroon-Plaçage' Myth of Antebellum New Orleans," 710, 718, 719; Clark, *The Strange Story of the American Quadroon*, 168, 176; Brasseaux, "Creoles of Color in Louisiana's Bayou Country," 69, 70.

39. Lachance, "Foreign French," 102–3, 119 (quote).

40. *Acts Passed at the First Session of the First Legislature of the Territory of Orleans*, Black Code XXXII (Section 40), 188, 190. All the acts were bilingual; the French version of Section 40 appears on 189 and 191.

41. Kennedy, *Population of the United States in 1860*, 194–95.

42. Mention of a "free black [family] in the records of the prairie posts" first appeared in 1766. Brasseaux, "Creoles of Color," 67 (quote in text)–68 (quote in note); Gehman, "Visible Means of Support," 208–22.

43. Johnson, "Colonial New Orleans," 19.

44. Maduell, *The Census Tables for the French Colony of Louisiana from 1699 through 1732*; Morlas, "La Madame et la Mademoiselle: Creole Women in Louisiana, 1718–1865," 17–19, 21; Hall, *Africans in Colonial Louisiana*, 3–7, 18; Johnson, "Colonial New Orleans," 36, 42–43; Havard and Vidal, *Histoire de l'Amérique française*, 403.

45. Brasseaux, *Acadian to Cajun*, 4–9, 92, 104–6.

46. Lachance, "The Foreign French," 128.

47. Eventually, despite the Creoles' efforts to protect and promote their culture and language, it went into a gradual decline and quasi-disappearance after the Louisiana Constitution of 1868 promulgated English as the only language of "laws, public records, and the judicial and legislative proceedings" and for "[t]he general exercises in the public schools," this last clause being repeated verbatim in the 1921 Constitution. *Constitution Adopted by the State Constitutional Convention of the State of Louisiana, March 7, 1868*, Title VI, Article 109 and Title VII, Article 138; *Constitution of the State of Louisiana Adopted in Convention at the City of Baton Rouge, June 18, 1921*, Article XII, Section 12.

48. Morlas, "La Madame et la Mademoiselle: Creole Women in Louisiana, 1718–1865," 112–13.

49. Domínguez, *White by Definition*, 141.

50. Tregle, "Creoles and Americans," 172. About the change in society, see also chapter 5, "Racial Polarization," in Domínguez, *White by Definition*.

51. Rebecca Scott, "Public Rights, Social Equality, and the Conceptual Roots of the Plessy Challenge," 782 (quotes); and Rebecca Scott, *Degrees of Freedom*, 41–42.

52. *Constitution Adopted by the State of Louisiana, 1868*, Title 1, Article 2.

53. Scott, "Public Rights," 783–89, 794 (quote 783). According to Scott, "[t]he origins of the phrase *public rights* are difficult to pin down. At least three lines of thought came together to give meaning to the concept: long-standing conceptions of personal honor, French and Caribbean revolutionary ideas of equality, and nineteenth-century European liberal codifications of rights. Ideas of honor underlay the belief that forced separation on the basis of color constituted what would today be called a dignitary injury. Egalitarian currents from the age of revolution provided a basis for arguing that all citizens had a standing of equality incompatible with the imposition of such dignitary injuries" (783). Indeed, "[t]he fundamental idea of differential public standing had been challenged by the 1789 French

Declaration of the Rights of Man and of the Citizen, which reflected a conscious assault on the allocation of rights and privileges according to birth, rank, and estate" (784). See also Scott, *Degrees of Freedom*, 42–47, 71, 88.

54. The Redeemers were a political group of White conservatives dedicated to preserving/re-establishing White supremacy in Louisiana, along with more radical and violent groups such as the White League/*La Ligue Blanche* and the Ku Klux Klan.

55. On January 5, 2022, Homer Plessy was formally pardoned by Louisiana Governor John Bel Edwards. At the time, Creole men also lost political rights by the introduction of many "qualifications"—such as the ability to read and write and the payment of a poll tax—required to be allowed to register as voters, as stipulated in the *Constitution of the State of Louisiana Adopted in Convention at the City of New Orleans, May 12, 1898*, Art. 197, Sec. 3 and 4, and Art. 198. Scott, "Public Rights", 795–804; Scott, *Degrees of Freedom*, 88 (quote in text)–93; "Gov. Edwards Signs the First and Historic Posthumous Pardon." John Bel Edwards—Office of the Governor (website). For more on the changes in race relations after the Civil War, see also Fairclough, *Race and Democracy, The Civil Rights Struggle in Louisiana, 1915–1972*, chapter 1; Somers, "Black and White in New Orleans: A Study in Urban Race Relations, 1865–1900"; Logsdon and Bell, "The Americanization of Black New Orleans 1850–1900"; Dollar, "Ethnicity and Jim Crow"; Brasseaux, "Creoles of Color"; and Scott, *Degrees of Freedom*, chapter 3, "Crisis and Voice—Southern Louisiana, 1874–1896," 61–93.

56. Anthony, "The Negro Creole Community in New Orleans," 150–52 (quote). For more about interracial relations in New Orleans, see also Boulard, "Blacks, Italians and the Making of New Orleans Jazz," 55; Somers, "Black and White in New Orleans"; and Campanella, *Geographies of New Orleans*, 298–302.

57. Zeno and Lewis interview by Russell and Allen (November 14, 1958), transcript 6 (quote); Zeno interview by Russell, Allen, and Oster (January 25, 1960), transcript by the author 22.

58. Zeno and Lewis interview by Russell and Allen (November 14, 1958), transcript 7–9; Zeno and Lewis interview by Russell and Allen (December 10, 1958), transcript 4–5; Zeno interview by Russell, Allen, and Oster (January 25, 1960), transcript by the author 23.

59. Zeno and Lewis interview by Russell and Allen (December 10, 1958), transcript 5–6 (quote), 14.

60. Zeno and Lewis interview by Russell and Allen (December 10, 1958), transcript 6–7, 12 (quote); Zeno and Lewis interview by Russell and Allen (November 14, 1958), transcript 1, 3.

61. Zeno interview by Russell, Allen, and Oster (January 25, 1960), transcript by the author 10 (quote), 11.

62. Zeno and Lewis interview by Russell and Allen (November 14, 1958), transcript 8–10 (quote 9); Zeno and Lewis interview by Russell and Allen (December 10, 1958), transcript 4.

63. Arguedas interview by Halpert (1939), LWO 4872, R 207-A, 43m26–46m50, transcript by the author 1 (block quotation), 1–2 (quotations in text).

64. Arguedas interview by Halpert (1939), LWO 4872, R 207-B, 15m29–15m55, transcript by the author 10.

CHAPTER 2. BLACK AMERICAN/FRENCH CREOLE FOLK MUSIC

1. At that time, an average of 26–27 percent of the population of New Orleans was of African descent, the Afro-French Creole and the Anglo-American Black communities combined. See table 1 "The New Orleans Population of Color" in chapter 1.

2. James Lincoln Collier used the term "black-American folk music" to describe the unique culture that enslaved Blacks developed as their musical practices began to be influenced by the "white culture in which it was embedded" (micromusics developing in a superculture as Slobin observed; see chapter 1). He called this period the "American transplantation." According to Gunther Schuller, the blues gradually emerged out of the synthesis of work songs, field hollers, and prison songs. Collier, *The Making of Jazz*, 16–17 (quotes in note), 19 (quotes in text); Schuller, *Early Jazz*, 36.

3. Among many others are Schuller, *Early Jazz*, 7–10, 16–18, 39–40, 46, 52; Collier, *The Making of Jazz*, 23–27, 103; Gioia, *The History of Jazz*, 9–13; Shipton, *A New History of Jazz*, 1, 6–7, 13; and Giddins and DeVeaux, *Jazz*, 12–13, 18–19, 79.

4. Ernest Borneman suggested that European and West African musics once had a "common source" and eventually developed their own "variants of the diatonic scale." Later a "clash between two stages of the same diatonic tradition" led to the "development of . . . Afro-European scales in [various] places . . . [such as] the 'spiritual' or 'shout scale,' comprising the tonic, mediant, dominant and part-sharpened subdominant [and] the 'blues scale,' a diatonic major with added or alternative minor thirds and diminished sevenths." Borneman, "The Roots of Jazz," 7 (quotes), 18; Borneman, "Creole Echoes," Part 1, 15.

5. Allen, Ware, and Garrison, *Slave Songs of the United States*, iv–vi, 113.

6. Nickerson, "Africo-Creole Music in Louisiana," 6.

7. "*Rythme binaire à 2/4. Avec la syncope sur le second temps succédant à un triolet irrégulier, pourrait donner l'impression d'un rythme nègre.*" (Translation by the author.) Pouinard, "Recherches sur la musique d'origine française en Amérique du Nord, Canada et Louisiane" 1: 237–38, 2: 157.

8. Caffery, *Traditional Music in Coastal Louisiana*, 102–3 (quote), 180–81, 237–39.

9. "*. . . j'acceptai la régie de l'Habitation de la Compagnie, qui devint peu de tems après l'Habitation du Roi. . . . tous les Dimanches il s'y trouvoit au moins quatre cent Negres sur l'Habitation . . . je convins avec les autres Habitans de ce que nous avions à faire pour empêcher ces assemblées.*" Le Page Du Pratz, *Histoire de la Louisiane*, 3: 226–27. (Translation by the author; French spelling as in the original but for the old ſ replaced by the modern s.)

"*. . . enfin, rien n'est plus à craindre que de voir les Nègres s'assembler les Dimanches, puisque sous prétexte de Calinda (ou de danse) on les verroit quelquefois s'assembler des trois à quatre cens ensemble faire un espèce de Sabbat qu'il est toujours prudent d'éviter, puisque c'est dans ces assemblées tumultueuses que . . . se forment les révoltes.*" Le Page Du Pratz, *Histoire de la Louisiane*, 1: 352. Translated in Le Page Du Pratz, *The History of Louisiana*, 366.

10. "*. . . on compte 35 habitations assez bien formez, mais surtout 15 a 20 très considérables tant par le nombre d'exclaves que par les bestes à cornes qui y sont. Depuis la Nlle Orléans en montant le fleuve jusqu'à 200 lieux on compte tant en habitations qu'en concession, 150, entre les quelles il y en à 20 a 25 fors riches, . . . qui composent ensemble plus de 560 negres et 1000 bestes a cornes, et plusieurs Exclaves Sauvages.*" French spelling as in the original. Caillot,

Relation du Voyage de la Louisianne [sic] *ou Nouvelle France*, 107–8. Translation by Teri F. Chalmers in Erin M. Greenwald, *A Company Man: The Remarkable French-Atlantic Voyage of a Clerk for the Company of the Indies: A Memoir by Marc-Antoine Caillot*, 85. Havard and Vidal suggest a number of 110 plantations around New Orleans in 1766. Havard and Vidal, *Histoire de l'Amérique française*, 287. This is not within the scope of this book, but the presence of both enslaved Native Americans and enslaved Africans surely allowed the encounter of their respective musical cultures.

11. Dawdy, *Building the Devil's Empire*, 185–86.

12. The game described seems to be *Le jeu du mouchoir* (drop the handkerchief). Clayton, *Mother Wit: The Ex-Slave Narratives*, 52–53.

13. Trist Family Papers, The Historic New Orleans Collection MSS 180, Folder 18, Box 3.

14. Russell, *My Diary, North and South*, 1: 370, 374. Russell was visiting André Bienvenue Roman, governor of Louisiana from 1831 to 1835 and 1839 to 1843. The Romans were a prominent family of French planters.

15. Allen, Ware, and Garrison, *Slave Songs of the United States*, 109–13 (all quotes 113).

16. Cable, "Creole Slave Songs," 821 (quotes in text), 822–23 (block quote).

17. In the beginning of the interview, Ms. Arguedas told "the very interesting story" about "this" mammy, Mona, who when a little girl had been given to her grandmother—whom she had always served—as a wedding gift in 1857. However, either the children called their Mammy with a surname, or there were two mammies, for later in the interview, Ms. Arguedas described Mammy Cavie as "not an old woman . . . about middle age." Arguedas interview by Halpert (1939), LWO 4872 R 207-A, 44m28–44m38, 46m01–46m25, and 208-A, 27m42–28m28, transcript by the author 1–2, 35 (quotes in notes).

18. Arguedas interview by Halpert (1939), LWO 4872, R 207-A, 53m45–53m59, transcript by the author 4.

19. Arguedas interview by Halpert (1939), LWO 4872 R 207 B, 8m20–9m43, 11m16–13m36, transcript by the author 8–9.

20. Dorothy Scarborough was an early member of the Texas Folklore Society, over which she presided in 1914–1915. Scarborough, *On the Trail of Negro Folk-Songs*, 10, 154, 212 (quotes), 213. Spelling of the Creole lyrics as in the text.

21. "For the shrimps Madam, for the shrimps." (Translation by the author.) Both Cable, in 1886, and Peterson (who wrote it from memory), in 1902, included another version of "Quand Mo Té Dans Grand Chemin," in their collection of Creole songs. However, only the lyrics of the first verse are the same as in Arguedas's version—enough to identify them as two variations based on the same song. Arguedas interview by Halpert (1939), LWO 4872, R 207-B, 5m04–6m44, transcript by the author 8; Peterson, *Creole Songs from New Orleans*, 3; Cable, "Creole Slave Songs," 824.

22. In an unpublished 1942 manuscript, Marcus Christian wrote: "Thirty years or more ago the cries of street-vendors became so common to the ears of New Orleanians that they merged into a jumble of varying sounds—Belle calas! tout chauds! Belle fromage! Belle chaurice! Confitures coco! Pralines-pistaches! Pralines-pacanes!—In those days when most of the street-vendors spoke Creole, everything sold was either "Belle" or "Bon." Italics inserted by Creecy, *Scenes in the South*, 39 (block quote); Marcus Christian, *The Black History of Louisiana*, Unpublished manuscript of *The Negro in Louisiana*, chapter 12, 8–9.

23. *Calas* were popular rice cakes often eaten at breakfast. Danny Barker was a banjo and guitar player, related to the famous Barbarin family through his mother. Danny Barker interview by Michael White (1992), 7.

24. *Pan Patat* is a sweet potato pudding, typical in New Orleans. Alice Zeno also spoke about it. Kennedy *Mellows*, 21; Edward Larocque Tinker, "Louisiana Gumbo" (*Yale Review* III no. 3, 1932) quoted in Sadler, "Creole Songs," 140; Zeno and Lewis interview by Russell and Allen (November 14, 1958), transcript 4 and (December 10, 1958), transcript 7.

25. Sadler also presented lyrics for "Les Oignons" and "Belles Calas." Sadler, "Creole Songs," 138–42; Scarborough, *On the Trail of Negro Folk-Songs*, 213 (italics in the text).

26. Lomax collected a rare sung version of the "Belles Calas" cry, very different from the one used in the song. Lomax, *John A. Lomax Southern States Collection, 1933–1937*.

27. The article presented only one verse of the song. The instruments described are similar to the ones described by Benjamin Latrobe at Congo Square in 1819 (more later in this chapter). "A Voudou Dance," *Times-Democrat*, June 24, 1884, 2.

28. Ms. Arguedas suggested that the wordless verse was "probably African words put into the song that really have no meaning to us." Arguedas interview by Halpert (1939), LWO 4872 R 207-A, 44m51–45m06, R 207-B, 28m01–38m41, transcript by the author 1, 15–17 (quote in note); and LWO 4872 R 208 A, 49m21, transcript by the author 41 (quote in text).

29. Cable, "Creole Slave Songs," 820–21. Few other excerpts have been collected, rarely with music. Starr, *Inventing New Orleans*, 76; Sadler, "Creole Songs," 132–37; Theard, *Old Songs of French and Creole Origin*, 273–74; Anderson, *The Voodoo Encyclopedia*, 353–59.

30. Alcée Fortier (1856–1914) grew up on Le Petit Versailles, a prominent sugar plantation owned by his grandfather Valcour Aimé. Théodore Pavie described dances and instruments that he could certainly have seen during his travels in the United States but, unfortunately, his account loses credibility when it comes to the dramatic story of an enslaved man's escape. Holmes, *An Account of the United States of America*, 332; Pavie, *Souvenirs atlantiques. Voyage aux États-Unis*, Tome Second, 318–20; Fortier, "Customs and Superstitions in Louisiana," 136–37.

31. Jerah Johnson points to the fact that the "formative stage of Afro-American culture involved a blending of African, Indian, and French, plus a few German and Spanish cultural elements." For more on the early developments of the square, see Johnson, *Congo Square in New Orleans*, 11–12, 43 (quote); and Johnson, "Colonial New Orleans," 42. Nowadays the square is in the southwest corner of Louis Armstrong Park, in Faubourg Treme, northwest of the French Quarter.

32. Evans, *Congo Square*, 2, 75 (block quote).

33. Some gatherings took place in St. Martinville—and perhaps in other rural areas—as Roger Baudier wrote that "Father Borella objected strenuously to the custom of the Congo Negro slaves gathering every Sunday in the open space before the church, where they conducted their weird and fantastic dances which they had brought with them from Africa." Baudier, *The Catholic Church in Louisiana*, 354.

34. "Congo Square: The Master of Ceremonies," *Daily Picayune*, March 22, 1846.

35. Latrobe also added drawings of the musical instruments he saw. Latrobe, *The Journal of Latrobe*, 179–82 (quotes 179 and 180); Johnson, *Congo Square in New Orleans*, 24–26; Evans, *Congo Square*, 64–70.

36. Creecy, *Scenes in the South*, 20–21.

37. Cable, "The Dance in Place Congo," *Century Magazine*, 517–32 (quotes 525 and 527).

38. Hearn also spoke about his experience in a letter to Henry E. Krehbiel dated January 1885, in which Hearn said that he had asked Cable to write down a melody for him. Hearn, "The Scenes of Cable's Romances," 41 (quote in text), 45 (block quote, my emphasis); Bisland, *The Life and Letters of Lafcadio Hearn*, 336–37.

39. Henry E. Krehbiel was the musical editor of the *New York Tribune* from 1880 to 1923, American editor of the second edition of the *Grove's Dictionary of Music and Musicians*, and author of *Afro-American Folksongs*. I don't quite understand Evans's and Starr's position: gatherings in Congo Square most likely lasted till the mid-1850s, and Cable would have been at least in his early teens when they stopped. Nonetheless, Starr agrees with Cable's biographer, Arlin Turner, who argued that Cable's descriptions were based on Médéric Moreau de Saint-Mery's books *Description typographique . . . de l'Isle de Saint-Domingue* and *De la danse*, published in 1797–98 and 1801 respectively, at the time of the arrival of Saint-Domingue refugees in New Orleans, who are indeed said to have greatly influenced the culture of the city. However, in his other article, "Creole Slave Songs," Cable does cite Saint-Méry (and other sources) when he uses some of his information about Voodoo, so one would expect he would have done the same here. Johnson, *Congo Square in New Orleans*, 32; Evans, *Congo Square*, 3 (quote), 31–32; Starr, *Louis Moreau Gottschalk*, 41–42; Cable, "The Dance in Place Congo," 529, and "Creole Slave Songs," 815.

40. Cable, "The Dance in Place Congo," 519–22.

41. Of the seven Creole songs included in *Slave Songs of the United States*, six appeared in Cable's article. According to Evans, the Bamboula was interchangeably called the Congo dance in New Orleans, although they appear to have been two different but closely related dances in other parts of the West Indies, where the Congo dance was also called the Chica. Evans, *Congo Square*, 93–94, 98–99, 103. About the Bamboula drum, see note 63 below.

42. Cable, "The Dance in Place Congo," 523.

43. Cable, "The Dance in Place Congo," 526.

44. Cable, "The Dance in Place Congo," 527–28; Saxon, Dreyer, and Tallant, *Gumbo Ya-Ya*, 429; Allen, Ware, and Garrison, *Slave Songs of the United States*, 111.

45. "À notre connaissance, cette chanson représente un des plus anciens textes publiés en créole louisianais." The boscugo or boscoyo refers either to something "ugly, hunchbacked, or decrepit" or—as bouscouyou—to "a very strange outgrowth of a cypress tree.... A parasite living in the water of cypress groves (. . .) ; a dwarf man." "[B]oscoyo . . . 'vilain, bossu, décrépit' et bouscouyou 'jet de cyprès, excroissance très curieuse. (. . .) Ce parasite croît dans l'eau de cyprières. (. . .); Homme nain.'" *Le Villageois/The Villager* was a bilingual weekly published in Marksville, Louisiana, from March 30, 1844, until April 23, 1859. Neumann-Holzschuh, *Textes anciens en créole louisianais*, 93–96. (Quote in text and in note, 93n1. Translation by the author, parentheses in the original).

46. Coleman, *Historical Sketch Book*, 158–60; Cable, "The Dance in Place Congo," 528; Fortier, "Bits of Louisiana Folk-Lore," 162; Krehbiel, *Afro-American Folksongs*, 151–53.

47. "New Orleans Court Locations: City Courts." Law Library of Louisiana (website).

48. Most of the information about Judge Préval's story comes from Edith Long's book *Along the Banquette* and "The Collins C. Diboll Vieux Carré Digital Survey" of The New Orleans

Historic Collection. Krehbiel noted that "old residents of New Orleans have told [him] that [Préval] was a magistrate," and Cable wrote that the song was about "a certain Judge Preval." Long, *Along the Banquette*, 6–8, 25; Maestri, *New Orleans City Guide*, 250; Krehbiel, *Afro-American Folksongs*, 151 (quote in text, and in note); Cable, "The Dance in Place Congo," 528.

49. Krehbiel devoted a whole chapter of his book on the "Satirical Songs of the Creoles" as found in both the West Indies and New Orleans. Cable, "Creole Slave Songs," 808; Allen, Ware, and Garrison, *Slave Songs of the United States*, 111, 113; Krehbiel, *Afro-American Folksongs*, 140–55; Saxon, Dreyer, and Tallant, *Gumbo Ya-Ya*, 429.

50. Cable, "The Dance in Place Congo," 527; Allen, Ware, and Garrison, *Slave Songs of the United States*, 111.

51. Flint, *Recollections of the Last Ten Years*, 140.

52. "The Congo Dance," *Daily Picayune*, October 18, 1843.

53. Evans, *Congo Square*, 31–32; Johnson, *Congo Square in New Orleans*, 47; Mead, "Memory Types of New Orleans," *Daily Picayune*, December 11, 1864.

54. Zeno interview by Russell, Allen, and Oster (January 25, 1960), reel 2, 928_01, 2m55, 8m40–9m09, 12m09–12m25, transcript by the author 13, 15, 17.

55. Zeno interview by Russell, Allen, and Oster (January 25, 1960), reel 2, 928_01, 2m28–2m38, 9m46–9m56, transcript by the author 13, 16. During this interview, she said that the Calinda was a song, not a dance (1m47–1m59, transcript 12–13). However, in a 1958 interview, she described the Calinda as a Creole dance in which women danced alone "hold[ing] their dress like that"; it is not clear if men were also dancing alone. See Zeno and Lewis interview by Russell and Allen (December 10, 1958), 926_01, reel 1, 11m58–12m38 (transcript 9–10).

56. Evans, *Congo Square*, 19, 30–31, 155; Kmen, *Music in New Orleans*, 52; Marquis, *In Search of Buddy Bolden*, 70.

57. Arguedas interview by Halpert (1939), LWO 4872 R 207 B, 15m29–15m55, transcript by the author 10.

58. Arguedas interview by Halpert (1939), LWO 4872 R 207 B, 16m–27m55, transcript by the author 10–14 (quote 25m43, transcript 13).

59. Arguedas interview by Halpert (1939), LWO 4872 R 207 B, 21m17–21m31, 22m12–22m29, and 22m44–22m59, transcript by the author 12, translation by the author.

60. I am grateful to Richard Campanella, who gave me the information about Esplanade Avenue and Delachaise Street. Arguedas interview by Halpert (1939), LWO 4872 R 207 B, 20m21–24m42, transcript by the author 12–13 (story and quote about Mazureau, 20m21–21m17, about Carondelet 21m39–21m56, about Delachaise 22m29–22m41); Cable, "The Dance in Place Congo," 528; Richard Campanella, "About Delachaise Street," email, December 6, 2020.

61. Not surprisingly, it was also sung outside of New Orleans. Ms. Arguedas and her cousin Mina Monroe, whose version appears in appendix 2, grew up on Labranche Plantation in St. Charles Parish. Monroe's version is among the very few that refers to both Préval and Mazuro and is the only one speaking about Madame Mazuro (verse 10). In "Bits of Louisiana Folklore," Alcée Fortier included the lyrics of a few songs "given by a St. Charles [Parish] Negro." The first one is "Michié Mazureau" but only the first verse is the same as Arguedas's version, while the refrain remains the same. Another version presented in appendix 2 was collected in St. John the Baptist Parish and another one in Baton Rouge. Arguedas interview

by Halpert (1939), LWO 4872 R 207 B, 18m39–19m25 (block quote, my emphasis, and first quote in text), 21m31–21m36 (second quote), transcript by the author 11–12; Monroe, *Bayou Ballads*, iii, vii, 40–55; Fortier, "Bits of Louisiana Folk-Lore," 164 (quote)–165.

62. As mentioned above, Saxon also wrote that "the Calinda was a voodoo dance." Warner, *Studies in the South and West*, 69–71; Saxon, Dreyer, and Tallant, *Gumbo Ya-Ya*, 429.

63. She also spoke about the Bamboula drum originating from Africa, where it was made out of large bamboo—hence the name—but, in Louisiana, was made with old barrels, which were plentiful thanks to the sugar industry. Arguedas interview by Halpert (1939), LWO 4872 R 207-B, 14m04–14m28, 17m52–18m32, transcript by the author 10–11. See also Evans, *Congo Square*, 102. About the "Cadja" song: LWO 4872 R 208-A, 46m27–50m43, transcript by the author 41 (quote)–42.

64. Zeno interview by Russell, Allen, and Oster (January 25, 1960), 928-01, reel 2, 4m51–5m28, 10m06–10m22, transcript by the author 14 (quote),16.

65. Both Mina Monroe and Freddi Evans wrote about one form of the Calinda as a war dance that included the ritual of men dancing with a bottle of water on their head. Bisland, *The Life and Letters of Lafcadio Hearn*, 297–98; Monroe, *Bayou Ballads*, vii; Evans, *Congo Square*, 101.

66. Zeno interview by Russell, Allen, and Oster (January 25, 1960), 928_01, reel 2 11m51–13m06, transcript by the author 17.

CHAPTER 3. FRENCH RELIGIOUS MUSIC

1. *Ordonnance de la Marine du mois d'aoust* (1681) prescribed that a chaplain had to be aboard each vessel (Book II, Section 2, Art. 1, 150); [Histoire de] *l'Aumonerie militaire française* (Paris, 1960), 128. Quoted in O'Neil, *Church and State in French Colonial Louisiana*, 8.

2. It is now St. Louis Cathedral in the French Quarter. Baudier, *The Catholic Church in Louisiana*, 55–58.

3. Madeleine Hachard, *Relation du voyage des Dames Religieuses Ursulines de Roüen [sic] à la Nouvelle Orleans [sic], Parties de France le 22 Février 1727 et arrivez [sic] à la Louisienne [sic] le 23 Juillet de la même année.* (Rouen: Antoine Le Prevost, 1728). Reproduced in *Relation du Voyage des Dames Religieuses Ursulines de Rouen à La Nouvelle-Orléans avec une introduction et des notes par Gabriel Gravier* (Paris: Maisonneuve et Ce, 1872), 54–55.

4. "Notre petite Communauté s'accroit . . . nous avons aussi sept Esclaves Pensionnaires à instruire pour le Bâtême & la première Communion, avec cela un grand nombre d'Externes, & des Négresses & Sauvagesses qui viennent deux heures par jours pour être instruites." Hachard, *Relation du voyage*, 97–98. See also 85 regarding the instruction the Ursulines offered to Black and Native American women. Translation taken from Clark, *Voices from an Early American Convent*, 82; and Costa, *Letters of Marie Madeleine Hachard*, 59, with slight modifications by the author. French spelling as in the original but for the old ſ replaced by the modern s.

5. "Ce Révérend Pere nous a fait la semaine Sainte une retraite & à nos Pensionnaires, plusieurs Dame de la Ville s'y sont renduës assiduës, elles se sont trouvées quelquefois aux Exhortations & Conférences jusqu'à prés de deux cens, nous avons eu les Leçons de Ténébres en musique & un Miserere chaque jour accompagné d'instrumens, notre Mere assistante, qui est madame le Boulenger, s'est signalée en cette occasion, le jour de Pâques, à la Messe & au

Salut nous y chantâmes des Motets à quatre parties, & la derniere des Fêtes de Pâques nous chantâmes la Messe entiere en musique, les Convents de France, avec tout leur brillant, n'en font pas tant." Hachard, *Relation du voyage*, 96. Translation from Clark, *Voices from an Early American Convent*, 81–82, and Myldred Masson Costa, *The Letters of Marie Madeleine Hachard*, 58, with slight modifications by the author. French spelling as in the original but for the old ſ replaced by the modern *s*.

6. Capuchin priests visited missions and plantations along the Mississippi, attending to both Whites and Blacks, planting the seeds for future parishes to develop. *Le Code Noir, ou Édit du Roy*, 1724, article II; Baudier, *Catholic Church in Louisiana*, 73–77, 189, 194; Pastor, "Black Catholicism," 79; Alberts, "Origins of Black Catholic Parishes," chapter 1, quote 15.

7. The number of enslaved workers owned by the Church comes from Ingersoll, *Manon and Mammon in Early New Orleans*, 43. Information about baptisms comes from Johnson, "Colonial New Orleans," 41 (quote); and Baudier, *Catholic Church*, 76.

8. Clark, *Voices from an Early American Convent*, 17–18 (quote); Baudier, *Catholic Church*, 183–84; Reinders, "The Churches and the Negro in New Orleans, 1850–1860," 242.

9. "Saint Augustine Church History," Saint Augustine Catholic Church (website).

10. Deggs, *No Cross, No Crown*, 3 (first two quotes), xxvi (third quote).

11. Josephine Charles, one of the founders, was Mother Superior 1870–82, followed by Marie Magdalene Alpaugh 1882–88. Even if Sister Deggs wrote the history of the congregation in English, most of the early nuns and students spoke little or no English. Deggs, *No Cross, No Crown*, 20, 24, 46, 51, and 88 (quote from the last two pages).

12. Alberts, "Origins of Black Catholic Parishes," 10–14; L. V. C., "The 'Old Timers': Saint Katherine's Golden Anniversary Celebration, 1945."

13. Reproduced in Lemmon, *French Baroque Music of New Orleans: Spiritual Songs from the Ursuline Convent (1736)*, who also wrote the introduction indicating in what year the manuscript was given to the Ursulines, vii.

14. For more on this practice, see Falck and Picker, "Contrafactum."

15. "The Ursuline nuns . . . provide the first evidence of elaborate religious music. One nun, Sister Claude Massy, *séculière de choeur* [sic], was especially trained in music." Baron, "Music in New Orleans, 1718–1792," 283.

16. Bucher, "Notes on the Performance," liner notes for *Manuscrit des Ursulines de la Nouvelle-Orléans*, 9.

17. Gipson, "From Secular Music to Sacred Poetry: The Textual Trajectory of *Nouvelles poésies*," 18 and 20.

18. All quotes from Justice, "Performance Practice," 24–25, 25n17. Fuller also points to the "rhythmic conventions [of jazz that] are remarkably reminiscent of the old French code [of *notes inégales*]." For more information on the history and use of *notes inégales*, see Fuller, "Notes Inégales," which Andrew Justice cites as a source for the passages quoted here.

19. ". . . *sur un air plaintif et dans le mode mineur.*" Brandon, "Moeurs [sic] et langue de la paroisse Vermillon," 1: 326 (quote, translation by the author); Saxon, Dreyer, and Tallant, *Gumbo Ya-Ya*, 427, 464.

20. I counted thirty-five (some fragmentary) out of some fifty recordings of *cantiques* in the collection Oster deposited at the Archives de folklore et d'ethnologie at Université Laval in Quebec City and five spirituals in English, performed by three singers. Oster, "Negro French Spirituals of Louisiana," 166.

21. Oster, "Negro French Spirituals of Louisiana," 166.

22. Gilbert Martin, age sixty-nine (born ca. 1888), recorded in New Roads, Pointe Coupée Parish, Louisiana, April 1957. "Tombeau, Tombeau Marie-Madeleine," Fonds Harry Oster, CD 1672, Track 45, and CD 1673, Track 26, Songs 189 and 224; Millien, *Chants et Chansons*, 34–36; Oster, "Negro French Spirituals of Louisiana," 167 (quotes).

23. Martin uses the same feet and hands percussion while singing an English spiritual. Martin, interview by Oster, Library of Congress (1963), 11m35–14m35, digest by the author, 1.

24. Ancelet, "Lomax in Louisiana: Trials and Triumph," 32 (online version, 1). See also Caffery, *Traditional Music in Coastal Louisiana*.

25. Nicholas Augustin Panique, age eighty-three (born ca. 1875), recorded in Léonville, St. Landry Parish, Louisiana, April 1958. Fonds Harry Oster, CD 1675, Track 5, and CD 1675, Track 18, Songs 262 and 282.

26. Millien, *Chants et Chansons*, xi, xii. "*S'il n'est pas toujours commode de noter la mélodie populaire, il est bien plus difficile de noter la façon de dire, la couleur, et le timbre*, la manière de quelques rares vieux chanteurs campagnards. C'est un mélange de petites notes, de grupetti plus ou moins rapides, de ports de voix avec crescendo ou diminuendo, de sons tremblés, de longs points d'orgue, etc." (Italics, here in roman, in the text, translation by the author.)

27. Nicholas Augustin Panique, Fonds Harry Oster, CD 1674, Track 35, and CD 1675, Track 8, Songs 262 and 272.

28. *La Clé du Caveau à l'usage de tous les Chansonniers français, des Amateurs, Auteurs, Acteurs de Vaudeville & tous les Amis de la Chanson*, no. 490, 215. The melody of "Que ne Suis-Je la Fougère" has been attributed to the Italian composer Giovanni Battista Pergolesi (1710–1736) or to Antonio Albanese (1729–1800), who made his career in France (Antoine Albanèse), lyrics by Charles-Henri Bouté. Performed by the ensemble Le Poème Harmonique, the song appears on *Plaisir d'amour: chansons et romances de la France d'autrefois* under the title of "Les Tendres Souhaits."

29. Up until the Second Vatican Council (1962–65), the Mass was sung in Latin. Fonds Harry Oster, CD 1675, Tracks 8, Songs 272; Oster, "Negro French Spirituals," 166 (quote). See texts and melodies in appendix 4, "Dans un Jardin Solitaire."

30. *Recueil de cantiques à l'usage des missions, des retraites et des catéchismes*, Tome Second, 92–95 (in which it is indicated to sing the hymn on "Que ne Suis-Je la Fougère" *before* the publication of the *Clé du Caveau*); *Manuel complet, à l'usage des catéchismes de Saint-Sulpice et autres paroisses de Paris*, 44–45 (under the name "La passion de Notre Seigneur Jésus-Christ"); *Nouveau recueil de cantiques, à l'usage du diocèse de Québec, avec tous les airs notés en musique dans le meilleur goût moderne*, 267–70 (under the name "Mystères de la Passion de N. S. J. C."). Some Ursulines came from Quebec to New Orleans in 1822; Chabot, "Les Ursulines de Québec en 1850," 91; Prévos, "Afro-French Spirituals about Mary Magdalene," 41–53 (quote 53n8).

31. Zeno interview by Russell, Allen, and Oster (January 25, 1960), reel 2, 928_01, 13m54–14m52, transcript by the author 18.

32. Zeno interview by Russell, Allen, and Oster (January 25, 1960), reel 1, 927_01, 15m28–16m20, transcript by the author 6; Nicholas Augustin Panique, Fonds Harry Oster, CD 1674, Track 36, and CD 1675, Track 11, Songs 263 and 275 (Marie-Madeleine Laissez-Moi Passer) and CD 1674, Track 34, and CD 1675, Track 10, Songs 260 and 274 (Dans un Brigatoire), both

recorded in 1958; Martin interview by Oster, Library of Congress (1963), AFC 1967003 AFS 12594, 0m12–1m57 (Marie Je Souviens Ti/Enfant de Jésus-Christ), recorded in 1963.

33. See appendix 5. In 1952, Brandon also interviewed Inez Catalon, spelling her name as Enes Catalan, then thirty-six, and her mother Léonore Catalan, seventy-two, from Kaplan, Louisiana, about whom Brandon noted that, indeed, she (Léonore) didn't speak English. Fonds Elizabeth Brandon, F208, CD 1173, Tracks 32, 33; Spitzer, liner notes for *Zodico: Louisiana Créole Music*, and side 1, Track 6.

34. Célestine Morton, seventy-six, Kaplan, Louisiana, recorded in December 1953. According to Brandon's note, Ms. Morton didn't speak English. Fonds Elizabeth Brandon, F208, CD 1173, Track 24, Song 25; Brandon, "Moeurs [sic] et langue de la paroisse Vermillon en Louisiane," 2: 156; Gilbert Martin, Fonds Harry Oster, CD 1673, Track 12, Song 211.

35. Wilson, "Traditional Louisiana-French Folk Music, 46. See appendix 6.

36. Oster, "Negro French Spirituals of Louisiana," 166.

CHAPTER 4. EUROPEAN MUSIC AND DANCES

1. Gore, *Memories of the Old Plantation Home*, 96.

2. "*nous passames non pas une Soirée, mais mesme toutte la nuit a chanter et a danser, . . . les Uns etoient en habits rouge, en amazonnes, les autres en habits gallonner, d'autres en femmes, pour moy j'estois En (Une) Bergere habillé de blanc, . . . j'avois mon Epoux qui etoit le marquis de Carnaval.*" Caillot, *Relation du Voyage*, 154–55. French spelling as in the original; Translation by Teri F. Chalmers in Greenwald, *A Company Man*, 134–35.

3. "*nos instruments et les autres remirent tout entrain . . . Mr de Perier qui avoit entendu parler de notre mascarade de la veille y vint, il nous fit l'honneur de gouter au vin, il densa deux menuets ou ensuitte il s'en alla, je dansay un passepied avec Mlle Cariere . . . et partimes Sur les 5 heures et ½ du matin qu'il Etoit en regrettant les jours gras.*" Caillot, *Relation du Voyage*, 161–63. French spelling as in the original; translation by Teri F. Chalmers in Greenwald, *A Company Man*, 140–41 (italics in text).

4. Gayarré, *History of Louisiana*, v. 2, 45 (second quote), 66–67 (first quote).

5. Kmen, *Music in New Orleans*, 5, 16 (quote)–17, 21.

6. Baron, *Concert Life in Nineteenth-Century New Orleans*, 10–12 (quotes 12).

7. Flint, *Recollections of the Last Ten Years*, 274.

8. Kmen explained that the "subscription or society balls" were organized by various groups who were "invited to subscribe to a series of balls in one of the public ballrooms." A committee was elected and managers chosen to organize the balls. Each series usually comprised "six to ten dances . . . at a cost of from nine to twenty dollars." Kmen, *Music in New Orleans*, 14.

9. Records and Deliberations of the Cabildo, Louisiana Reference Vault, AB301, 1779–84, vol. 2, 47–48, New Orleans Public Library—Central—Louisiana Division; whole quote in Smith, *Mardi Gras Indians*, 78.

10. Kmen, *Music in New Orleans*, 10–15, 23 (about mask and clothing), 43 (first quote)–46, 51–52 (second and third quote); Couch, "The Public Masked Balls," 403–4. For more about the Quadroon balls, see also Baron, "Music in New Orleans, 1718–1792," 287; Clark, *The Strange Story*, 175, 177–78; Aslakson, "Quadroon-Plaçage," 709, 715, 719–22.

11. Kmen cites Berquin-Duvallon, *Vue de la colonie espagnole du Mississippi . . . en l'année 1802*, in which a ball is described where the musicians were "*cinq ou six Bohêmes ou gens de couleur, râclant fortement du violon*" ("The musicians are half a dozen gypsies, or else people of colour [sic], scraping their fiddle with all their might"), and Bernhard, Duke of Saxe-Weimar, who attended a White ball in 1826, where "the music was performed by negroes and coloured [sic] people and was pretty good." Kmen, *Music in New Orleans*, 230–31 (quote); Berquin-Duvallon, *Vue de la colonie espagnole du Mississippi*, 32; Berquin-Duvallon, *Travels in Louisiana and the Floridas*, 26–27; Bernhard, *Travels Through North America*, v. 2, 58; Cable, "Creole Slave Songs," 808.

12. For more about the refugees from Saint-Domingue in the early nineteenth century, see chapter 1. Baron, *Concert Life*, 565n3 (first quote); Kmen, *Music in New Orleans*, 13, 21–22, 40 (second quote); Dessens, *From Saint-Domingue to New Orleans*, 22–31; Lachance, "The Foreign French," 103–5, 117.

13. "*Cette collection donne un large aperçu de ce qui se jouait dans les salons de la Nouvelle-Orléans durant la deuxième moitié du XIXe siècle.*" Zagala, "Le 'trois sur quatre,'" 88 (translation by the author).

14. Zeno and Lewis interview by Russell and Allen (November 14, 1958), transcript reel 1, 21.

15. Baron, *Concert Life*, 21 (second quote), 98, 101–2, 272 (third quote), 303 (first quote). Baron notes (19) that the acoustics of the opera hall were so good that the venue also "served for major concerts."

16. Such an ensemble would surely not have had segregated seating imposing on the "colored" part of its audience to sit in the back. Kmen, *Music in New Orleans*, 234–36; Trotter, *Music and Some Highly Musical People*, 350–52 (quotes 351); Davis, *Louisiana: A Narrative History*, 227. Although he doesn't cite a source, Davis gives 1838 as the year of the *Société's* incorporation.

17. For more about nineteenth-century composers in New Orleans, see Trotter, *Music and Some Highly Musical People*; Wyatt, "Six Composers of Nineteenth-Century New Orleans"; and Sullivan, "Composers of Color of Nineteenth-Century New Orleans" in which Barès is discussed 63–70.

18. In her compilation, Clara Gottschalk Peterson specified that her brother used the above-mentioned melodies, with the exception of the songs used in Le Mancenillier, of which only "Ou Som Somroucou" is included and about which she only noted that it was "sung in a Negro story called 'Bouqui et Lapin.'" "Pauv' Piti Mam'zelle Zizi" appears as "Lolotte" in Allen, Ware, and Garrison, *Slave Songs of the United States*, 112; Peterson, *Creole Songs from New Orleans*, 1 (quote in text), 3, 6, 9, 11 (quote in note), 15; Starr, *Louis Moreau Gottschalk*, 74–75, 446–48.

19. *Il s'agit d'autant de motifs particulièrement rares dans la musique publiée de cette époque. Plus encore: ils sont ici tous simultanés. En outre, ce passage apparaît quatre fois durant le morceau. Les quatre mesures l'intégrant sont en effet immédiatement répétées, puis l'ensemble formé par ces huit mesures est entendu à nouveau à la reprise du thème, tout comme dans le ragtime.* Zagala, "Le 'trois sur quatre,'" 211 (translation by the author). See chapter 2 for more about the tresillo.

20. Zagala, "Le 'trois sur quatre,'" 217, 405. Further research would be needed to establish if there is a relation with Gottschalk's piano style in "The Banjo," but Lafcadio Hearn's

observation (written in a letter to H. E. Krehbiel in 1881) is striking: "Did you ever hear negroes [sic] play the piano by ear? . . . They use the piano exactly like a banjo. It is good banjo-playing, but no piano-playing." Bisland, *The Life and Letters of Lafcadio Hearn*, 232.

21. "Allen Toussaint: A Saint for All Seasons," December 7, 2016, Hour 1, Segment 1-Allen Toussaint 1998, 8m15–9m35 (transcript by the author). Quote in text from the website.

22. Starr, *Louis Moreau Gottschalk*, 74–77 (quote, 75); Starr and Lowens, "Louis Moreau Gottschalk," Oxford Music Online.

23. Stewart, "The Other Professors," 1–2, 4, 22 (quotes); Stewart, "Paul Sarebresole and New Orleans's First Rag."

24. Lemmon, "Music in Colonial Louisiana," 2; Conrad, *First Families of Louisiana*, 46, 109.

25. E. Clark, *Voices from an Early American Convent*, 125–26.

26. Mary Theresa Austin Carroll, *The Ursulines in Louisiana, 1727–1824* (New Orleans, 1886), 20, quoted in Baron, "Music in New Orleans," 285 (first and second quote), 290n19 (third quote). Baron writes that "[t]here were regularly 100 drummers and fifers in New Orleans from at least 1770, although the number might have decreased by 1778" (285).

27. By rule, each military unit was to be provided with a fife and a drum for operations on the battlefield, but Kinzer's research indicates that they most likely always had a drum but not always a fife. Kinzer, "Tio Family: Four Generations," 43–46, 52–54 (quotes 54), 60n39.

28. Hare, *Negro Musicians and Their Music*, 265; Ellison, "African-American Music and Musket," 310; Hollandsworth, *Louisiana Native Guards*, 70. The *Corps d'Afrique* was later integrated into the United States Colored Infantry. Weidman, "Black Soldiers in the Civil War," 1.

29. Cable, "Creole Slave Songs," 815 (translation in text).

30. Cable, "Creole Slave Songs," 815 (translation by the author).

31. Sakakeeny, *Roll with It*, 17 (quote); Trotter, *Music and Some Highly Musical People*, 351; Schafer, Brass Bands, 27–28.

CHAPTER 5. EARLY JAZZ CREOLE MUSICIANS

1. Brothers, *Louis Armstrong's New Orleans*, 173–74. Louis Armstrong was born in New Orleans in 1901 and died in New York City in 1971.

2. Located on the upriver limit of the French Quarter, Canal Street marks the division between the uptown and downtown sectors of New Orleans.

3. Alex Bigard (brother of Barney Bigard) interview by Russell and Allen (April 30, 1960), reel 2, 42m45–43m12, digest, 10; Armstrong, *Satchmo: My Life in New Orleans*, 182; Brothers, *Louis Armstrong's New Orleans*, 252; Gara, *The Baby Dodds Story*, 13.

4. Russell, *New Orleans Style*, 23. For more on segregation not being the cause of the musical encounter, see Jerah Johnson, "Jim Crow Laws of the 1890s and the Origins of New Orleans Jazz: Correction of An Error," *Popular Music* 19, no. 2 (2000): 243–51.

5. They were called "fakers" in English by opposition to the "readers." Interestingly, an old French dictionary, *Le Littré* (published in 1873–1874), indicates the second meaning of *routinier* as a musical term designating a person that plays or sings "by routine," without having learned music: "*Terme de musique. Celui qui joue ou chante de routine sans avoir appris la musique*" (translation by the author). Dominique interview by Russell (1958), reel 1, track 1, 19m–19m07 and 19m55–20m05, transcript 13–14; Louis Tio interview by Russell,

Collins, and Dejan (1960), 831_01, reel 2, 4m59–5m19, digest 6. For more about the opinion of some Creoles on uptown Blacks, see Leonard Bechet interview by Lomax in Morton and Lomax, *Transcript of the 1938 Recordings*, 144–45.

6. Kinzer, "The Tio Family: Four Generations," 201. When jazz emerged, the word *jazz* was not used to designate the new music. For more about the musical encounters between downtown and uptown musicians, see in chapter 5, the short biographies of the Tio family, especially about Lorenzo Tio Jr. and others bridging the gap between the two musical approaches; Jelly Roll Morton's early recollection of Afro-French pianist Mamie Desdunes playing the blues; Kid Ory, who belonged more to the uptown Anglo-American musicians; and Sidney Bechet as being part of the "Creole Rebels." See also Leonard Bechet interview by Lomax in Morton and Lomax, *Transcript of the 1938 Recordings*, 150–53.

7. The musicians presented in this chapter are but a few of the many Creole musicians active during the formative years of jazz.

8. For more about intercultural phenomena, and the use of the word *Creole* as a free-floating signifier, see chapter 1.

9. Among the monographs available are McCusker, *Creole Trombone: Kid Ory and the Early Years of Jazz* (2012); Lomax, *Mister Jelly Roll: The Fortunes of Jelly Roll Morton, New Orleans Creole and "Inventor of Jazz"* (1950); Bechet, *Treat It Gentle: An Autobiography* (1960); and Chilton, *Sidney Bechet: The Wizard of Jazz* (1987). About other Creole musicians, born a little later than the musicians discussed in this chapter—George Lewis (1900–1968), Barney Bigard (1906–1980), Don Albert (1908–1980) and Danny Barker (1909–1994)—see Tom Bethell, *George Lewis: A Jazzman from New Orleans*; Barney Bigard, *With Louis and the Duke: The Autobiography of a Jazz Clarinetist*; Christopher Wilkinson, *Jazz on the Road—Don Albert's Musical Life*; and Danny Barker, *A Life in Jazz*.

10. Nonetheless, the family has been little documented, the main source to this day being Charles Kinzer's PhD dissertation "The Tio Family: Four Generations of New Orleans Musicians, 1814–1933," to which I am greatly in debt for this section.

11. Antoinette Tio also taught guitar. Kinzer, "The Tio Family: Four Generations," 168; Louis Tio interview by Russell, Collins, and Dejan (1960), 832_01, reel 3, 2m11; quote, transcription by the author, 3.

12. Kinzer, "The Tio Family: Four Generations," 1 (quote), 15; "Hazeur, Jean-François," in *Dictionnaire biographique du Canada*.

13. Kinzer, "The Tio Family: Four Generations," 13–14, 82 and 82n2 (quote), 95–96.

14. The Tios lived in the French-speaking colony of Eureka, and later in the city of Tampico, where they relocated in 1859–60 in the hope of escaping the increasingly harsh conditions in the South. Kinzer, "The Tio Family: Four Generations," 71–72, 101, 104–5, 107–8, 112, 114, 121.

15. Louis Tio interview by Russell, Collins, and Dejan (1960), 830_01, reel 1, 2m57–3m50, digest, 1; Kinzer, "The Tio Family: Four Generations," 137, 193, 200, 201, 204, 301, 313.

16. "Hot" and "ratty" were used to designate the syncopated music of uptown musicians. Louis Tio interview by Russell, Collins, and Dejan (1960), 830_01, reel 1, 3m50–4m, digest 1; Kinzer, "The Tio Family: Four Generations," 217 (second quote), 219–22, 225, 232–33 (first quote). More about the Eagle Band later in this chapter.

17. As unique and informative as they are, these recordings don't fully represent the Piron Orchestra's sound and repertoire for two main reasons. First, the acoustical recording

technology was limited in terms of capturing all the instruments properly so as to faithfully reproduce the sound of live performances. Second, in order to maximize booking, the band would cover a wide range of music, and, to a certain extent, adapt its sound to satisfy whomever their patrons—and dancers on the floor—would be, whether White or "Colored," or whether in New Orleans or in New York City. For further details about Piron's orchestra and in-depth musical analysis with transcriptions, see Kinzer, "The Tio Family: Four Generations," 255–81 (260 second quote, 266 first quote, 270–71 and 271n61 block quote), 357–81. About recording technology and the need to adapt to various audiences, see Raeburn, "New Orleans Jazz Styles of the 1920s," xv–xvii.

18. Kinzer is quoting jazz historian John Steiner, "Chicago," in *Jazz*, edited by Nat Hentoff and Albert McCarthy. Kinzer also argues that "[b]y extension backward to the antebellum activities of Thomas Tio and Louis Hazeur, it becomes possible to view the Tio family as prime structural agents of a century-long continuum in the transmission of a characteristic manner of music-making on the clarinet." Kinzer, "The Tio Family: Four Generations," 297 (first quote and quote in note), 322, 330 (second quote).

19. Bigard, *With Louis and the Duke*, 64.

20. Jelly Roll was a self-chosen nickname with sexual connotations. Gushee argues that Morton would be the anglicization of *Mouton*, the family name of his stepfather. Gushee, "A Preliminary Chronology of the Early Career," 393.

21. Mardi Gras Indians are "tribes" of African Americans who dress in Native American–inspired regalia to perform their own parades and celebrations on Mardi Gras and St. Joseph's Day. For more on the Mardi Gras Indians, see Morton and Lomax, *Transcript of the 1938 Recordings*, 102–3; Smith, *Mardi Gras Indians*; Lewis and Breunlin, *House of Dance and Feathers*; and Sakakeeny, "Mardi Gras Indians."

22. As Bruce Raeburn put it, "In these neighborhoods, music pervaded the streets . . . so everyone within earshot could absorb musical innovations readily." Raeburn, "Beyond the 'Spanish Tinge,'" 23; Morton and Lomax, *Transcript of the 1938 Recordings*, 52–53.

23. Morton's recollection of his youth points to him being born in 1885. Morton and Lomax, *Transcript of the 1938 Recordings*, 8–9 (quotes), 10, 12 (about his date of birth), 174. See also Reich and Gaines, *Jelly's Blues*, 271–73.

24. However, as Gushee points out, we don't know whether Morton's claims were based on shame, ignorance, or the perception that the peculiar status and history of the Creoles "would not be understood elsewhere." Moreover, toward the end of Reconstruction and the removal of federal troops in 1877, segregation was on the rise, giving place to violent episodes such as the Battle of Liberty Place fought by the White League in 1874, and the Robert Charles Riot in 1900 which young Ferdinand witnessed. Such a situation might have led individuals or families to "adapt" their ancestry and family history, and/or to anglicize their names. Gushee, "A Preliminary Chronology," 391 (quote in note)–393 (quotes in text).

25. Morton and Lomax, *Transcript of the 1938 Recordings*, 9.

26. Garrett, *Struggling to Define a Nation*, 54 (quote); Morton and Lomax, *Transcript of the 1938 Recordings*, 104.

27. Garrett, *Struggling to Define a Nation*, 64–65.

28. Garrett (*Struggling to Define a Nation*, 58) is quoting Russell (*New Orleans Style*, 23), in which Dodds added, "When we used to play blues for a dance long ago, it was so draggy, sometimes people would say it sounded like a dead march"; Gara, *The Baby Dodds Story*, 11.

29. In the version he played at the Library of Congress, Morton also sang some lyrics, explaining that this is how he "used to sing it in the Elite" (a nightclub in Chicago). Schuller, *Early Jazz*, 137 (quote in text). Morton and Lomax, *Transcript of the 1938 Recordings*, 57 and 57n21 (quote in note), 58.

30. Mamie Desdunes was the natural daughter of Rodolphe Desdunes, a prominent member of the Creole community, who played an active role in the *Comité des Citoyens* that challenged the Separate Car Act (see chapter 1). As Bunk Johnson recalled, "[s]he was a hustlin' woman. A blues-singing poor gal." Lomax, *Mister Jelly Roll*, 20–21 (quote in note); Raeburn, "Beyond the 'Spanish Tinge,'" 24 (quote in text).

31. Collier, *The Making of Jazz*, 107.

32. Thanks to John McCusker, the gap has been filled with the publication of *Creole Trombone: Kid Ory and the Early Years of Jazz* in 2012.

33. McCusker, *Creole Trombone*, 9, 11–13, 22; Ory interview by Ertegun and Campbell (1957), reel 1, 13m41–14m04, transcript 11.

34. McCusker, *Creole Trombone*, 83–84 (quotes), 101, 106–8, 112.

35. Armstrong, *Satchmo: My Life in New Orleans*, 137, 139.

36. In the beginning of the twentieth century, the slide trombone gradually replaced the valve trombone, which allowed for the development of new instrumental techniques. Ory bought his first slide trombone in 1909. The usual tale is that the term *tailgate trombone* comes from the position the trombone player occupied at the back (the tailgate) when dances and picnics were advertised by musicians playing in wagons, with signs on the side. David Sager, "A Tale of the Slide Trombone in Early Jazz," 2 (quote), 10; McCusker, *Creole Trombone*, 70; Herbert, *The Trombone*, 217–23, 263–71. More about early jazz in the section about the revival recordings of Creole songs in chapter 6.

37. Ory's Sunshine Orchestra/Spikes' Seven Pods of Pepper Orchestra, "Ory's Creole Trombone," 1922, reissued on *Kid Ory and His Creole Jazz Band 1922–1947*. Kid Ory (trombone), Mutt Carey (cornet), Dink Johnson (clarinet), Fred Washington (piano), Ed Garland (bass), Ben Borders (drums).

38. Wilbur Sweatman and his Jass Band recorded for Pathe, in late 1916 or 1917. Sager, "Ory's Creole Trombone—Kid Ory (June 1922)," 1; McCusker, *Creole Trombone*, 144–50; Levin, "Kid Ory's Legendary Nordskog/Sunshine Recordings"; Schuller, *Early Jazz*, 74; Gioia, *The History of Jazz*, 41; Berresford, "Wilbur Sweatman," Oxford Music Online.

39. Sager, "A Tale of the Slide Trombone," 11 (quote); McCusker, *Creole Trombone*, 145–47.

40. McCusker, *Creole Trombone*, 177 (quote), 194–96.

41. T-Bone Walker's "Blues for Marili" was written for Morden. McCusker, *Creole Trombone*, 186; Ginell, *Hot Jazz for Sale*, 37–39, 121–23; Tucker, "A Feminist Perspective," 96.

42. Griffiths, *Hot Jazz*, 20 (quotes in text). The word "raddy" also appears in the 1940 interviews of the women involved in the formation of the Million Dollar Baby Dolls social club ca. 1912 that led to the Mardi Gras tradition of costuming as Baby Dolls. "They were known for 'walking raddy' (a kind of strut that would end with the steps needed to 'shake on down') . . . They were 'raddy' women who did not care about what others who devalued them thought of them." Similarly, in the 1992 interview by Michael White, Danny Barker spoke about "the boss drummer everybody respected. Jean Vigne. They called him 'Raddy.' . . . Raddy means you don't give a damn. . . . just everything he did, he did with a rhythm."

He also made a distinction between *raddy* and *ratty*, which means that you do "rat things," although, in *A Life in Jazz* (first published in 1986), he had explained that "ratty music is bluesy, folksy music that moves you and exhilarates you, makes you dance." Saxon, Dreyer, and Tallant, *Gumbo Ya-Ya*, 9, 11; Vaz, *The "Baby Dolls,"* 14 and 20 (first quote in note), 128; Danny Barker interview by Michael White, 68; Barker, *A Life in Jazz*, 30.

43. Although Miles also wrote to Griffiths that her "mother never taught [her] anything about singing," two of Miles's later LPs also hint at her mother's constant singing as an early influence: *Hot Songs My Mother Taught Me* and *Torchy Lullabies My Mother Sang Me*, both released in 1956. Miles interview by Allen (1951), reel 1, 0m45–0m55 (first quote) and digest, 1; Goreau, "An Evening with Lizzie Miles," 9 (second quote); Griffiths, *Hot Jazz*, 26 (quote in note).

44. Griffiths, *Hot Jazz*, 20.

45. Miles interview by Allen (1951), reel 1, 1m03–2m07, 2m44–3m18 (quote in text and block quote), and digest, 1.

46. Miles interview by Allen, reel 1 (1951), 2m07–2m26, and digest, 1; Abbott and Seroff, "Lizzie Miles: Her Forgotten Career," 58, 60 (quotes), 61.

47. The slang word "Bam" probably evolved referentially from Alabama, and it can refer to Alabama or to the Deep South Cotton Belt states in general. "Lizzie Miles: Her Forgotten Career," quotes from 61, 63, 65; Abbott and Seroff, *The Original Blues*, 59 (about the slang word "Bam"); Miles interview by Allen (1951) reel 1, 12m50–13m44.

48. Miles interview by Allen (1951) reel 1, 7m44–8m13, 10m14–11m33, 13m44–14m04 (13m46–13m48, quote), and digest 3–4; Manetta interview by Russell (1957), 2h24m31; Abbott and Seroff, "Lizzie Miles: Her Forgotten Career," 68.

49. Anderson, "The Genesis of King Oliver's Creole Jazz Band," 287–93.

50. "Muscle Shoals Blues" and "She Walked Right Up and Took My Man Away" (OKeh 8031, A & B). Reissued on *Lizzie Miles: Complete Recorded Works in Chronological Order* vol. 1 (DOCD-5458).

51. Miles interview by Allen (1951), reel 1:15m21–21m02, digest 4–5, and reel 2:1m47–3m32, digest 9; Goreau, "An Evening with Lizzie Miles, 9 (quote); Griffiths, *Hot Jazz*, 23–24.

52. *Lizzie Miles: Complete Recorded Works in Chronological Order* presents her recordings from 1922 to 1939 (vol. 1, DOCD 5458; vol. 2, DOCD-5459; vol. 3, DOCD-5460).

53. Dahl, *Stormy Weather: The Music and Lives of a Century of Jazzwomen*, 104; Gioia, *The History of Jazz*, 16.

54. "I Hate a Man Like You" and "Don't Tell Me Nothin' 'Bout My Man" (Victor V-38571, A & B; reissued on *Lizzie Miles: Complete Recorded Works*, vol. 3, Docd-5460).

55. However, on the oral history tape, Miles didn't mention going back to Chicago, suggesting that her mother's long illness kept her in New Orleans, so it's most likely that she didn't stay steadily in Chicago. Miles interview by Allen (1951), reel 2:3m32–6m13, digest 10; Griffiths, *Hot Jazz*, 24.

56. *Moans and Blues* (1956); *Hot Songs My Mother Taught Me* (1956); and *Torchy Lullabies My Mother Sang Me* (1956). Accompaniment by Red Camp (piano), Tony Almerico's All Stars, or his Parisian Room Band, guest appearances from Albert French (banjo). Miles interview by Allen (1951), reel 2:6m14–9m04, and digest 10–11; Abbott, liner notes for *Lizzie Miles: Complete Recorded Works*, vol. 3; Griffiths, *Hot Jazz*, 24–27.

57. This list doesn't pretend to be exhaustive, but the bilingual songs I have found on recordings are: "A Good Man Is Hard to Find" (*A Night in Old New Orleans*, 1956); "Basin

Street Blues" (*Lizzie Miles*, 1994 [previously unissued]); "Bill Bailey, Won't You Please Come Home?" (*A Night in Old New Orleans*, 1956; *Lizzie Miles*, 1994 [recorded in 1953]; *Hot Songs My Mother Taught* Me, 1956); "Can't Help Loving That Man of Mine" (*Moans and Blues* 1956); "Darktown Strutters' Ball" (*A Night in Old New Orleans*, 1956; *Torchy Lullabies My Mother Sang Me*, 1956); "Jelly Roll/I Ain't Gonna Give Nobody None of This Jelly Roll" (*Sharkey and His Kings of Dixieland*, 2008 [recorded in 1952]; *Sharkey Bonano At Lenfant's Lounge*, 1991 [recorded in 1952]; *Moans and Blues*,1956).

58. Bechet, *Treat It Gentle*, 69, 73, 77–81, 197; Chilton, *Sidney Bechet: Wizard of Jazz*, 6–7, 10–11; Morton and Lomax, *Transcript of the 1938 Recordings*, 137, from where I am taking the full name of the band, which is often called only Silver Bells (or Bell) Band.

59. Brothers, *Louis Armstrong's New Orleans*, 189–93 (first quote 192, second quote 189); Bechet, *Treat It Gentle*, 79; Chilton, *Sidney Bechet: Wizard of Jazz*, 7–8.

60. See the passage earlier in this chapter about Tio and the Eagle Band. Bechet himself gave various dates as to exactly when he joined the band (1908, 1911, 1914); Chilton suggested around 1913 and Kinzer wrote that when Tio Jr. quit the band "probably sometime late in 1912, he was replaced by his young friend Sidney Bechet." Bechet, *Treat It Gentle*, 83, 90; Chilton, *Sidney Bechet: Wizard of Jazz*, 15 (quote in text); Kinzer, "The Tio Family: Four Generations," 225 (quote in note).

61. Leonard Bechet interview by Lomax, in Morton and Lomax, *Transcript of the 1938 Recordings*, 144 (first quote), 151 (second quote).

62. Balliett, "Le Grand Bechet," 37–38.

63. Self-taught conductor Ernest Ansermet was the principal director of the Ballets Russes orchestra in 1915; he had made his North American debut with them in New York in 1916, and his South American debut in 1917. He also premiered works by Prokofiev, Satie, and Stravinsky. In 1918, he founded the Orchestre de la Suisse Romande, which he directed until 1967–68. The article "Sur un orchestre nègre" was reissued in 1938 in *Hot Jazz—Revue Internationale de la Musique de Jazz*, where it appeared alongside the English translation by Walter E. Schaap. Ansermet, "Sur un orchestre nègre," 9. Excerpts from the article are also quoted in Bechet, *Treat It Gentle*, 127; and Chilton, *Sidney Bechet: Wizard of Jazz*, 40.

64. Levin, "Barney Bigard—The Great New Orleans Clarinetist," 24 (first quote); Bigard, *With Louis and the Duke*, 71 (second quote). Both quotes are also found in Chilton, *Sidney Bechet: Wizard of Jazz*, 58.

65. The Blue Five were Thomas Morris (cornet), John Mayfield (trombone), Sidney Bechet (soprano sax), Buddy Christian (banjo), and Clarence Williams (piano). For more about Bechet performances on "Wild Cat Blues" and "Kansas City Man Blues," see Chilton, *Sidney Bechet: Wizard of Jazz*, 57–58.

66. Bechet's solos predate the Louis Armstrong Hot Five and Hot Seven sessions (1925–28), traditionally regarded as having ushered in the age of the jazz soloist. However, Armstrong too was already improvising before these sessions. For more about his earlier solos, see Brian Harker, "'Telling a Story': Louis Armstrong and Coherence in Early Jazz."

67. Sarrusophones are a family of brass instruments resembling the saxophone, but played with a double reed—although it is possible that Bechet used a single-reed mouthpiece (like a saxophone). I am not counting the pieces for which there are some doubts about Bechet

actually playing, based on the discographies compiled by David Mylne in Bechet, *Treat It Gentle*, 221–40; and by Mel Collins, "Recordings of Sidney Bechet," 13–14. Chilton, *Sidney Bechet: Wizard of Jazz*, 66, 235; Collins, Blaikley, "Sarrusophone," Oxford Music Online; Baines, *Woodwind Instruments and Their History*, 166–67.

68. Mamie Smith (vocals), Sidney Bechet (sax soprano), Buddy Christian (banjo), Clarence Williams (piano).

69. Eva Taylor and the Clarence Williams' Blue Five: Eva Taylor (vocals), Louis Armstrong (cornet), Charlie Irvis (trombone), Sidney Bechet (bass [contrabass] sarrusophone), Buddy Christian (banjo), Clarence Williams (piano).

70. "Achin' Hearted Blues," same personnel as note 65. Sippie Wallace accompanied by Clarence Williams' Trio: Sippie Wallace (vocals), Sidney Bechet (clarinet), Buddy Christian (banjo), Clarence Williams (piano). For a full discussion on these recordings and various solos, see Chilton, 59–61, 66. Interestingly, Schuller has analyzed Bechet's last twelve bars on "New Orleans Hop Scop Blues" as a "foreground solo" with which he "dared to end" the final chorus. Schuller, *Early Jazz*, 197.

71. In 1925, *La Revue Nègre* featured Josephine Baker as its star singer and dancer. Chilton, *Sidney Bechet: Wizard of Jazz*, 75–79 (quote 77).

72. Chilton, *Sidney Bechet: Wizard of Jazz*, 216 (quote), 234; Bechet, *Treat It Gentle*, 191–200.

CHAPTER 6. THE EARLY JAZZ REVIVAL AND THE CREOLE SONGS

1. "Hot jazz" or "hot" record collectors were thus named because they were collecting early jazz in the style emanating from New Orleans, which they saw as the "real" and authentic jazz rather than jazz styles of the thirties and beyond. A thorough examination of the history and ideology of "hot" jazz collectors can be found in Raeburn, *New Orleans Style*, chapter 2; for a short description, see 1–5 of his introduction.

2. Brown, "Farewell to Basin Street," 9, 51.

3. Russell quoted in Raeburn, *New Orleans Style*, 117.

4. Active between late 1941 and 1954, the Jazz Man label specialized in the recording of early jazz. The musicians were Bunk Johnson (trumpet), George Lewis (clarinet), Jim Robinson (trombone), Walter Decou (piano), Lawrence Marrero (banjo), Austin Young (Lester Young's uncle, bass), and Ernest Rogers (drums). Raeburn, *New Orleans Style*, 115–16; Ginell, *Hot Jazz for Sale*, 301–11, with details about Johnson's sessions, 303–4.

5. For more on Russell, see Hazeldine, *Bill Russell's American Music*. The chapter "American Music" presents a short chronological history of the label (xiii–xv), followed by an index of the various sessions in chronological order. The New Orleans sessions are discussed on 1, 11–87, and 111–33.

6. The Jazz Man Record Shop was founded by David Stuart, to whom Morden was married in February 1941. They apparently separated after only twenty-five days but remained business partners. She filed for divorce in November 1942, and when it was finalized in 1944, she got to keep the shop—which she already had been managing before the wedding—as part of the divorce settlement. Ginell, *Hot Jazz for Sale*, 40–44, 121–29 (about Orson Welles Almanac and the All Star Jazz Group).

7. The musicians were Mutt Carey (trumpet); Jimmy Noone, Barney Bigard, Omer Simeon, or Darnell Howard (clarinet); Bud Scott (banjo/guitar); Buster Wilson (piano); Ed Garland (bass); and Zutty Singleton, Alton Redd, or Minor Hall (drums). Ginell, *Hot Jazz for Sale*, xv, 133–34, 141, 144–45, 305–6, 312; McCusker, *Creole Trombone*, 186, 197–99; Raeburn, *New Orleans Style*, 127–30.

8. Ginell, *Hot Jazz for Sale*, 156–58.

9. Blesh, liner notes for *Baby Dodds Trio/Jazz A' La Creole* [sic]; Blesh, *Shining Trumpets: A History of Jazz*, 337–38.

10. Raeburn, *New Orleans Style*, 91–97, 107–11, 118–20; chapters 3 and 4, 111–81, provide a detailed account of the emergence of the early jazz revival.

11. Zagala, "Le 'trois sur quatre,'" 88, 195 (quotes, second one in English in the text).

12. Cable himself performed a few Creole songs during the "Twins of Genius" tour with Mark Twain between November 1884 and February 1885. Cable, "Creole Slave Songs" and "The Dance in Place Congo"; Railton, "Touring with Cable and Huck."

13. Peterson, *Creole Songs from New Orleans*, 1.

14. Ms. Le Jeune's collection appeared as an article in the *Louisiana Historical Quarterly*, but it seems to have been the reproduction of an address she had given the year before, at the thirty-ninth annual meeting of the Music Teachers' Association, where indeed, Mrs. Edouard May sang. Ms. Le Jeune also noted that the songs were accompanied by "an empty barrel, a gourd filled with peas, and the rattling of bones . . . and sustained by another . . . which was the delight of my tender years, and could . . . be made to imitate the violin . . . a comb wrapped in tissue paper." Hare performed songs in lecture-recitals with baritone William Richardson. And ten of the twelve songs from Monroe's *Bayou Ballads* appeared on the 1941 record *Bayou Ballads of the Louisiana Plantations*, sung by Marguerite Castellanos-Taggart with Edna McLaughlin (piano); Le Jeune, "Creole Folk Songs," 456–57 (quote in note); Cable, "Creole Slave Songs," 824–25; "Music and Art," 244 (about Le Jeune's address); Hare, *Six Creole Folk-Songs*; Hare, *Negro Musicians and Their Music*; Wright, "Hare, Maud Cuney"; Monroe, *Bayou Ballads*, iv (quote in text).

15. Levine, *Highbrow Lowbrow*, 146.

16. Arguedas interview by Halpert (1939), LWO 4872 R 207-B, 2m53–4m17 (quote 2m53–2m55, 3m38–4m07), transcript by the author 7.

17. Kinzer, "Tio Family: Four Generations," 159–61, 164, 206, 211. For more on the Tio and Doublet String Band, see 162–65.

18. Nickerson, "Africo-Creole Music in Louisiana," 4.

19. Nickerson. *Five Creole Songs*; McGinty, "Conversation with . . . Camille Nickerson," 88 (quote); Anne Key Simpson, "Camille Lucie Nickerson, the Louisiana Lady." For more about Camille Nickerson's career and work as a teacher see the recent MA thesis "Her People and Her History: How Camille Lucie Nickerson Inspired the Preservation of Creole Folk Music and Culture, 1888–1982" by Shelby N. Loyacano (2019).

20. The band members were Bill Johnson, founder (bass), Jimmy Palao (violin), George Baquet (clarinet)—later replaced by Louis "Big Eye" Nelson—Freddie Keppard (cornet), Eddie Vincent/Vinson/Venson (trombone), Norwood Williams (guitar), Ollie "Dink" Johnson (drums). Gushee, *Pioneers of Jazz*, 47 (first quote), 93–94 (second quote), 97, 274, 295.

21. Armontine Palao was the wife of Jimmy Palao. Gushee, *Pioneers of Jazz*, 94.

22. Morton and Lomax, *Transcript of the 1938 Recordings*, 31. Also revealing is the 1918 anonymous editorial "Jass and Jassism" published in the *Times-Picayune*, in which the author refused to accept the idea of New Orleans as the birthplace of jazz. Speaking about "this particular form of musical vice," he concluded that "we do not recognize the honor of parenthood." As Raeburn points out, not everybody agreed with this point of view, as can be read in the "Letters to the Editor" sent by various readers following the publication of the editorial. "Jass and Jassism," New Orleans *Times-Picayune* (quotes); Raeburn, *New Orleans Style*, 219–20.

23. A note in the transcript specifies that the can-can was "a variation on the quadrille and polka [that] was first danced in France in the 1820s and [was] subsequently banned by the police as indecent." Indeed, in the late nineteenth century, the French can-can involved women lifting their dress to kick their legs high up, revealing their legs and garters, which men surely found exciting. However, both Johnny St. Cyr and Leonard Bechet also mentioned having played this song, and according to Bechet, can-can is "like a Hoodoo [a variant practice of the Voodoo, if this is what he is referring to] ... like a gossip like, in a way, ... like, a person, ... that's spreading [nasty] gossip." Accordingly, Marguerite B. Wogan's 1931 short play was called *Cancans Kisinieres "Cooks Gossip."* Morton and Lomax, *Transcript of the 1938 Recordings*, 106–7 (quote in text, my emphasis, bracketed comments in original), 106, note 29 (quote in note); St. Cyr interview by Lomax, Association for Cultural Equity (1949); Bechet interview by Lomax, Association for Cultural Equity (1949), 0m50–1m30.

24. St. Cyr's verses (one about going to the market and the other about Mam'zelle Josephine [*sic*]) are similar to verses sung by Lizzie Miles and Danny Barker (discussed later in the chapter). St. Cyr interview by Lomax, in Morton and Lomax, *Transcript of the 1938 Recordings*, 140–43 (italics and bracketed comments in the original).

25. Lomax, *Mister Jelly Roll*, 72.

26. Picou interview by Russell, Rose, and Collins (1958), digest reel 1, p. 2, and reel 3, p. 2. First quote on reel 3, 10m18–10m28; Hobson, *Creating Jazz Counterpoint*, 88 (second quote)–90. Charters, *A Trumpet around the Corner*, 62.

27. Picou interview by Russell, Rose, and Collins (1958), digest reel 2, p. 1, exact quote on reel 2, 3m34–3m57.

28. The English translations of the titles are from Picou interview by Russell, Rose, and Collins (1958), reel 2, 5m30–6m40, digest, reel 2, pp. 1–2 (for the titles of the songs); Picou interview by Russell and Collins (1960), reel 2, 3m02–3m40 (quote), digest, reel 2, p. 4.

29. Lomax, *Mister Jelly Roll*, 73, 74; Picou and Dominguez interview by Lomax (1949).

30. Barbarin interview by Russell and Allen (1959), transcript reel 1, 21–24, quotes 21, 23–24. Stories about men cross-dressing also appear in accounts by Sybil Kein (see later in this chapter) and Alice Zeno, creating a direct link with Marc-Antoine Caillot's narration of the 1730 Mardi Gras celebration at a home on Bayou St. John, in which he was disguised as a shepherdess (see chapter 4). Zeno and Lewis interview by Russell and Allen (November 14, 1958), transcript reel 1, p. 14, and reel 2, transcript 29.

31. Vaz, *The "Baby Dolls,"* 8, 68–69; for more about men cross-dressing see 86, 87–91.

32. Bechet interview by Lomax (1949), 10; Danny Barker interview by Allen (1959), 38m45–40m18, summary, 11.

33. Head arrangements were not written in advance (though some rough sketches might have been); they were put together and memorized during rehearsals (or even performances). For more about the downtown Creoles/uptown Black musicians, see chapter 5.

34. Ory's Sunshine Orchestra/Spikes' Seven Pods of Pepper Orchestra, "Ory's Creole Trombone," 1922, reissued on *Kid Ory and His Creole Jazz Band 1922–1947*. "Ory's Creole Trombone" was also recorded in 1927 during the seminal Louis Armstrong Hot Five sessions with Kid Ory (trombone), Johnny Dodds (clarinet), Johnny St. Cyr (banjo), and Lil Hardin (piano) in a similar arrangement.

35. Sager, "A Tale of the Slide Trombone in Early Jazz," 1–3, 10–12; Herbert, *The Trombone*, 217–23, 263–71. See also the section about Kid Ory in chapter 5, where the tailgate trombone style is discussed.

36. As noted by Lawrence Gushee, "The much-discussed question of two-beat versus four-beat rhythm is related to the transition from ragtime [traditionally in 2/4] to jazz . . . Perhaps the most distinctive rhythmic feature was a pervasive but relaxed playing off the beat, particularly at the slower foxtrot or slow drag tempo." These last two were among the "new" dances that were becoming popular among the young generation at the turn of the nineteenth century, eventually replacing the "old" European dance suites. Gushee, "New Orleans Jazz," Oxford Music Online (quote in note). About the changes in dance styles and suites, see Gushee, "The Nineteenth-Century Origins of Jazz," 15–22; Szwed and Marks, "Afro-American Transformation," 33.

37. Kid Ory's Creole Jazz Band, "Ory's Creole Trombone," Crescent 6, November 1945, reissued on *Kid Ory's Creole Jazz Band 1944/1945. The Legendary Crescent Recordings Sessions*. Kid Ory (trombone), Mutt Carey (trumpet), Darnell Howard (clarinet), Buster Wilson (piano), Bud Scott (guitar), Ed Garland (bass), and Minor Hall (drums).

38. Moreover, Mutt Carey (cornet [1922]/trumpet) and Ed Garland (bass) played on both the 1922 and 1945 recordings of "Ory's Creole Trombone," on the 1946 and 1947 recordings of "Eh La Bas," and on the 1945 recording of "Blanche Touquatoux" (discussed later).

39. Kid Ory and His Creole Jazz Band, "Eh La Bas," reissued on *The Complete Kid Ory Columbia Session 1946*; "Eh La Bas," recorded in 1947, issued on *Kid Ory at the Green Room* Vol. 2.

40. Even if the chorus comes first, I am labeling it as B and the verse as A, which is what is most often seen. It should also be noted that I am not indicating variations on the same section as A' or B', but rather aiming to describe musical forms and overall arrangements more than the specific details of the performances.

41. Kid Ory, "Eh La Bas" (1946): Mutt Carey (trumpet), Barney Bigard (clarinet), Kid Ory (trombone/vocals), Buster Wilson (piano), Bud Scott (guitar), Ed Garland (bass), Minor Hall (drums).

42. "Eh La Bas," recorded in 1960, issued on *The Complete Kid Ory Verve Sessions*, Disc 7. Teddy Buckner (trumpet), Bob McCracken (clarinet), Kid Ory (trombone/vocals), Lionel Reason (piano), Frank Haggerty (guitar), Morty Corb (bass), Jesse Sailes (drums).

43. Lizzie Miles, "Eh La Bas," on *The Great Bob Scobey and His Frisco Band*, 1956, reissued on Bob Scobey, *The Great Bob Scobey and His Frisco Band* Vol. 2: Bob Scobey (trumpet), Clancy Hayes (banjo), Bill Napier (clarinet), Jack Buck (trombone), Hal McCormick (bass), Fred Higuera (drums).

44. Dede Pierce claimed to have originated the song. However, there are other origin stories for "Eh La Bas" that are quite different. Richard Allen, liner notes for *Gulf Coast Blues*; Dede and Billie Pierce interview by Allen (1959, 1960, and 1963); Paul and Emile Barnes interview by Russell and Collins (1959); Alcide "Slow Drag" Pavageau interview by Russell and Allen (1958).

45. Transcription (minor variations in the 1960 version not indicated) and translation of the three versions included by the author, using several sources some translations are dictated by the changing context of the lyrics: Ashforth, liner notes for Emile Barnes, *The Louisiana Joymakers*; Billie and Dede Pierce interview by Allen (January 10, 1960), 14m45–31m05; Van Wey, *Street Cries and Creole Songs of New Orleans*; Louisiana Creole Dictionary (website).

46. About men cross-dressing, see chapter 6n30 above. Kein, *Creole: The History and Legacy*, 124.

47. Neumann-Holzschuh, *Textes anciens en créole louisianais*, 96–97. Other scholars have collected songs they usually called "Mon Cher Cousin" or "Maison Denise," which present only a few verses from "Denise Lacage." Theard, *Old Songs of French and Creole Origin*, 220; Wehrmann, *Creole Songs of the Deep South*, 7; Albertine Hilaire Alexis (born in 1865) in Arguedas interview by Halpert (1939), LWO 4872 R 207 B, 44m27–46m21, transcript by the author 20.

48. Line 3 of the verse: "Since the mulatto (been) in the kitchen, There's no more bones for the dogs" (translation by the author). Tiersot spent two days on a plantation, where he "heard all the repertoire of yesteryears sung by an old Negress, Philomène Butler, born enslaved, . . . had remained in the service of her former masters" after the emancipation. Tiersot adds that he met some "young ladies to whom she would have rocked the early days . . . Mesdames Wogan, Beugnot [Jeanne Wogan Arguedas's mother was née Beugnot] and Lejeune." This is similar to the story told by Ms. Arguedas (born in 1886, she might have been one of the "young ladies") about her mammy Mona, who had been given as a wedding gift to her grandmother in 1857. (See chapter 1.) Tiersot, *Notes d'ethnographie musicale*, 1, 76–78 (quote in note, 76: "*entendre chanter tout le répertoire d'autrefois par une vieille négresse, Philomène Butler, née esclave, puis, après sa libération, demeurée au service de ses anciens maîtres; . . . de jeunes dames dont elle avait bercé les premiers jours . . . Mesdames Wogan, Beugnot et Lejeune*") (translation by the author).

49. Saxon, Dreyer, and Tallant, *Gumbo Ya-Ya*, 432.

50. The "Toucoutou Affair" took place when Anastasie Desarzant sued Pierre LeBlanc and Eglantine Desmaziliere, for slander for having publicly called her a "woman of color"—which, at the time, bore a lot of significance with regard to (White only) social rights and privileges. Desdunes, *Nos hommes et notre histoire*, 38–39; Thompson, "'Ah Toucoutou, ye conin vous'"; Thompson, *Exiles at Home*, 1–6, 67 (quote in note)–70.

51. *Paul Barbarin and His New Orleans Jazz*, reissued on Collectables Records. Louis Nelson and His Palm Court Jazz Band: Danny Barker (banjo/vocals), Louis Nelson (trombone), Wendell Brunious (trumpet), Sammy Rimington (clarinet), Butch Thompson (piano), Chester Zardis (bass), Stanley Stephens (drums).

52. Transcription and translation by the author. Apart from "Sullied woman" found in Harriet Janis's liner notes for *Jazz a la Creole* [sic], and the double-entendre about the word "to to" (toe or backside) that comes from Stearns, *The Story of Jazz*, 11.

53. Danny Barker, *New Orleans Jazz Man and Raconteur*. See note 51.

54. Actually, Barker also sang "Salee Dame," in which the two verses have the same lyrics as the second and third verses of his version of "Eh La Bas."

55. For more about the "Spanish tinge" in early jazz, see chapters 2 (about the habanera and tresillo) and 5; Russell, *New Orleans Style*, 23; Garrett, *Struggling to Define a Nation*, 58.

56. Desdunes, *Nos Hommes et Notre Histoire*, 38–39.

57. Translation by Sister Dorothea Olga McCants in Desdunes, *Our People and Our History*, 63–64; alternative translation (closer to the original) from Saxon, Dreyer, and Tallant, *Gumbo Ya-Ya*, 428.

58. Transcription and translation by the author. Many thanks to Étienne Viator for his time and invaluable help in deciphering and translating Ory's lyrics in both the 1945 and 1960 versions. The author doesn't claim these transcriptions to be definitive.

59. Kid Ory and His Creole Jazz Band, "Blanche Touquatoux," Decca 25134, 1945, reissued on *Kid Ory and His Creole Jazz Band 1922–1947*. Mutt Carey (trumpet), Joe Darenbourg (clarinet), Buster Wilson (piano), Bud Scott (guitar), Ed Garland (bass), Minor Hall (drums), Kid Ory (trombone/vocals), Cecile Ory (vocals).

60. Borneman, "Creole Echoes," Part 1, 14. See chapter 2 for more about the tresillo.

61. "Blanche Touquatoux" previously unissued, *The Complete Kid Ory Verve Sessions*, Disc 7—same musicians as note 42. The "'Rhythm changes" come from the 1930 George Gershwin song "I Got Rhythm," which became a standard and a commonly used chord progression during the 1930s and 1940s.

62. However, Saxon removed a verse and omitted to indicate that the first verse he gave is, in fact, the refrain. Desdunes's version is the most complete, but an earlier version was published by Alcée Fortier in 1887. Fortier, "Bits of Louisiana Folk-Lore," 167; Desdunes, *Nos Hommes et Notre Histoire*, 38–39; Saxon, Dreyer, and Tallant, *Gumbo Ya-Ya*, 428.

63. Kid Ory, *The Complete Kid Ory Verve Sessions*, Disc 7.

64. The songs were: "Au clair de la lune," "Auprès de ma blonde," "Frère Jacques," "Il était une bergère," "L'alouette," "Le roi Dagobert," "Marlborough s'en va-t-en guerre," "Sur le pont d'Avignon." (These are also part of the children's repertoire of French Canada.) *The Complete Kid Ory Verve Sessions*, Disc 7.

65. Hadlock, liner notes for *The Complete Kid Ory Verve Sessions*, 9 (emphasis in the text).

66. Irma Henry also recalled having played that game. I am using her spelling for the second phrase although there are two alternate spellings: "C'est li ci, c'est li ça" (Hare) or "C'est de-ci, c'est de-là" (Theard). Zeno and Lewis interview by Russell and Allen (November 14, 1958), transcript 14–15, reel 1, 21m31–21m48 (quote); Henry, "A Bibliography of Louisiana Negro Creole Folk Music," 114, 120; Sadler, "Creole Songs," 142; Hare, *Negro Musicians and Their Music*, 94; Theard, *Old Songs of French and Creole Origin*, 158.

67. "Les Ognons" first issued on the Circle 78 rpm album *Jazz a la Creole* [sic]: Albert Nicholas (clarinet and vocals), James P. Johnson (piano), Danny Barker (guitar and vocals), Pops Foster (bass). Blesh, liner notes for 2000 edition *Baby Dodds Trio/Jazz A' La Creole* [sic].

68. About calas, see chapter 2, pages 35–36 and 41–43. Verses transcribed and translated by the author. Interlude quoted from Harriet Janis's liner notes for *Jazz a la Creole*.

69. Bechet also recorded it in 1952 and 1955, accompanied by the Claude Luter Orchestra, and one last time in 1958 with unidentified musicians. Bechet, *Treat It Gentle*, 231, 234, 237, 240.

70. Collier also indicated that work songs were often "insult songs" or "songs of derision" (see chapter 2). Janis, liner notes for *Jazz a la Creole* [sic], first issued in 1947; Collier, *The Making of Jazz*, 19.

71. Stearns, *The Story of Jazz*, 11; Van Dam, "The influence of the West African Songs of Derision in the New World," 53.

72. Herskovits, *The Myth of the Negro Past*, 157–58.

73. Wilson said he "was 'bout eighteen years old when the Civil War come." Fifteen of the seventy interviewees of Vol. 16, Texas, part 4, 1936–1938 of the *Federal Writers' Project* had close links to Louisiana, where they themselves or their parents had been born and/or enslaved. Wash Wilson, interview for the *Federal Writers' Project*, 195 (quote in note)–200 (quote in text, 198, my italics; also quoted in Gates, *The Signifying Monkey*, 68).

74. In the late 1960s and early 1970s, Claudia Mitchell-Kernan studied the conversational aspect of signifying in Oakland, California, that involved "implicit content or function" used to conceal a message, its receiver, or its intent. Working from a different perspective, Henry Louis Gates worked on the use of signifying in African American literature in his 1988 book *The Signifying Monkey: A Theory of African-American Literary Criticism*. Mitchell-Kernan, "Signifying and Marking" (quote in note, 166); Gates, *The Signifying Monkey*, 51–70.

75. According to Kein, "[t]here are approximately eighty extant Creole songs, most of which have survived with musical notation intact." However, the list that I have gathered—which does not presume to be exhaustive—includes oral material and even a few fragments of songs. Songs have been collected, in both French and Creole French, in New Orleans and all the parishes along the Gulf Coast of southwest Louisiana. Not surprisingly, there are also a lot of variations in lyrics and melodies, and deeper analysis and research (beyond the scope of this book) would be needed to assess the exact number of songs collected. Kein, *Creole: The History and Legacy*, 125.

76. Alcée Fortier made a similar comment about the songs published in Cable's 1886 articles, as once "well known to all Louisianians." Nickerson, "Africo-Creole Music in Louisiana," 8; Fortier, "Bits of Louisiana Folk-Lore," 161.

77. Blesh included them in his list of the formative elements of early jazz and mentioned the "Creole Song (C'est l'Autre Can-Can)" performed by Morton and Ory; Stearns mentioned "Sali Dame" as a "signifying song" (see above); Schuller mentioned Morton's rendition of "C'été 'n aut' can-can, payé donc" [sic] to exemplify his ability to jazz up any tunes. Finally, Shipton includes them in his chapter about the precursors of jazz. Blesh, *Shining Trumpets: A History of Jazz*, 175, 179; Stearns, *The Story of Jazz*, 11; Schuller, *Early Jazz*, 139; Shipton, *A New History of Jazz*, 18–19.

78. I refer to America in its original meaning as a continent, so that "Franco-American" represents all of the French communities of the American continent—French Canada, the French West Indies, French Guiana, and so on.

EPILOGUE

1. Shannon Powell (drums), Christian Winther (clarinet), Wendell Brunious (trumpet), Leroy Jones (trumpet), Seva Venet (banjo), Kyle Roussel (piano), Chris Severin (bass).

APPENDIX 1. MORE ABOUT CREOLIZATION AND CREOLE IDENTITY

1. —*Hétéronomie d'un projet colonial marqué par la prépondérance d'une économie de plantation « à moteur externe », car vouée à la satisfaction de besoins extérieurs, ceux de la métropole;*
—*Disparition (« désapparition »), dans le cas des Antilles, ou absence (dans le cas de l'océan Indien) d'une population autochtone; tous les hommes viennent donc d'ailleurs: à côté du colonisateur européen, le flux prépondérant de peuplement est constitué par l'immigration forcée en provenance d'Afrique, du fait de l'appel en main d'œuvre servile que génère la plantation* [The use of "disparition (« désapparition »)" suggests both meanings of the word "disappearance": ceasing to exist, or ceasing to be visible];
—*La diversité des apparences physiques chez les arrivants sert de matériau à une idéologie hiérarchique: la « race » permet de justifier les ordonnancements sociaux (le « préjugé de couleur »).* Bonniol, "Situations créoles," 51–52 (translation by the author).

2. Cultural contacts and exchanges between Africa and Europe started long before the founding of *La Louisiane*. European colonial projects were often carried out by companies formed in the many colonizing countries who also established enclaves in the West African countries where they operated. Not surprisingly, new cultural practices emerged in these enclaves where Africans, Europeans, and Euro-Africans lived on the Atlantic littoral. Moreover, Gioia suggests that "traces" of the Moorish presence in the Iberian peninsula (from 711 to 1492) "may have laid the groundwork for the blossoming of African American jazz." Similarly, Hall also noted that from the end of the eleventh century up to the mid-twelfth century, the "Almoravides empire, [sic]" having conquered the empire of Ghana (located south of the Sahara between the Senegal and Niger Rivers) "united Spain, North Africa and Senegambia [from where a lot of the enslaved people in Louisiana came] under its political dominance." Berlin, "From Creole to African"; Berlin, *Many Thousands Gone*, 17–28; Gioia, *The History of Jazz*, 5 (quote in note); Hall, *Africans in Colonial Louisiana*, chapter 2 (quotes in note, 29).

3. Bonniol, "Situations créoles," 51. Stuart Hall suggests to think of creolization in the Caribbean "in terms of three 'presences': *présence africaine, présence européenne, and présence américaine*, . . . referring to an older concept—'America' as the New World." Hall, "Creolité and the Process of Creolization," 16–17. For more information and various case studies about creolization, see Baron and Cara, *Creolization as Cultural Creativity*; Stewart, *Creolization: History, Ethnography, Theory*; Gutiérrez Rodríguez and Tate, *Creolizing Europe: Legacies and Transformations*.

4. Herskovits, *Acculturation: The Study of Culture Contact*, 1938, 1–5 (quote 1, 5, italics in the text).

5. Herskovits, *Acculturation*, 10. This definition first appeared in the "Memorandum for the Study of Acculturation" published in 1936 by Robert Redfield, Ralph Linton, and Melville J. Herskovits, while working as a committee for the Social Science Research Council. For a later perspective on the concept of acculturation, see Margaret Kartomi, "The Processes and Results of Musical Culture Contact: A Discussion of Terminology and Concepts."

6. Robert Baron views Herskovits as a "proto-creolist" who "developed the concepts of syncretism and reinterpretation, referring to the reconciliation of cultural elements and

beliefs from cultures in contact with one another and the processes that give old meanings to new forms and retain old forms with new meanings." Herskovits, *The Myth of the Negro Past*, 161–65, 246–51, 297–98 (quotes, 298); Baron and Cara, *Creolization*, 16–17 (quotes in note).

7. In 1943, both Herskovits and Ortiz were involved in the establishment of the Instituto Internacional de Estudios Afroamericanos (International Institute of Afro-American Studies) in Mexico City. Ortiz, *Cuban Counterpoint*, 97–98 (quote), 102–3. Originally in Spanish, *Contrapunteo cubano del tabaco y del azúcar* was published in 1940, translated into English in 1995, and into French in 2011. "*Introducción*," *Afroamérica: La tercera raíz* (website).

8. Rutherford, "The Third Space: Interview with Homi Bhabha," 211.

9. "It is a peculiar sensation, this double-consciousness.... One ever feels his twoness,—an American, a Negro; two souls, two thoughts, two unreconciled strivings; two warring ideals in one dark body, whose dogged strength alone keeps it from being torn asunder." Gilroy, *The Black Atlantic*, 1–2; Du Bois, *The Souls of Black Folk*, 9 (quote in note).

10. Gilroy, *The Black Atlantic*, 1–2, 75.

11. Bernabé, Chamoiseau, and Confiant, *Éloge de la Créolité/In Praise of Creoleness*, 75 (first published in French in 1989). For the authors, *Creoleness* "involves a double process:
 – the adaptation of Europeans, Africans, and Asians to the New World; and
 – the cultural confrontation of these peoples within the same space, resulting in a mixed culture called Creole." 93.

12. Several African American writers contributed to *La Revue du Monde Noir*, such as Alain Locke and Langston Hughes. Smith, "Black Like That: Paulette Nardal and the Negritude Salon," 57–59, 59n11.

13. The term *Négritude* was coined in the magazine *L'Étudiant Noir* in 1935 by Aimé Césaire, who later "confess[ed] that [he did] not always like the word." Diagne, "Négritude" (quote in note); Ashcroft, Griffiths, and Tiffin, *Post-Colonial Studies*, 144 (quote in text), 145.

APPENDIX 2. CHANSON DU VIÉ BOSCUGO/MICHIÉ PRÉVAL (DANSEZ CALINDA)

1. According to *Textes anciens*, the "Romaine" was a "kind of robe made like a soutane," ("*sorte de robe de la forme d'une soutane*"). Neumann-Holzschuh, *Textes anciens*, 95n1 (translation by the author).

2. As noted by the authors of *Textes anciens*, Coleman adds the verb *fait*—"Yé té fait nègue payé." Neumann-Holzschuh, *Textes anciens*, 95n4.

APPENDIX 3. TOMBEAU, TOMBEAU MARIE-MADELEINE

1. Last verse with no repeat as in the text. Millien, *Chants et Chansons*, 36.

BIBLIOGRAPHY

Abbott, Lynn. Liner notes for *Lizzie Miles: Complete Recorded Work in Chronological Order*. Volume 1 (ca. 24 February to 25 April 1923). Vienna, Austria: Soundborn Studios, Document Records, 1996. Docd-5458.

Abbott, Lynn. Liner notes for *Lizzie Miles: Complete Recorded Work in Chronological Order*. Volume 2 (25 April 1923 to 29 February 1928). Vienna, Austria: Soundborn Studios, Document Records, 1996. Docd-5459.

Abbott, Lynn. Liner notes for *Lizzie Miles: Complete Recorded Work in Chronological Order*. Volume 3 (2 May 1928 to 7 October 1939). Vienna, Austria: Soundborn Studios, Document Records, 1996. Docd-5460.

Abbott, Lynn, and Doug Seroff. "Lizzie Miles: Her Forgotten Career in Circus Side-Show Minstrelsy 1914–1918." *78 Quarterly* 1, no. 7 (1992): 57–70.

Abbott, Lynn, and Doug Seroff. *The Original Blues: The Emergence of the Blues in African American Vaudeville, 1899–1926*. Jackson: University Press of Mississippi, 2017.

Acts Passed at the First Session of the First Legislature of the Territory of Orleans, begun and held in the city of New Orleans, on the 25th day of January, in the year of our Lord one thousand eight and six, and of the independence of the United States of America, the thirtieth. Black Code XXXII. New Orleans, LA: Bradford & Anderson, 1807. Accessed April 4, 2019. https://babel.hathitrust.org/cgi/pt?id=mdp.35112203962842;view=1up;seq=7.

Alberts, John Bernard. "Origins of Black Catholic Parishes in the Archdiocese of New Orleans, 1718–1920." PhD diss., Louisiana State University, 1998. New Orleans: The Historic New Orleans Collection, BX1407 N4 N49, 1998.

Alexis, Albertine Hilaire, in Jeanne Wogan Arguedas interview by Herbert Halpert. New Orleans, LA. *1939 Southern Recordings Expedition*. American Folklife Center, Library of Congress, Washington, DC. AFC 1939/005–AFS 3119 to 3134.

"Allen Toussaint: A Saint for All Seasons." Interview by Nick Spitzer on *American Routes*, December 7, 2016: Hour 1, Segment 1–Allen Toussaint 1998. Accessed November 19, 2021. http://americanroutes.wwno.org/archives/show/986/Allen-Toussaint-A-Saint-for-All-Seasons.

Allen, Richard. Liner notes for *Gulf Coast Blues*. Arhoolie Production 488, 1971 and 2000.

Allen, William Francis, Charles Pickard Ware, and Lucy McKim Garrison, eds. *Slave Songs of the United States: The Classic 1867 Anthology*. New York: Dover, 1995 [1867].

An Act to Prohibit the Importation of Slaves into any Port or Place Within the Jurisdiction of the United States, From and After the First Day of January, in the Year of our Lord One Thousand Eight Hundred and Eight (Approved March 2, 1807). Accessed April 26, 2018. http://avalon.law.yale.edu/19th_century/sl004.asp.

"An Act to Regulate the Conditions and Forms of the Emancipation of Slaves, approved March 9, 1807." In *A New Digest of the Statutes Laws of the State of Louisiana from the Change of Government to the Year 1841 Inclusive*, compiled by Henry H. Bullard and Thomas Curry. New Orleans, LA: E. Johns, Stationer's Hall, 1842: 427–29.

Ancelet, Barry Jean. "Lomax in Louisiana: Trials and Triumph." *Louisiana Folklore Miscellany* 9 (2009): 32–52. Accessed June 6, 2017. http://www.louisianafolklife.org/LT/Articles_Essays/LFMlomax.html.

Ancelet, Barry Jean. *Cajun and Creole Folktales—The French Oral Tradition of South Louisiana*. Jackson: University Press of Mississippi, 1994.

Anderson, Gene. "The Genesis of King Oliver's Creole Jazz Band." *American Music* 12, no. 3 (Autumn 1994): 283–303. Accessed May 17, 2020. https://www.jstor.org/stable/3052275.

Anderson, Jeffrey, E., ed. *The Voodoo Encyclopedia: Magic, Ritual, and Religion*. Santa Barbara, CA: ABC-CLIO, 2015.

Ansermet, Ernest. "Sur un orchestre nègre/On a Negro Orchestra." Translated by Walter E. Schaap. *Hot Jazz—Revue Internationale de la Musique de Jazz/International Review of Jazz Music* 4, no. 28 (Novembre–Décembre 1938): 4–9.

Anthony, Arthé Agnes. "The Negro Creole Community in New Orleans, 1880–1920: An Oral History." PhD diss., University of California, Irvine, Louisiana Research Collection, Tulane University, 1978.

Arguedas, Jeanne Wogan. Interview by Herbert Halpert. New Orleans, LA. *1939 Southern Recordings Expedition*. American Folklife Center, Library of Congress, Washington, DC. AFC 1939/005–AFS 3119 to 3134.

Armstrong, Louis. *Satchmo: My Life in New Orleans*. Cambridge, MA: Da Capo Press, 1986 [1954].

Ashcroft, Bill, Gareth Griffiths, and Helen Tiffin. *Post-Colonial Studies: The Key Concepts*. 2nd ed. New York: Routledge, 2007 [2000].

Ashforth, Alden. Liner notes for Emile Barnes, *The Louisiana Joymakers Introducing DeDe & Billie Pierce*. American Music Records AMCD-13, 1995.

Aslakson, Kenneth. "The 'Quadroon-Plaçage' Myth of Antebellum New Orleans: Anglo-American (Mis)interpretations of a French-Caribbean Phenomenon." *Journal of Social History* 45, no. 3 (2012): 709–34. Accessed October 5, 2013. https://doi.org/10.1093/jsh/shr059.

"A Voudou Dance." *Times-Democrat*, New Orleans, Louisiana, June 24, 1884. Accessed November 1, 2021. https://www.newspapers.com/image/130933861.

Baines, Anthony. *Woodwind Instruments and Their History*. New York: Dover, 1991 [1967].

Balliett, Whitney. "Le Grand Bechet." In *Jelly Roll, Jabbo and Fats: 19 Portraits in Jazz*, 31–41. New York: Oxford University Press.

Barbarin, Paul. Interview by William Russell and Richard B. Allen. January 7, 1959. Hogan Jazz Archive, Tulane University, New Orleans. Item 8, ID: 66–67. Accessed May 15, 2019. http://musicrising.tulane.edu/listen/detail/484/Paul-Barbarin-1959-01-07.

Barker, Danny. Interview by Richard B. Allen. June 30, 1959. Hogan Jazz Archive, Tulane University, New Orleans. Item 8, ID: 66–67. Accessed October 31, 2021. https://musicrising.tulane.edu/listen/interviews/danny-barker-1959-06-18/.

Barker, Danny. Interview by Michael White. July 21–23, 1992. Smithsonian Jazz Oral History Program, NEA Jazz Master Interview, Transcript. Accessed October 8, 2012. https://amhistory.si.edu/jazz/Barker-Danny/Barker_Danny_Transcript.pdf.

Barker, Danny. *A Life in Jazz*, edited by Alyn Shipton. New Orleans: The Historic New Orleans Collection, 2016 [1986].

Barnes, Paul, and Emile Barnes. Interview by William Russell and Ralph Collins. October 1, 1959. Hogan Jazz Archive, Tulane University, New Orleans. November 1, 2021. https://musicrising.tulane.edu/listen/interviews/emile-barnes-and-paul-barnes-1959-10-01/.

Baron, John H. *Concert Life in Nineteenth-Century New Orleans: A Comprehensive Reference*. Baton Rouge: Louisiana State University Press, 2013.

Baron, John H. "Music in New Orleans, 1718–1792." *American Music* 5, no. 3 (1987): 282–90. Accessed May 19, 2017. http://www.jstor.org/stable/3051737?seq=1.

Baron, Robert, and Ana C. Cara, eds. *Creolization as Cultural Creativity*. Jackson: University Press of Mississippi, 2011.

Baudier, Roger. *The Catholic Church in Louisiana*. New Orleans, LA: A. W. Hyatt Stationery, 1939.

Bauer, Craig A. *Creole Genesis: The Bringier Family and Antebellum Plantation Life in Louisiana*. Lafayette: University of Louisiana at Lafayette Press, 2011.

Bechet, Leonard. Interview by Alan Lomax. April 4–14, 1949. Association for Cultural Equity, Lomax Digital Archive: New Orleans Jazz Interview, 1949. Accessed November 28, 2021. https://archive.culturalequity.org/node/52725.

Bechet, Leonard. Interview by Alan Lomax. April 1949. In *Jelly Roll Morton and Alan Lomax: Transcript of the 1938 Library of Congress Recordings*, 144–45, 150–53.

Bechet, Sidney. *Treat It Gentle: An Autobiography*. Cambridge, MA: Da Capo Press, 2002 [1960].

Benoist, Jean. "La créolisation : locale ou mondiale?" *Archipelie* 3–4 (2012): 12–30.

Berendt, Joachin E., and Gunther Huesmann. *The Jazz Book: From Ragtime to the 21st Century*. Translated by H. and B. Bredigkeit, Dan Morgenstern, and Tim Nevill. Chicago: Lawrence Hill Books, 2009 [1953].

Berlin, Ira. *Many Thousands Gone: The First Two Centuries of Slavery in North America*. Cambridge, MA: Belknap Press of Harvard University Press, 1998.

Berlin, Ira. "From Creole to Africa: Atlantic Creoles and the Origins of African-American Society in Mainland North America." *William and Mary Quarterly* Third Series, 53, no. 2 (April 1996): 251–88. Accessed November 17, 2020. https://www.jstor.org/stable/2947401.

Bernabé, Jean, Patrick Chamoiseau, and Raphaël Confiant. *Éloge de la Créolité/In Praise of Creoleness*. Paris: Gallimard, 1993.

Bernhard, Duke of Saxe-Weimar Eisenach. *Travels Through North America During the Years 1825 and 1826*. 2 vols. Philadelphia: Carey, Lea & Carey, 1828.

Berquin-Duvallon. *Travels in Louisiana and the Floridas in the Year 1802*. Translated by John Davis. New York: R. Riley, 1806.

Berquin-Duvallon. *Vue de la colonie espagnole du Mississipi ou des provinces de la Louisiane et Floride occidentale en l'année 1802, par un observateur resident sur les lieux*. Paris: À l'Imprimerie Expeditive, 1803.

Berresford, Mark. "Wilbur Sweatman." *Oxford Music Online*. Oxford University Press. Accessed April 30, 2020. https://www.oxfordmusiconline.com.

Bethell, Tom. *George Lewis: A Jazzman from New Orleans*. Berkeley: University of California Press, 1977.

Bhabha, Homi. *The Location of Culture*. New York: Routledge, 1994.

Bigard, Alex. Interview by William Russell and Richard B. Allen. April 30, 1960. Hogan Jazz Archive, Tulane University, New Orleans. Sub-series 2-B, Item 50, ID: 120–24. Accessed April 9, 2020. https://musicrising.tulane.edu/listen/interviews/alexander-bigard-1960-04-30/.

Bigard, Barney. *With Louis and the Duke: The Autobiography of a Jazz Clarinetist*. London: MacMillan, 1985.

Bisland, Elizabeth. *The Life and Letters of Lafcadio Hearn*, vol. 1. Boston and New York: Houghton, Mifflin, 1907. Accessed May 17, 2020. https://archive.org/details/lifeandletters l04heargoog/page/n14/mode/2up.

Blaikley, D. J. Revised by Antony C. Baines and William Waterhouse. "Sarrusophone." *Oxford Music Online*. Oxford University Press. Accessed October 15, 2021. https://www.oxford musiconline.com.

Blesh, Rudi. Liner notes for *Baby Dodds Trio/Jazz A' La Creole* [sic]. Reissued with Harriet Janis original liner notes on GHB Records BCD-50, 2000. First issued 1947.

Blesh, Rudi. *Shining Trumpets: A History of Jazz*. New York: Alfred A. Knopf, 1946.

Blesh, Rudi. *Shining Trumpets: A History of Jazz*. New York: Alfred A. Knopf, 2nd ed., revised and enlarged 1958. New York: Da Capo Paperback, 1975.

Bonniol, Jean-Luc. "Situations créoles, entre culture et identité." In *Situations créoles: Pratiques et représentations*, edited by Carlo A. Celius, 49–60. Montréal: Éditions Nota bene, 2006.

Borders, Florence E. "Researching Creole and Cajun Musics in New Orleans." *Black Music Research Journal* 8, no. 1 (1988): 15–31.

Borneman, Ernest. "Creole Echoes, Part 1." *Jazz Review* 2, no. 8 (Sept. 1959): 13–15.

Borneman, Ernest. "Creole Echoes, Part 2." *Jazz Review* 2, no. 10 (Nov. 1959): 26–27.

Borneman, Ernest. "The Roots of Jazz." In Hentoff, Nat, and Albert J. McCarthy, eds., *Jazz: New Perspectives on the History of Jazz by Twelve of the World's Foremost Jazz Critics and Scholars*. New York: Da Capo Press, 1978 [1959].

Bossu, Jean-Bernard. *Nouveaux voyages aux Indes Occidentales*. Paris: Le Jay, 1768.

Boulard, Gary. "Blacks, Italians and the Making of New Orleans Jazz." *Journal of Ethnic Studies* 16, no. 1 (Spring 1988): 53–65.

Brandon, Elizabeth. "Moeurs [sic] et langue de la paroisse Vermillon en Louisiane." PhD diss., Université Laval, Québec, 1955.

Brandon, Elizabeth. Fonds Elizabeth Brandon, F208, Archives de folklore et d'ethnologie, Université Laval, Québec, 1952–1954.

Brasseaux, Carl A. "A New Acadia: The Acadian Migrations to South Louisiana, 1764–1803." *Acadiensis* 15, no. 1 (Oct. 1985): 123–32. Accessed July 2, 2017. https://journals.lib.unb.ca/index.php/Acadiensis/article/view/12083/12927.

Brasseaux, Carl A. *Acadian to Cajun: Transformation of a People 1803–1877*. Jackson: University Press of Mississippi, 1992.

Brasseaux, Carl A. "Creoles of Color in Louisiana's Bayou Country, 1766–1877." In *Creoles of Color of the Gulf South*, edited by James H. Dormon, 67–86. Knoxville: University of Tennessee Press, 1996.

Brothers, Thomas. *Louis Armstrong's New Orleans*. New York: W. W. Norton, 2006.

Brown, John Mason. "Song of the Slaves." *Lippincott's Magazine* 2 (December 1868): 617–23.
Brown, Sterling A. "Farewell to Basin Street." *Record Changer* 3 (December 1944): 7–9, 51.
Bucher, Anne Catherine. "Notes on the Performance." Liner notes for *Manuscrit des Ursulines de la Nouvelle-Orléans*. France: K617134, 2002, ℗ 2001.
Buisseret, David. Introduction to *Creolization in the Americas*, edited by David Buisseret and Steven G. Reinhardt, 3–17. College Station: Texas A&M University Press, 2000.
Cable, George W. "Creole Slave Songs." *Century Magazine* 31, no. 6 (April 1886): 807–28.
Cable, George W. "The Dance in Place Congo." *Century Magazine* 31, no. 4 (February 1886): 517–32.
Cable, George W. *Old Creole Days*. Gretna, LA: Pelican Publishing, 2009 [1879].
Caffery, Joshua Clegg. *Traditional Music in Coastal Louisiana: The 1934 Lomax Recordings*. Baton Rouge: Louisiana State University Press, 2013. Accessed March 25, 2018. Audio recordings available at https://www.lomax1934.com/.
Caillot, Marc-Antoine. *Relation du Voyage de la Louisianne [sic] ou Nouvelle France fait par le Sr. Caillot en l'Année 1730*. New Orleans: The Historic New Orleans Collection, MSS 596.
"Camille Nickerson." Smithsonian Online Virtual Archives, Archives Center, National Museum of American History. Accessed November 2, 2021. https://sova.si.edu/details/NMAH.AC.0618.S04.01-ref1059.
Campanella, Richard. *Geographies of New Orleans: Urban Fabrics Before the Storm*. Lafayette: Center for Louisiana Studies, 2006.
Carney, Court. "New Orleans and the Creation of Early Jazz." *Popular Music and Society* 29, no. 3 (2006): 299–315.
Carré, Claude. "Les haïtiens et la naissance du jazz à la Nouvelle-Orléans." *CaribCreole News*, 2011. Accessed May 25, 2017. http://haitirectoverso.blogspot.ca/2011/09/haiti-les-haitiens-et-la-naissance-du.html.
Cathedral-Basilica Saint-Louis King of France (website). "Our History." Accessed December 21, 2016. http://www.stlouiscathedral.org/our-history.
Celius, Carlo A., ed. *Situations créoles: Pratiques et représentations*. Montréal: Éditions Nota bene, 2006.
Chabot, Marie-Emmanuel. "Les Ursulines de Québec en 1850." *Sessions d'étude: Société canadienne d'histoire de l'Église catholique* 36 (1969): 75–92.
Charters, Samuel. *A Trumpet around the Corner: The Story of New Orleans Jazz*. Jackson: University Press of Mississippi. 2008.
Charters, Samuel Barklay. *Jazz: New Orleans 1885–1963—An Index to the Negro Musicians of New Orleans*. Rev. ed. New York: Oak Publications, 1963.
Chaudenson, Robert. *La créolisation: théorie, applications, implications*. Paris: Éditions L'Harmattan, 2003.
Chilton, John. *Sidney Bechet: The Wizard of Jazz*. London: First Da Capo Press, 1996.
Christian, Marcus. *The Black History of Louisiana*. Unpublished manuscript of *The Negro in Louisiana* (1942), Louisiana and Special Collections, Earl K. Long Library, Marcus Christian Collection, Louisiana Digital Library, University of New Orleans, 2011. Accessed July 5, 2021. https://louisianadigitallibrary.org/islandora/object/uno-p15140coll42%3A28.
Civil Code of the State of Louisiana with the Statutory Amendments from 1825 to 1853, Inclusive. Compiled and edited by Thomes Gibbes Morgan. Title VI, Chapter 3. New Orleans, LA: Bloomfield & Stell, 1863.

Clark, Emily. "'By All the Conduct of Their Lives': A Laywomen's Confraternity in New Orleans, 1730–1744." *William and Mary Quarterly* 54, no. 4 (1997): 769–94. Accessed June 7, 2017. https://www.jstor.org/stable/2953882.

Clark, Emily. "Creoles, Catholics, and Color Lines." *Journal of Africana Religions* 2, no. 2 (2014): 263–70. Accessed June 7, 2017. https://muse.jhu.edu/article/542263/pdf.

Clark, Emily. *The Strange Story of the American Quadroon: Free Women of Color in the Revolutionary Atlantic World*. Chapel Hill: University of North Carolina Press, 2013.

Clark, Emily. *Masterless Mistresses: The New Orleans Ursulines and the Development of a New World Society, 1727–1834*. Omohundro Institute of Early American History and Culture, Williamsburg, VA. Chapel Hill: University of North Carolina Press, 2007.

Clark, Emily, ed. *Voices from an Early American Convent: Marie Madeleine Hachard and the New Orleans Ursulines, 1727–1760*. Baton Rouge: Louisiana State University Press, 2007.

Clayton, Ronnie W. *Mother Wit: The Ex-Slave Narratives of the Louisiana Writers' Project*. University of Kansas Humanistic Studies, 51–61. New York: Peter Land, 1990.

Code Noir ou Loi municipale servant de reglement pour le gouvernement & l'administration de la justice, police, discipline & le commerce des esclaves négres [sic], dans la province de la Louisianne [sic]: entreprit par délidération [sic] du Cabildo en vertu des ordres du Roi, que Dieu garde, consignés dans sa lettre faite à Aranjuez le 14 de mai 1777. Nlle. Orléans: Antoine Boudousquié, imprimeur du Roi, & du Cabildo, 1788.

Cohen, Robin. "Creolization and Cultural Globalization: The Soft Sounds of Fugitive Power." *Globalizations* 4, no. 3 (September 2007): 369–84.

Cohn, Lawrence, ed. *Nothing but the Blues: The Music and the Musicians*. New York: Abbeville, 1993.

Coleman, Will H. *Historical Sketch Book and Guide of New Orleans and Environs*. New York: Will H. Coleman, 1885.

Collier, James Lincoln. *The Making of Jazz: A Comprehensive History*. New York: Dell, 1978.

Collins, Mal. "The Recordings of Sidney Bechet." June 2011, The Sidney Bechet Society (website). Accessed June 3, 2019. http://www.sidneybechet.org/discography/.

Collins, Peter. "Camille Nickerson." In *https://64parishes.org Encyclopedia of Louisiana*, edited by David Johnson. Louisiana Endowment for the Humanities, 2010. Article published August 8, 2013. Accessed July 24, 2014. https://64parishes.org/entry/camille-nickerson.

Complete National Recording Registry Listing, Library of Congress. Accessed April 29, 2020. https://www.loc.gov/programs/national-recording-preservation-board/recording-registry/complete-national-recording-registry-listing/.

"Congo Square: The Master of Ceremonies." *Daily Picayune*, March 22, 1846, 2.

Conrad, Glenn R. *The First Families of Louisiana*. Vol. 2, translated and compiled by Glenn R. Conrad. Baton Rouge, LA: Claitor's Publishing, 1970.

Conrad, Glenn R. "The History of New Iberia." City of New Iberia, LA (website). Accessed April 14, 2018. http://www.cityofnewiberia.com/site403.php.

Constitution Adopted by the State Constitutional Convention of the State of Louisiana, March 7, 1868. New Orleans, LA: Republican Office, 1868.

Constitution of the State of Louisiana Adopted in Convention at the City of New Orleans, May 12, 1898. New Orleans, LA: H. J. Hearsey, Convention Printer, 1898.

Constitution of the State of Louisiana Adopted in Convention at the City of Baton Rouge, June 18, 1921. Baton Rouge, LA: Ramires-Jones Printing, 1921.

Costa, Myldred Masson. *The Letters of Marie Madeleine Hachard 1727–1728.* Translated by Myldred Masson Costa. New Orleans, LA: Laborde Printing, 1974.

Couch, R. Randall. "The Public Masked Balls of Antebellum New Orleans: A Custom of Masque Outside the Mardi Gras Tradition." *Louisiana History* 35, no. 4 (Autumn 1994): 403–31.

"Créolisation." Édouard Glissant (website). Accessed November 9, 2020. http://www.edouardglissant.fr/creolisation.html.

Creecy, James R. *Scenes in the South, and Other Miscellaneous Pieces.* Washington, DC: T. McGill, 1860.

"Dagmar Adelaide Renshaw LeBreton (1891–1994): Oral History Interviews from the 1980s by Adele Ramos Salzer, Anneke Himmele, and Susan Tucker." In *Newcomb College 1886–2006: Higher Education for Women in New Orleans,* edited by Susan Tucker and Beth Willinger, 347–60. Baton Rouge: Louisiana State University Press, 2012.

Dahl, Linda. *Stormy Weather: The Music and Lives of a Century of Jazzwomen.* New York: Limelight, 1984.

Davis, Edwin Adams. *Louisiana: A Narrative History.* Baton Rouge, LA: Claitor's, 1971.

Dawdy, Shannon Lee. *Building the Devil's Empire: French Colonial New Orleans.* Chicago: University of Chicago Press, 2008.

Deggs, Sister Mary Bernard. *No Cross, No Crown: Black Nuns in Nineteenth-Century New Orleans,* edited by Virginia Meacham Gould and Charles E. Nolan. Bloomington: Indiana University Press, 2001.

Delanglez, Jean. "The French Jesuit in Lower Louisiana, 1700–1763." PhD diss., Catholic University of America, 1935. *Studies in American Church History* 21, 1935.

Desdunes, Rodolphe Lucien. *Nos hommes et notre histoire.* Montréal: Arbour & Dupont, 1911.

Desdunes, Rodolphe Lucien. *Our People and Our History.* Translated by Sister Dorothea Olga McCants. Baton Rouge: Louisiana State University Press, 1973.

Dessens, Nathalie. *From Saint-Domingue to New Orleans: Migration and Influence.* Gainesville: University Press of Florida, 2007.

Dessens, Nathalie. "Les migrants de Saint-Domingue en Louisiane avant la guerre de Sécession: de l'intégration civique à l'influence politique." *Revue Française d'Études Américaines, Immigration et citoyenneté aux États-Unis* 75 (Janvier 1998): 34–36.

Diagne, Souleymane Bachir. "Négritude." *The Stanford Encyclopedia of Philosophy* (Summer 2018 ed.), edited by Edward N. Zalta. Accessed November 4, 2020. https://plato.stanford.edu/archives/sum2018/entries/negritude/.

Diderot, Denis, and Jean le Rond d'Alembert. "Negre." [sic] *Encyclopédie ou Dictionnaire raisonné des Sciences, des Arts et Métier,* Paris, 1751–1772. Accessed May 27, 2017. http://encyclopédie.eu/index.php/ naturelle/7544183-NEGRE.

"Doby, Frances." In Ronnie W. Clayton, *Mother Wit: The Ex-Slave Narratives of the Louisiana Writers' Project.* University of Kansas Humanistic Studies, 51–61. New York: Peter Land, 1990.

Dollar, Susan E. "Ethnicity and Jim Crow: The Americanization of Louisiana Creoles." In *Louisiana Beyond Black and White: New Interpretation of Twentieth-Century Race and*

Race Relations, edited by Michael S. Martin, 1–16. Lafayette: University of Louisiana at Lafayette Press, 2011.

Domínguez, Virginia R. *White by Definition: Social Classification in Creole Louisiana*. New Brunswick, NJ: Rutgers University Press, 1986.

Dominique, Natty. Interview by William Russell. May 31, 1958. Hogan Jazz Archive, Tulane University, New Orleans. Sub-series 4-D Item 35, ID: 286. Accessed April 7, 2020. https://musicrising.tulane.edu/listen/interviews/natty-dominique-1958-05-31/.

Dormon, James, H. ed. *Creoles of Color of the Gulf South*. Knoxville: University of Tennessee Press, 1996.

Du Bois, W. E. B. *The Souls of Black Folk*. Hazelton: Pennsylvania State University, 2006 [1903].

Duhé, Lawrence. Interview by William Russell. June 9, 1957. Hogan Jazz Archive, Tulane University, New Orleans. Sub-series 4-D, Item 39, ID 923, Accessed May 15, 2019. http://musicrising.tulane.edu/listen/detail/192/Lawrence-Duhe-1957-06-09.

Dumont de Montigny, Jean-François Benjamin. *Mémoires historiques sur la Louisiane*. Tome Second. Paris: J. B. Bauche, 1753.

Duron, Jean. Introduction to *French Baroque Music of New Orleans: Spiritual Songs from the Ursuline Convent (1736)*, edited by Alfred E. Lemmon, viii–xii. New Orleans: The Historic New Orleans Collection, 2014.

Eccles, William J. *The Canadian Frontier, 1534–1760*. Albuquerque: University of New Mexico Press, 1983 [1969].

Ellison, Mary. "African-American Music and Musket in Civil War in New Orleans." *Louisiana History* 35, no. 3 (Summer 1994): 285–319.

Epstein, Dena J. "African Music in British and French America." *Musical Quarterly* 59, no. 1 (1973): 61–91.

Evans, Freddi W. *Congo Square: African Roots in New Orleans*. Lafayette: University of Louisiana at Lafayette Press, 2011.

Fairclough, Adam. *Race and Democracy, The Civil Rights Struggle in Louisiana, 1915–1972*. Athens: University of Georgia Press, 1995.

Falck, Robert, and Martin Picker. "Contrafactum." *Oxford Music Online*. Oxford University Press. Accessed November 25, 2016. https://www.oxfordmusiconline.com.

Fiehrer, Thomas. "From Quadrille to Stomp: The Creole Origins of Jazz." *Popular Music* 10, no. 1 (1991): 21–38.

Fisher, Miles M. *Negro Slave Songs in the United States*. New York: Citadel, 1953.

Flint, Timothy. *Recollections of the Last Ten Years, Passed in Occasional Residences and Journeyings in the Valley of the Mississippi, from Pittsburg and the Missouri to the Gulf of Mexico, and from Florida to the Spanish Frontier: in a Series of Letters to the Rev. James Flint, of Salem, Massachusetts*. Boston: Cummings, Billiard, 1826.

Floyd, Samuel A., Jr. "Ring Shout! Black Music, Black Literary Theory, and Black Historical Studies." *Black Research Music Journal* 11, no. 2 (Autumn 1991): 265–87. Accessed Nov. 29, 2020. https://www.jstor.org/stable/779269?seq=1.

Fortier, Alcée. *Louisiana Folk-Tales—in French Dialect and English Translation*. Boston and New York: Published for the American Folk-Lore Society by Houghton, Mifflin, 1895.

Fortier, Alcée. "Bits of Louisiana Folk-Lore." *Transactions and Proceedings of the Modern Language Association of America* 3 (1887): 100–168.

Fortier, Alcée. "Customs and Superstitions in Louisiana." *Journal of American Folklore* 1, no. 2 (1888): 136–40.

Fournier, Robert. "Le Mythe créole." In *Situations créoles: Pratiques et représentations*. Edited by Carlo A. Celius, 23–48. Montréal: Éditions Nota Bene, 2006.

Francis, W. T., and Chatah-Imah. "Zozo Mokeur." New Orleans, LA: Louis Crumewald, 1887.

Fuller, David. "Notes Inégales." *Oxford Music Online*. Oxford University Press. Accessed November 27, 2016. https://www.oxfordmusiconline.com.

Furetière, Antoine. *Dictionnaire universel, Contenant generalement tous les mots françois, tant vieux que modernes, & les Termes de toutes les Sciences et des Arts*. Tome Premier, 1690. Accessed May 27, 2017. https://gallica.bnf.fr/ark:/12148/bpt6k50614b.

Gara, Larry. *The Baby Dodds Story as Told to Larry Gara*. Rev. ed. Alma, MI: Rebeats Publications, 2002 [1959].

Garrett, Charles H. *Struggling to Define a Nation: American Music and the Twentieth Century*. Berkeley: University of California Press, 2008.

Gates, Henry Louis, Jr. *The Signifying Monkey: A Discovery of African-American Literary Tradition*. New York: Oxford University Press, 1989.

Gayarré, Charles. *Histoire de la Louisiane*. Vol. 1. Nouvelle-Orléans: Imprimé par Magne & Weisse, 1846.

Gayarré, Charles. *Histoire de la Louisiane*. Vol. 2. Nouvelle-Orléans: Imprimé par Magne & Weisse, 1847.

Gayarré, Charles. *History of Louisiana: The French Domination*. Vol. 2. New York: Redfield, 1854.

Gehman, Mary. "Visible Means of Support: Businesses, Professions, and Trades of Free People of Color." In *Creole: The History and Legacy of Louisiana's Free People of Color*, edited by Sybil Kein, 208–22. Baton Rouge: Louisiana State University Press, 2000.

Giddins, Gary, and Scott DeVeaux. *Jazz*. New York: W. W. Norton, 2009.

Gilroy, Paul. *The Black Atlantic: Modernity and Double Consciousness*. Cambridge, MA: Harvard University Press, 1993.

Ginell, Cary. *Hot Jazz for Sale: Hollywood's Jazz Man Record Shop*. Origin Jazz Library and Lulu.com, 2010.

Gioia, Ted. *The History of Jazz*. New York: Oxford University Press, 2011.

Gipson, Jennifer. "From Secular Music to Sacred Poetry: The Textual Trajectory of *Nouvelles poésies*." In *French Baroque Music of New Orleans: Spiritual Songs from the Ursuline Convent (1736)*, edited by Alfred E. Lemmon, 14–21. New Orleans: The Historic New Orleans Collection, 2014.

Goffin, Robert. *Jazz: From Congo to the Metropolitan*. Translated by Walter Schaap and Leonard G. Feather. Garden City, NY: Doubleday, Doran, 1944.

Goodwin, Noël. "Ernest Ansermet." *Oxford Music Online*. Oxford University Press. Accessed June 1, 2019. https://www.oxfordmusiconline.com.

Gore, Laura Locoul. *Memories of the Old Plantation Home*. Vacherie, LA: Zoë Company, 2007.

Goreau, Laurraine. "An Evening with Lizzie Miles." *Jazz Journal* 17, no. 1 (January 1964): 8–9.

Gould, Virginia Meacham, and Charles E. Nolan. Introduction to *No Cross, No Crown: Black Nuns in Nineteenth-Century New Orleans*, by Sister Mary Bernard Deggs, ix–xxxvi. Bloomington: Indiana University Press, 2001.

"Gov. Edwards Signs the First and Historic Posthumous Pardon of Civil Rights Leader Mr. Homer A. Plessy." John Bel Edwards—Office of the Governor (website). Accessed January 6, 2022. https://gov.louisiana.gov/index.cfm/newsroom/detail/3521.

Grider, Sylvia. "Scarborough, Emily Dorothy." *Handbook of Texas Online*, Texas Historical Association. Accessed May 20, 2020. http://www.tshaonline.org/handbook/online/articles/fsco1.

Griffiths, David. *Hot Jazz: From Harlem to Storyville*. Studies in Jazz 28, Institute of Jazz Studies, Rutgers University. Lanham, MD: Scarecrow, 1998.

Greenwald, Erin M., ed. *A Company Man: The Remarkable French-Atlantic Voyage of a Clerk for the Company of the Indies: A Memoir by Marc-Antoine Caillot*. Translated by Teri F. Chalmers. New Orleans: The Historic New Orleans Collection, 2013.

Gushee, Lawrence. "A Preliminary Chronology of the Early Career of Ferdinand 'Jelly Roll' Morton." *American Music* 3, no. 4 (Winter 1985): 389–412.

Gushee, Lawrence, and Harry Carr. "How the Creole Band Came to Be." *Black Music Research Journal* 8, no. 1 (1988): 83–100. Accessed January 29, 2014. https://www.jstor.org/stable/779504?origin=JSTOR-pdf&seq=1.

Gushee, Lawrence. *Pioneers of Jazz: The Story of the Creole Jazz Band*. New York: Oxford University Press. 2005.

Gushee, Lawrence. "The Nineteenth-Century Origins of Jazz." *Black Music Research Journal* 14, no. 1 (Spring 1994): 1–24.

Gushee, Lawrence. "New Orleans Jazz." *Oxford Music Online*. Oxford University Press. Accessed May 19, 2020. https://www.oxfordmusiconline.com.

Gutiérrez Rodríguez, Encarnación, and Shirley Anne Tate, eds. *Creolizing Europe: Legacies and Transformations*. Liverpool, UK: Liverpool University Press, 2005.

Hachard, Madeleine. *Relation du voyage des Dames Religieuses Ursulines de Roüen [sic] à la Nouvelle Orleans [sic], Parties de France le 22 Février 1727 et arrivez [sic] à la Louisienne [sic] le 23 Juillet de la même année*. Rouen: Chez Antoine Le Prevost, rue Saint Vivien 1728. Reproduced in *Relation du voyage des Dames Religieuses Ursulines de Rouen à la Nouvelle-Orléans avec une introduction et des notes par Gabriel Gravier*. Paris: Maisonneuve et Cᵉ, Quai Voltaire 15, 1872. Accessed April 4, 2019. https://archive.org/details/relationduvoyagoohachgoog.

Hadlock, Richard. Liner notes for *The Complete Kid Ory Verve Sessions*. Mosaic: MD8–189, 1999.

Hall, Gwendolyn Midlo. *Africans in Colonial Louisiana: The Development of Afro-Creole Culture in the Eighteenth Century*. Baton Rouge: Louisiana State University Press, 1992.

Hall, Gwendolyn Midlo. "The Formation of Afro-Creole Culture." In *Creole New Orleans*, edited by Arnold R. Hirsh and Joseph Logsdon, 58–87. Baton Rouge: Louisiana State University Press, 1992.

Hall, Stuart. "Créolité and the Process of Creolization." In *Creolizing Europe: Legacies and Transformations*, edited by Encarnación Gutiérrez Rodríguez and Shirley Anne Tate, 12–25. Liverpool, UK: Liverpool University Press, 2005.

Halpert, Herbert. Interview with Jeanne Wogan Arguedas, New Orleans, LA. *1939 Southern Recordings Expedition*. American Folklife Center, Library of Congress, Washington, DC. AFC 1939/005—AFS 3119 to 3134. https://lccn.loc.gov/2008700314.

Hammond, John Craig. "Slavery, Settlement, and Empire: The Expansion and Growth of Slavery in the Interior of the North American Continent 1770–1820." *Journal of the Early Republic* 32, no. 2 (Summer 2012): 175–206.

Hanger, Kimberly S. *Bounded Lives, Bounded Places: Free Black Society in Colonial New Orleans 1769–1803*. Durham, NC: Duke University Press, 1997.

Hanger, Kimberly S. "Origins of New Orleans's Free Creoles of Color." In *Creoles of Color of the Gulf South*, edited by James H. Dormon, 1–25. Knoxville: University of Tennessee Press, 1996.

Hannerz, Ulf. "The World in Creolisation." *Africa: Journal of the International African Institute* 57, no. 4 (1987): 546–59.

Hare, Maud Cuney. *Negro Musicians and Their Music*. Washington, DC: Associated Publishers, 1943 [1935]. Accessed May 28, 2020. http://digital.library.upenn.edu/women/cuney-hare/musicians/musicians.html.

Hare, Maud Cuney. *Six Creole Folk-Songs with Original Creole and Translated English Texts*. New York: Carl Fisher, 1921.

Harker, Brian. "'Telling a Story': Louis Armstrong and Coherence in Early Jazz." *Current Musicology* (1997): 46–83. Accessed May 18, 2020. https://openmusiclibrary.org/article/48775/.

Havard, Gilles, and Cécile Vidal. *Histoire de l'Amérique française*. Paris: Flammarion, 2003.

Hazeldine, Mike, ed. *Bill Russell's American Music*. New Orleans, LA: Jazzology, 1993.

"Hazeur, Jean-François." In *Dictionnaire biographique du Canada*. Accessed November 24, 2017. http://www.biographi.ca/fr/bio/hazeur_jean_francois_2E.html.

Hearn, Lafcadio. "The Scenes of Cable's Romances." *Century Magazine* 27, no. 1 (November 1883): 40–47.

Henry, Irma Louise. "A Bibliography of Louisiana Negro Creole Folk Music." Master's thesis, Juilliard School, 1949.

Hentoff, Nat, and Albert J. McCarthy, eds. *Jazz: New Perspectives on the History of Jazz by Twelve of the World's Foremost Jazz Critics and Scholars*. New York: Da Capo Press, 1978 [1959].

Herbert, Trevor. *The Trombone*. New Haven, CT: Yale University Press, 2006.

Hersch, Charles. *Subversive Sounds: Race and the Birth of Jazz in New Orleans*. Chicago: University of Chicago Press, 2007.

Herskovits, Melville J. *Acculturation: The Study of Culture Contact*. New York: J. J. Augustin, 1938.

Herskovits, Melville J. *The Myth of the Negro Past*. New York: Harper & Brother, 1941.

Hirsh, Arnold R., and Joseph Logsdon, eds. *Creole New Orleans*. Baton Rouge: Louisiana State University Press, 1992.

"History of the Catholic Press." *Clarion Herald*, New Orleans, Louisiana. Accessed April 2, 2021. https://clarionherald.org/news/history-of-the-catholic-press.

"History/Historia." Los Isleños Heritage and Cultural Society (website). Accessed April 4, 2018. http://www.losislenos.org.

Hobbs, Holly. "Adams, Dolly Douroux." In *64parishes.org Encyclopedia of Louisiana*, edited by David Johnson. Louisiana Endowment for the Humanities, 2010. Article published November 8, 2013. Accessed May 14, 2019. https://64parishes.org/entry/dolly-adams.

Hobson, Vic. *Creating Jazz Counterpoint: New Orleans, Barbershop Harmony, and the Blues*. Jackson: University Press of Mississippi. 2014.

Hollandsworth, James G. *The Louisiana Native Guards: The Black Military Experience During the Civil War*. Baton Rouge: Louisiana University Press, 1998.

Holmes, Isaac. *An Account of the United States of America: Derived from Actual Observation, During a Residence of Four Years in That Republic, Including Original Communications*. London: Caxton, 1823.

Huber, Leonard V. *Mardi Gras: A Pictorial History of Carnival in New Orleans*. Gretna: Pelican, 1977.

Ingersoll, Thomas N. "Free Blacks in a Slave Society: New Orleans, 1718–1812." *William and Mary Quarterly* 48, no. 2 (April 1991): 173–200.

Ingersoll, Thomas N. *Manon and Mammon in Early New Orleans: The First Slave Society in the Deep South 1718–1819*. Knoxville: University of Tennessee Press, 1999.

Ingersoll, Thomas N. "The Slave Trade and the Ethnic Diversity of Louisiana's Slave Community." *Louisiana History* 37, no. 2 (Spring 1996): 133–61.

"Introducción." *Afroamérica. La tercera raíz* (website). Accessed November 1, 2020. http://www.nacionmulticultural.unam.mx/afroamerica/.

Janis, Harriet. Liner notes for *Jazz a la Creole* [sic]. Reissued with Harriet Janis's original LP liner notes on GHB Records BCD-50, 2000. First issued in 1947.

"Jass and Jassism." *New Orleans Times-Picayune*, June 20, 1918. Reproduced in *African American Review* 29, no. 2 (1995): 231–32. Accessed June 1, 2020. https://www.jstor.org/stable/3042296?seq=1.

Johnson, Jerah. "Colonial New Orleans." In *Creole New Orleans*, edited by Arnold R. Hirsh and Joseph Logsdon, 12–57. Baton Rouge: Louisiana State University Press, 1992.

Johnson, Jerah. *Congo Square in New Orleans*. 1991. Reprint, New Orleans: Louisiana Landmarks Society, 1995.

Johnson, Jerah. "New Orleans's Congo Square: An Urban Setting for Early Afro-American Culture. " *Louisiana History: The Journal of the Louisiana Historical Association* 32, no. 2 (Spring 1991): 117–57. Accessed July 10, 2013. https://www.jstor.org/stable/4232877?origin=JSTOR-pdf&seq=1.

Johnson, Jerah. "Jim Crow Laws of the 1890s and the Origins of New Orleans Jazz: Correction of An Error." *Popular Music* 19, no. 2 (2000): 243–51.

Justice, Andrew. "Performance Practice: Crafting a Historically Informed Interpretation of *Nouvelles poésies*." In *French Baroque Music of New Orleans: Spiritual Songs from the Ursuline Convent (1736)*, edited by Alfred E. Lemmon, 22–26. New Orleans: The Historic New Orleans Collection, 2014.

Kartomi, Margaret J. "The Processes and Results of Musical Culture Contact: A Discussion of Terminology and Concepts." *Ethnomusicology* 25, no. 2 (1981): 227–49.

Kein, Sybil, ed. *Creole: The History and Legacy of Louisiana's Free People of Color*. Baton Rouge: Louisiana State University Press, 2000.

Kein, Sybil. "The Use of Louisiana Creole in Southern Literature." In *Creole: The History and Legacy of Louisiana's Free People of Color*, edited by Sybil Kein, 117–54. Baton Rouge: Louisiana State University Press, 2000.

Kennedy, Joseph C. G., Superintendent of Census. *Population of the United States in 1860; Compiled From the Original Returns of the Eighth Census*. Washington, DC: Government Printing Office, 1864. Accessed May 24, 2019. https://archive.org/details/populationofusinoookennrich/page/n3.

Kennedy, R. Emmet. *Mellows: A Chronicle of Unknown Singers*. New York: Albert and Charles Boni, 1925.

Kinzer, Charles E. "The Tio Family: Four Generations of New Orleans Musicians, 1814–1933." Vols. 1–2. PhD diss., Louisiana State University and A&M College, 1993. Ann Arbor, MI: University Microfilms International, 1994.

Kmen, Henry A. *Music in New Orleans: The Formative Years 1791–1841*. Baton Rouge: Louisiana State University Press, 1966.

Kmen, Henry A. "The Root of Jazz and the Dance in Place Congo: A Re-Appraisal." *Anuario Interamericano de Investigation Musical* 8 (1972): 5–16.

Knörr, Jacqueline. "Towards Conceptualizing Creolization and Creoleness." Max Planck Institute for Social Anthropology, Working Paper 100. Halle/Saale, Germany, 2008.

Krehbiel, Henry Edward. *Afro-American Folksongs: A Study in Racial and National Music*. New York: G. Schirmer, 1914.

La Clé du Caveau à l'usage de tous les Chansonniers français, des Amateurs, Auteurs, Acteurs de Vaudeville & tous les Amis de la Chanson. Paris: Capelle et Renard, 1811. Accessed January 1, 2017. https://ia802604.us.archive.org/8/items/laclducaveauoocape/laclducaveauoocape.pdf.

Lachance, Paul F. "The Foreign French." In *Creole New Orleans*, edited by Arnold R. Hirsh and Joseph Logsdon, 101–30. Baton Rouge: Louisiana State University Press, 1992.

Latrobe, Benjamin Henry. *The Journal of Latrobe. Being the Notes and Sketches of an Architect, Naturalist and Traveler in the United States from 1796 to 1820*. Introduction by J. H. B. Latrobe. New York: D. Appleton, 1905.

Laussat, Pierre-Clément de. *Mémoirs of My Life*. Translated by Agnes-Josephine Pastwa. Edited and with a foreword by Robert D. Bush. Baton Rouge: Louisiana State University Press, 2003.

Le Code noir, ou Édit du Roy servant de règlement pour le gouvernement et l'administration de la justice, police, discipline et le commerce des esclaves nègres dans la province et colonie de la Loüisianne. Donné à Versailles au mois de Mars 1724. Bibliothèque nationale de France/Gallica (website). Accessed April 22, 2017. http://gallica.bnf.fr/ark:/12148/btv1b86086055/f1.item.r=code+noir.langFR.

Le Jeune, Emilie. "Creole Folk Songs." *Louisiana Historical Quarterly* 2, no. 4 (October 1919): 454–62.

Le Page Du Pratz, Antoine Simon. *Histoire de la Louisiane*, Tome Premier. Paris: De Bure, Delaguette, and Lambert, 1758. Accessed February 26, 2017. https://ia600302.us.archive.org/14/items/cihm_36373/cihm_36373.pdf.

Le Page Du Pratz, Antoine Simon. *Histoire de la Louisiane*, Tome Second. Paris: De Bure, Delaguette, and Lambert, 1758. Accessed February 26, 2017. https://archive.org/details/cihm_36374.

Le Page Du Pratz, Antoine Simon. *Histoire de la Louisiane*, Tome Troisième. Paris: De Bure, Delaguette, and Lambert, 1758. Accessed February 26, 2017. https://archive.org/details/cihm_36375.

Le Page Du Pratz, Antoine Simon. *The History of Louisiana or of the Western Parts of Virginia and Carolina*. Translated from the French by M. Le Page Du Pratz. London: T. Beckett, 1774.

Leblanc, Phyllis E. "Église catholique française en Louisiane (19e-20e siècles)." *Encyclopédie du Patrimoine de l'Amérique Française*. Accessed August 3, 2014. http://www.amerique francaise.org/fr/.

Lemmon, Alfred A., ed. *French Baroque Music of New Orleans: Spiritual Songs from the Ursuline Convent (1736)/Musique française baroque à la Nouvelle-Orléans: Recueil d'airs spirituels des Ursulines (1736)*. New Orleans: The Historic New Orleans Collection, 2014.

Lemmon, Alfred E. "Music in Colonial Louisiana." In *French Baroque Music of New Orleans: Spiritual Songs from the Ursuline Convent (1736)*. Edited by Alfred E. Lemmon, 1–6. New Orleans: The Historic New Orleans Collection, 2014.

Lemmon, Alfred E. "Music in Eighteenth-Century New Orleans." Liner notes to *Manuscrit des Ursulines de la Nouvelle-Orléans*. France: K617134, 2002, ℗ 2001.

Lemuel, Berry. "The Impact of Creole Music on Jazz." *Second Line* 38–39 (Fall/Winter 1986–87): 9–13.

Le Propagateur Catholique 1, 1842–1843. Accessed May 14, 2019. https://babel.hathitrust.org/cgi/pt?id=wu.89076979970;view=1up;seq=9;size=75.

Levin, Floyd. "Barney Bigard—The Great New Orleans Clarinetist." *Second Line* 24 (Fall 1972): 23–25.

Levin, Floyd. "Kid Ory's Legendary Nordskog/Sunshine Recordings." *Jazz Journal International* 46, no. 7 (July 1993): 6–10. Accessed April 16, 2020. http://www.doctorjazz.co.uk/page35.html.

Levine, Lawrence W. *Highbrow Lowbrow: The Emergence of Cultural Hierarchy in America*, Cambridge, MA: Harvard University Press, 2002 [1990].

Lewis, Ronald, and Rachel Breunlin. *The House of Dance and Feathers*. New Orleans, LA: University of New Orleans Press, 2009.

Littré, Emile. *Dictionnaire de la langue française*. Paris: L. Hachette, 1873–1874. Electronic version created by François Gannaz. Accessed May 19, 2020. http://www.littre.org.

Loyacano, Shelby N. "Her People and Her History: How Camille Lucie Nickerson Inspired the Preservation of Creole Folk Music and Culture, 1888–1982." PhD diss., University of New Orleans, 2019. Accessed May 30, 2020. https://scholarworks.uno.edu/td/2624.

Logsdon, Joseph, and Caryn Cossé Bell. "The Americanization of Black New Orleans 1850–1900." In *Creole New Orleans*, edited by Arnold R. Hirsh and Joseph Logsdon, 201–61. Baton Rouge: Louisiana State University Press, 1992.

Lomax, Alan. *Mister Jelly Roll: The Fortunes of Jelly Roll Morton, New Orleans Creole and "Inventor of Jazz."* New York: Grosset and Dunlap, 1950.

Lomax, John. *John A. Lomax Southern States Collection, 1933–1937*. Archive of Folk Culture, American Folklife Center, Library of Congress, Washington, DC. AFC 1935/002.

Long, Edith E. *Along the Banquette: French Quarter Buildings and Their Stories*. 1st ed. New Orleans: Vieux Carré Property Owners, Residents and Associates, 2004.

Louisiana Creole Dictionary (website). Accessed October 26, 2021. https://www.louisianacreoledictionary.com/Default.aspx.

L. V. C. "The 'Old Timers': Saint Katherine's Golden Anniversary Celebration, 1945." Creole Genealogical and Historical Association, November 1, 2012. Accessed March

26, 2019. http://www.creolegen.org/2012/11/01/the-old-timers-st-katherines-50th-ann iversary-celebration-1945/.

M***. *Mémoires sur la Louisiane et la Nouvelle-Orléans*. Paris: Ballard, 1804.

Maduell, Charles R. *The Census Tables for the French Colony of Louisiana From 1699 Through 1732*. Compiled and translated by Charles R. Maduell Jr. Baltimore, MD: Genealogical Publishing, 1972.

Maestri, Robert. Co-operating sponsor, *New Orleans City Guide*. Written and compiled by the Federal Writers' Project of the Work Progress for the City of New Orleans. American Guide Series. Boston: Houghton Mifflin, 1938.

Manetta, Manuel. Interview by William Russell. March 28, 1957. New Orleans: The Historic New Orleans Collection, MSS 530.2.2.

Manetta, Manuel. Interview by William Russell. April 21, 1959. New Orleans: The Historic New Orleans Collection, MSS 530.2.53.

Manuel complet, à l'usage des catéchismes de Saint-Sulpice et autres paroisses de Paris. Paris: Legrand, 1813. Accessed May 9, 2019. https://books.google.ca/books?id=L7d1iZ4qN3oC.

Marquis, Donald M. *In Search of Buddy Bolden: First Man of Jazz*. Baton Rouge: Louisiana State University Press, 2005 [1978].

Martin, Gilbert. Interview by Harry Oster. June 15, 1963. Harry Oster collection of Louisiana, Mississippi, and Iowa recordings, Archives of Folk Culture, American Folklife Center, Library of Congress, Washington, DC. AFC 1967003-AFS 12594.

Maryland Historical Society. Collections Online, "Benjamin Henri Latrobe," Items MS 2009. Accessed May 27, 2019. http://www.mdhs.org/digital-images?SearchTitles=&field _creator_value=&field_collection_.

Mattern, Mark. "Let the Good Times Unroll: Music and Race Relations in Southwest Louisiana." *Black Music Research Journal* 17, no. 2 (Autumn 1997): 159–68.

McCusker, John. *Creole Trombone: Kid Ory and the Early Years of Jazz*. Jackson: University Press of Mississippi, 2012.

McGinty, Doris E. "Conversation with . . . Camille Nickerson—The Louisiana Lady." *Black Perspectives in Music* 7, no. 1 (Spring 1979): 81–94.

McKnight, Mark. "Louisiana Baroque: Bibliographical Details of *Nouvelles poésies*." In *French Baroque Music of New Orleans: Spiritual Songs from the Ursuline Convent (1736)*, edited by Alfred E. Lemmon, 7–13. New Orleans: The Historic New Orleans Collection, 2014.

Mead. "Memory Types of New Orleans." *Daily Picayune*. December 11, 1864, 1.

Miles, Lizzie. Interview by Richard Allen. January 18, 1951. Hogan Jazz Archive, Tulane University, New Orleans. Item 45, ID: 598–99.

Miller, Gene. "Blacks, Creoles and the Roots of Jazz." *Mississippi Rag* 17, no. 8 (1990): 1–2.

Miller Surrey, Nancy M. *The Commerce of Louisiana during the French Régime 1699–1763*. Tuscaloosa: University of Alabama Press, 2006 [1916].

Millien, Achille. *Chants et Chansons*, Tome Premier. Paris: Ernest Leroux, 1906.

Mitchell-Kernan, Claudia. "Signifying and Marking: Two Afro-American Speech Acts." In *Directions in Sociolinguistics: The Ethnography of Communication*, edited by John J. Gumpertz and Dell Hymes. Hoboken, NJ: Wiley-Blackwell, 1991 [1972].

Monroe, Mina. *Bayou Ballads: Twelve Folk-Songs From Louisiana*. New York: G. Schirmer, ca. 1921.

Morlas, Katy Frances. "La madame et la mademoiselle: Creole women in Louisiana, 1718–1865." Master's thesis, Louisiana State University, 2005. Accessed April 4, 2019. https://digitalcommons.lsu.edu/cgi/viewcontent.cgi?article=1907&context=gradschool_theses.

Morton, Jelly Roll, and Alan Lomax. *Jelly Roll Morton: The Complete Library of Congress Recordings by Alan Lomax*. Recorded 1938. Transcript included. Rounder Records, 2006. Library of Congress. Accessed April 4, 2019. https://lccn.loc.gov/2007659420.

Morton, Jelly Roll. *The "Jelly Roll" Blues*. Chicago: Will Rossiter, 1915.

Mufwene, Salikoko Sangol. "Creole Languages." In *Encyclopedia Britannica*, published 2017. Accessed November 9, 2020. https://www.britannica.com/topic/creole-languages.

"Music and Art." *The Crisis* 15, no. 5 (March 1918): 244. Accessed October 16, 2021. https://www.marxists.org/history/usa/workers/civil-rights/crisis/0300-crisis-v15n05-w089.pdf.

Nash, Gary B. *Red, White, and Black: The Peoples of Early America*. Upper Saddle River, NJ: Prentice-Hall, 1974.

Natsis, James J. "Legislation and Language: The Politics of Speaking French in Louisiana." *French Review* 73, no. 2 (December 1999): 325–31.

Neumann-Holzschuh, Ingrid, ed. *Textes anciens en créole louisianais*. Hamburg: Helmut Buske Verlag, 1987.

"New Orleans Court Location: City Courts." Law Library of Louisiana (website). Accessed December 27, 2020. https://lasc.libguides.com/c.php?g=952398&p=6922006.

Neyrat, Abbé A. Stanislas. *Cantiques du Petit Séminaire de la Primatiale de Lyon, recueillis, harmonisés ou composés par l'abbé A. Stanislas Neyrat*. Paris: F. Girard, 1867.

Nickerson, Camille. "Africo-Creole [sic] Music in Louisiana: A Thesis on the Plantation Songs Created by the Creole Negroes of Louisiana." Master's thesis, Oberlin Conservatory of Music, Oberlin College Libraries, 1932.

Nickerson, Camille. *Five Creole Songs Harmonized and Arranged by Camille Nickerson*. Boston: Boston Music Company, 1942.

Nouveau recueil de cantiques, à l'usage du diocèse de Québec, avec tous les airs notés en musique dans le meilleur gout moderne. Québec: Nouvelle Imprimerie, Hall des Francs-Maçons, 1819. Accessed May 9, 2019. https://archive.org/details/nouveaurecueildeoodaul.

O'Neil, Charles E. *Church and State in French Colonial Louisiana: Policy and Politics to 1732*. New Haven, CT: Yale University Press, 1966.

Ordonnance de la Marine du mois d'aoust 1681 Commentée & Conferée sur les anciennes Ordonnances, le Droit Romain & les nouveaux Reglemens, Livre Second, Titre 2. Paris: Charles Osmond, 1714. Reproduction, Bibliothèque nationale de France. Accessed May 23, 2018. http://gallica.bnf.fr/ark:/12148/bpt6k95955s/f1.item.zoom.

Ortiz, Fernando. *Cuban Counterpoint: Tobacco and Sugar*. Translation by Harriet de Onís. Durham, NC: Duke University Press, 1995.

Ortiz, Fernando. *Controverse cubaine entre le tabac et le sucre: leurs contrastes agraires, économiques, historiques et sociaux, leur ethnographie et leur transculturation*. Translated by Jean-Jacques Bonaldi. Montréal: Mémoire d'encrier, 2011.

Ory, Edward "Kid." Interview by Nesuhi Ertegun and Bob Campbell. April 20, 1957. Hogan Jazz Archive, Tulane University, New Orleans. Item 623, ID: 658–61.

Oster, Harry. "Negro French Spirituals of Louisiana." *Journal of the International Folk Music Council* 14 (1962): 166–67.

Oster, Harry. Fonds Harry Oster, F901, Archives de folklore et d'ethnologie, Université Laval, Québec, 1956–1961.

Oster, Harry. Harry Oster Collection of Louisiana, Mississippi, and Iowa recordings, Archive of Folk Culture, American Folklife Center, Library of Congress, Washington, DC. Box 20, AFC 1967/003. Accessed April 4, 2019. https://lccn.loc.gov/2012655246.

Pasquier, Michael. "Creole Catholicism before Black Catholicism: Religion and Slavery in French Colonial Louisiana." *Journal of Africana Religions* 2, no. 2 (2014): 271–79.

Pasquier, Michael. "'Though Their Skin Remains Brown, I Hope Their Souls Will Soon Be White': Slavery, French Missionaries, and the Roman Catholic Priesthood in the American South, 1789–1865." *Church History* 77, no. 2 (2008): 337–70.

Pastor, Lori Rene. "Black Catholicism: Religion and Slavery in Antebellum Louisiana." Master's thesis, Louisiana State University, 2005. Accessed April 4, 2019. https://digitalcommons.lsu.edu/cgi/viewcontent.cgi?article=2863&context=gradschool_theses.

Pavageau, Alcide. "Slow Drag." Interview by William Russell and Richard B. Allen. December 10, 1958. Hogan Jazz Archive, Tulane University, New Orleans. Accessed November 1, 2021. https://musicrising.tulane.edu/listen/interviews/alcide-slow-drag-pavageau-1958-12-10/.

Pavie, Théodore. *Souvenirs atlantiques. Voyage aux États-Unis et au Canada*, Tome Second. Paris: Roret, 1833.

Peterson, Clara Gottschalk. *Creole Songs from New Orleans in the Negro Dialect*. New Orleans, LA: L. Grunewald, 1902.

Picone, Michael D. "Anglophone Slaves in Francophone Louisiana." *American Speech* 78, no. 4 (Winter 2003): 404–32.

Picou, Alphonse. Interview by William Russell, Al Rose, and Ralph Collins. April 4, 1958. Hogan Jazz Archive, Tulane University, New Orleans. Sub-series 16–9, Item 24, ID: 691–93. Accessed April 2, 2022. http://musicrising.tulane.edu/listen/detail/34/Alphonse-Picou-1958-04-04.

Picou, Alphonse. Interview by William Russell and Ralph Collins. November 3, 1960. Hogan Jazz Archive, Tulane University, New Orleans. Sub-series 16–9, Item 25, ID: 1171, 1173. Accessed April 2, 2022. http://musicrising.tulane.edu/listen/detail/35/Alphonse-Picou-1960-11-03.

Picou, Alphonse, and Paul Dominguez. Interview by Alan Lomax. April 3, 1949. Association for Cultural Equity, Lomax Digital Archive: New Orleans Jazz Interview, 1949. Accessed November 28, 2021. https://archive.culturalequity.org/node/997.

Pierce, Dede, and Billie Pierce. Interview by Richard Allen. October 7, 1959. Hogan Jazz Archive, Tulane University, New Orleans. Accessed October 28, 2021. https://musicrising.tulane.edu/listen/interviews/billie-and-dede-pierce-1959-10-07/.

Pierce, Dede, and Billie Pierce. Interview by Richard Allen. January 10, 1960. Hogan Jazz Archive, Tulane University, New Orleans. Accessed October 28, 2021. https://musicrising.tulane.edu/listen/interviews/dede-pierce-1960-01-10/.

Pierce, Dede, Billie Pierce, Israel Gorman, and Joseph "Kid Twat" Butler. Interview by Richard Allen. November 20, 1963. Hogan Jazz Archive, Tulane University, New Orleans. Accessed October 28, 2021. https://musicrising.tulane.edu/listen/interviews/pierce-band-billie-pierce-de-de-pierce-israel-gorman-joseph-kid-twat-butler-1963-11-20/.

Pouinard, Alfred A. "Recherches sur la musique d'origine française en Amérique du Nord, Canada et Louisiane" vols. 1–2. PhD diss., Université Laval, Québec, 1950.

Prévos, André. "Afro-French Spirituals about Mary Magdalene." Louisiana Folklore Society. *Louisiana Folklore Miscellany* 4 (1976–80): 41–53.

Raeburn, Bruce B. "Beyond the 'Spanish Tinge': Hispanics and Latinos in Early New Orleans Jazz." In *Eurojazzland: Jazz and European Sources, Dynamics, and Context*, edited by Luca Cerchiari, Laurent Cugny, and Franz Kerschbaumer, 21–42. Boston: Northeastern University Press, 2012.

Raeburn Bruce B. "New Orleans Jazz Style of the 1920s: Sam Morgan's Jazz Band." In *Sam Morgan's Jazz Band, Complete Recorded Works in Transcription*, edited by John J. Joyce Jr., Bruce Boyd Raeburn, and Anthony M. Cummings, xv–xxiv. MUSA 24, Middleton, WI: A-R Editions, 2012.

Raeburn, Bruce B. *New Orleans Style and the Writing of American Jazz History*. Ann Arbor: University of Michigan Press, 2009.

Raeburn, Bruce B. "Stars of David and Sons of Sicily: Constellations Beyond the Canon in Early New Orleans Jazz." *Jazz Perspective* 32 (August 2009): 123–52.

Raeburn, Bruce B. "'That Ain't No Creole, It's a ...!': Masquerade, Marketing, and Transgressions Against the Color Line in New Orleans Jazz." Lecture given at New Orleans Jazz National Historical Park, Old US Mint, New Orleans, LA, October 27, 2012.

Railton, Stephen. "Touring with Cable and Huck." On Mark Twain and His Time (website). Accessed May 29, 2020. https://twain.lib.virginia.edu/huckfinn/hftourhp.html#a.

Ramsey, Frederic, Jr., and Charles Edward Smith, eds. *Jazzmen*. New York: Harcourt Brace Jovanovich, 1977 [1939].

Recueil de cantiques à l'usage des missions, des retraites et des catéchismes. Seconde édition, Tome Second. Québec: John Neilson, 1796.

Redfield, Robert, Ralph Linton, and Melville J. Herskovits. "Memorandum for the Study of Acculturation." *American Anthropologist* 38, no. 1 (January–March 1936): 149–52.

Reich, Howard, and William H. Gaines. *Jelly's Blues: The Life, Music, and Redemption of Jelly Roll Morton*. Cambridge, MA: Da Capo Press, 2003.

Reinders, Robert C. "The Churches and the Negro in New Orleans, 1850–1860." *Phylon* 22, no. 3 (3rd Qtr. 1961): 241–48. Accessed March 26, 2019. https://www.jstor.org/stable/274198?seq=1#page_scan_tab_contents.

"Remembering Danny Barker." *Music Inside Out with Gwen Thompkins*. New Orleans: WWNO 89.9 FM, 2016. Accessed November 19, 2021. http://musicinsideout.wwno.org/danny-barker/.

"Remembering the Corps d'Afrique in the American Civil War." *USCT Chronicle* (website). Accessed July 24, 2014. http://usctchronicle.blogspot.ca/2011/05/remembering-corps-dafrique-in-american.html.

Russell, Bill. *New Orleans Style*. Compiled and edited by Barry Martyn and Mike Hazeldine. New Orleans, LA: Jazzology, 1994.

Russell, William H. *My Diary, North and South*. London: Bardbery and Evans, 1863.

Rutherford, Jonathan. "The Third Space: Interview with Homi Bhabha." In *Identity: Community, Culture, Difference*, edited by Jonathan Rutherford, 208–21. London: Lawrence and Wishart, 1990.

Sadler, Cora. "Creole Songs." PhD diss., University of Michigan, 1939.

Sager, David. "A Tale of the Slide Trombone in Early Jazz." *Jazz Archivist* III, no. 1–2 (November 1987): 1–3, 10–12. Hogan Jazz Archive, Tulane University, New Orleans. Accessed April 4, 2019. https://jazz.tulane.edu/sites/default/files/jazz/docs/jazz_archivist/Jazz_Archivist_vol3no1_1988.pdf.

Sager, David. "Ory's Creole Trombone—Kid Ory (June 1922)." Complete National Recording Registry Listing, Library of Congress. Accessed April 29, 2020. https://www.loc.gov/static/programs/national-recording-preservation-board/documents/OrysCreoleTrombone.pdf.

"Saint Augustine Church History." Saint Augustine Catholic Church (website). Accessed April 3, 2019. https://www.staugchurch.org/blog/saint-augustine-church-history.

Sakakeeny, Matt. "Jazz Funerals and Second Line Parades." In *64parishes.org Encyclopedia of Louisiana*, edited by David Johnson. Louisiana Endowment for the Humanities, 2010–. Article published October 2, 2017. Accessed November 11, 2017. http://www.knowlouisiana.org/entry/jazz-funerals-and-second-line-parades.

Sakakeeny, Matt. "Mardi Gras Indians." *Oxford Music Online*. Accessed June 27, 2018. https://www.oxfordmusiconline.com.

Sakakeeny, Matt. *Roll with It: Brass Bands in the Street of New Orleans*. Durham, NC: Duke University Press, 2013.

Sanchirico, Andrew. "Is Conventional Jazz History Distorted by Myths?" *Journal of Jazz Studies* 8, no. 1 (2012): 55–81.

Sandke, Randall. *Where the Dark and the Light Folks Meet: Race and the Mythology, Politics, and Business of Jazz*. Toronto, Ontario: Scarecrow, 2010.

Saxon, Lyle, Edward Dreyer, and Robert Tallant, eds. *Gumbo Ya-Ya: A Collection of Louisiana Folktales*. Boston: Riverside, 1945.

Scarborough, Dorothy. *On the Trail of Negro Folk-Songs*. Cambridge, MA: Harvard University Press, 1925.

Schafer, J. William, with assistance from Richard B. Allen. *Brass Bands and New Orleans Jazz*. Baton Rouge: Louisiana University Press, 1977.

Schuller, Gunther. *Early Jazz: Its Roots and Musical Development*. New York: Oxford University Press, 1986 [1968].

Scott, Rebecca J. "Public Rights, Social Equality, and the Conceptual Roots of the Plessy Challenge." *Michigan Law Review* 106, no. 5 (2008): 777–804.

Scott, Rebecca J. *Degrees of Freedom*. Cambridge, MA: Belknap Press of Harvard University Press, 2005.

Scott, Rebecca J. "Se battre pour ses droits: Écritures, litiges et discrimination raciale en Louisiane (1888–1899)." Translated by Jean Hébrard. *Cahiers du Brésil Contemporain* (Paris) 53/54 (2003): 175–210.

Seck, Ibrahima. *Bouki fait Gombo*. New Orleans, LA: University of New Orleans Press, 2014.

Shapiro, Nat, and Nat Hentoff, eds. *Hear Me Talkin' to Ya*. New York: Dover, 1966 [1955].

Shipton, Alyn. *A New History of Jazz*. New York: Continuum, 2001.

Simpson, Anne Key. "Camille Lucie Nickerson, 'The Louisiana Lady.'" *Louisiana History: Journal of the Louisiana Historical Association* 36, no. 4 (Autumn 1995): 431–51.

Slobin, Mark. *Subcultural Sounds: Micromusics of the West*. Lebanon, NH: University Press of New England, 1993.

Smith, Harrison. "Lizzie Miles: 'Last Press Notice.'" *Coda: Canadian Jazz Magazine* 5, no. 9 (April 1968): 22.
Smith, Michael P. *Mardi Gras Indians*. Gretna, LA: Pelican Publishing, 2007 [1994].
Smith, Robert P. "Black Like That: Paulette Nardal and the Negritude Salon." *CLA Journal* 45, no. 1 (September 2001): 53–68. Accessed November 9, 2020. http://www.jstor.org/stable/44325093.
Somers, Dale A. "Black and White in New Orleans: A Study in Urban Race Relations, 1865–1900." *Journal of Southern History* 40, no. 1 (1974): 19–42.
Soniat Du Fossat, Guy. *History of Louisiana, From the Founding of the Colony to the End of the Year 1791*. Translated by Charles T. Soniat. Louisiana Historical Society, ca. 1903. Accessed April 14, 2019. https://archive.org/details/synopsisofhistoroosoni/page/n4.
Sonnier, Austin, Jr. *Jazzmen of Southwest Louisiana, 1900–1950*. Louisiana Life Series #3, Center for Louisiana Studies. Lafayette: University of Southwestern Louisiana, 1989.
Spear, Jennifer M. *Race, Sex, and Social Order in Early New Orleans*. Baltimore, MD: Johns Hopkins University Press, 2009.
Spitzer, Nicholas R. "Creolization as Cultural Continuity and Creativity in Postdiluvian New Orleans and Beyond." *Southern Spaces*, 28 November 2011. Accessed July 24, 2014. http://www.southernspaces.org/2011/creolization-cultural-continuity-and-creativity-postdiluvian-new-orleans-and-beyond.
Spitzer, Nicholas R. "Monde Creole: The Cultural World of French Louisiana Creoles and the Creolization of World Cultures." *Journal of American Folklore* 116 (Winter 2003): 459.
Spitzer, Nicholas R. Liner notes for *Zodico: Louisiana Créole Music*. Rounder Records #6009. Somerville, MA: Rounder Records, 1976.
St. Cyr, Johnny. Interview by Alan Lomax. April 2, 1949. Association for Cultural Equity, Lomax Digital Archive: New Orleans Jazz Interview, 1949. Accessed November 28, 2021. https://archive.culturalequity.org/node/61836.
St. Cyr, Johnny. Interview by Alan Lomax. April 1949. In *Jelly Roll Morton and Alan Lomax: Transcript of the 1938 Library of Congress Recordings*, 140–43.
Starr, S. Frederick, ed. *Inventing New Orleans: Writings of Lafcadio Hearn*. Jackson: University Press of Mississippi, 2001.
Starr, S. Frederick. *Louis Moreau Gottschalk*. Chicago: University of Illinois Press, 1995.
Starr, S. Frederick, and Irvin Lowens. "Louis Moreau Gottschalk." *Oxford Music Online*, Oxford University Press. Accessed June 5, 2018. https://www.oxfordmusiconline.com.
Stearns, Marshall W. *The Story of Jazz*. New York: Oxford University Press, 1956.
Stewart, Charles, ed. *Creolization: History, Ethnography, Theory*. Walnut Creek, CA: Left Coast Press, 2007.
Stewart, Jack. "Paul Sarebresole and New Orleans's First Rag." *Jazz Archivist* XII, no. 1 (May 1997): 12–20. Hogan Jazz Archive, Tulane University, New Orleans. Accessed June 1 2020. https://jazz.tulane.edu/sites/default/files/jazz/docs/jazz_archivist/Jazz_Archivist_vol12_May_1997.pdf#paul.
Stewart, Jack. "The Other Professors." *Jazz Archivist* XI, no. 1 (May 1996): 1–31. Hogan Jazz Archive, Tulane University, New Orleans. Accessed May 25, 2020. https://jazz.tulane.edu/sites/default/files/jazz/docs/jazz_archivist/Jazz_Archivist_vol11_May_1996.pdf#other.

Sturtevant, Edward. *Edward Lewis Sturtevant Letters.* New Orleans: The Historic New Orleans Collection, MSS 390.

Sublette, Ned. *Cuba and Its Music.* Chicago: Chicago Review, 2004.

Sublette, Ned. *The World That Made New Orleans.* Chicago: Chicago Review, Lawrence Hill Books, 2008.

Sullivan, Lester. "Composers of Color of Nineteenth-Century New Orleans: The History Behind the Music." *Black Music Research Journal* 8, no. 1 (1988): 51–82. This article also appears in Kein, Sybil, ed. *Creole: The History and Legacy of Louisiana's Free People of Color,* 71–100. Baton Rouge: Louisiana State University Press, 2000.

Szwed, John F., and Morton Marks. "The Afro-American Transformation of European Set Dances Suites." *Dance Research Journal* 20, no. 1 (Summer 1988): 29–36.

Taylor, Joe G. "The Foreign Slave Trade in Louisiana after 1808." *Louisiana History* 1, no. 1 (Winter 1960): 36–43.

"The Collins C. Diboll Vieux Carré Digital Survey." A Project of The New Orleans Historic Collection. Accessed February 12, 2021. https://www.hnoc.org/vcs/index.php.

"The Congo Dance." *Daily Picayune,* October 18, 1843, 2.

"The Congo Dance: A Glimpse of the Old Square of a Sunday Afternoon Sixty Years Ago." *Daily Picayune,* October 12, 1879, 2.

Theard, Marie. *Old Songs of French and Creole Origin Collected in Louisiana.* Unpublished manuscript prepared for the Louisiana Federation of Music Clubs, ca. 1935.

Thompson, Shirley. "'Ah Toucoutou, ye conin vous': History and Memory in Creole New Orleans." *American Quarterly* 53, no. 2 (June 2001): 232–66.

Thompson, Shirley. *Exiles at Home: The Struggle to Become American in Creole New Orleans.* Cambridge, MA: Harvard University Press, 2009.

Tiersot, Julien. *Notes d'ethnographie musicale (Deuxième série)—La musique chez les peuples indigènes de l'Amérique du Nord (États-Unis et Canada).* Paris: Librairie Fischbacher, Breitkopf et Haertel Éditeurs, 1909.

Tio, Louis. Interview by William Russell, Ralph Collins, and Harold Dejan. October 26, 1960. Hogan Jazz Archive, Tulane University, New Orleans. Sub-series 20-T, Item 14, ID: 830-32. Accessed April 7, 2020. https://musicrising.tulane.edu/listen/interviews/louis-tio-1960-10-26/.

Tovey, Michael, and Barry Kernfeld. "Lawrence Duhé." *Oxford Music Online.* Oxford University Press. Accessed May 15, 2019.

Tregle, Joseph G., Jr. "Creoles and Americans." In *Creole New Orleans,* edited by Arnold R. Hirsh and Joseph Logsdon, 131–85. Baton Rouge: Louisiana State University Press, 1992.

Tregle, Joseph G., Jr. "On That Word 'Creole' Again: A Note." *Louisiana History* 23, no. 2 (Spring 1982): 193–98.

Trist Family Papers: 1625–1952. New Orleans: The Historic New Orleans Collection, MSS 180.

Trotter, James M. *Music and Some Highly Musical People.* Boston: Lee and Shepard, 1881. Accessed November 4, 2017. http://www.gutenberg.org/ebooks/28056.

Tucker, Sherrie, Principal Investigator. "A Feminist Perspective on New Orleans Jazzwomen." Research Study Submitted to New Orleans Jazz National Historical Park, National Park Service, New Orleans. September 30, 2004. Accessed April 10, 2020. https://www.nps.gov/jazz/learn/historyculture/upload/New_Orleans_Jazzwomen_RS-2.pdf.

Usner, Daniel H., Jr. "The Facility Offered by the Country: The Creolization of Agriculture in the Lower Mississippi Valley." In *Creolization in the Americas*, edited by David Buisseret and Steven G. Reinhardt, 35–62. College Station: Texas A&M University Press, 2000.

Usner, Daniel H., Jr. "From African Captivity to American Slavery: The Introduction of Black Laborers to Colonial Louisiana." *Louisiana History* 20, no. 1 (1979): 25–48.

Van Dam, Theodore. "The influence of the West African Songs of Derision in the New World." *African Music* 1, no. 1 (1954): 53–56.

Vaz, Kim Marie. *The "Baby Dolls": Breaking the Race and Gender Barriers of the New Orleans Mardi Gras Tradition*. Baton Rouge: Louisiana State University Press, 2013.

Vogel, Claude L. "The Capuchins in French Louisiana (1722–1766)." PhD diss., Catholic University of America, Washington, DC, 1928. Accessed May 14, 2019. https://archive.org/details/capuchinsinfrencoovoge.

Warner, Charles Dudley. *Studies in the South and West, with Comments on Canada*. New York: Harper & Brothers, 1889.

Wegmann, Andrew N. "The Vitriolic Blood of a Negro: the Development of a Racial Identity and Creole Elitism in New Spain and Spanish Louisiana, 1763–1803." *Journal of Transatlantic Studies* 13, no. 2 (April 2015): 204–25. Accessed March 30, 2020. https://doi.org/10.1080/14794012.2015.1022373.

Wehrmann, Henri. *Creole Songs of the Deep South*. New Orleans, LA: Philip Werlein, 1946.

Weidman, Budge. "Black Soldiers in the Civil War: Preserving the Legacy of the United States Colored Troops." National Archives (website). Accessed May 15, 2019. https://www.archives.gov/education/lessons/blacks-civil-war/article.html.

Wells, Lise W. Liner notes for *Creole Songs Sung and Played by Lise Wells*. New Orleans: The Historic New Orleans Collection, Library of Congress Catalog no. 81-750-444, 1981.

Wharton, Edward C. *A History of the Proceedings in the City of New Orleans, on the Occasion of the Funeral Ceremonies in Honor of James Abram Garfield*. New Orleans, LA: Hyatt, 1881.

White, Amos. Interview by William Russell. August 23, 1958. Hogan Jazz Archive, Tulane University, New Orleans. Sub-series 23-W, Item 14, ID: 82–885.

"'Wide Wide World' Visits N. O. Sunday." *New Orleans Item*, Sunday, February 2, 1958. New Orleans: The Historic New Orleans Collection, MSS 536: Miles, Lizzie. Folder 9.

Wilkinson, Christopher. *Jazz on the Road: Don Albert's Musical Life*. Berkeley: University of California Press, 2001.

Wilson, Mary Louise Lewis. "Traditional Louisiana-French Folk Music: An Argument for its preservation and Utilization as a State Cultural Heritage." PhD diss., University of Pittsburgh (PA), 1977. Ann Arbor, MI: University Microfilms International, 1978.

Wilson, Wash. Interview for the *Federal Writers' Project: Slave Narrative Project*, Vol. 16, Texas, Part 4, 1936–1938. Published in 1941. Accessed November 27, 2020. https://www.loc.gov/item/mesn164/.

Wogan, Marguerite B. "Mother's Book." Unpublished manuscript, May 1952.

Wogan, Marguerite B. *Cancan Kisinieres "Cooks Gossip."* New Orleans: Rogers Printing, 1931.

Wood, Berta. "Lizzie Miles from New Orleans." *Jazz Journal* 10, no. 6 (June 1957): 1–2.

Wright, Josephine. "Hare, Maud Cuney." *Oxford Music Online*. Oxford University Press. Accessed May 28, 2020. https://www.oxfordmusiconline.com.

Wyatt, Lucius R. "Six Composers of Nineteenth-Century New Orleans." *Black Music Research Journal* 10, no. 1 (Spring 1990): 125–40.

Zagala, Mathilde. "Le 'trois sur quatre' dans la musique écrite en circulation à la Nouvelle-Orléans d'avant le jazz enregistré, 1835–1917." PhD diss., Université Paris-Sorbonne, 2016.

Zeno, Alice. Interview by William Russell, Richard B. Allen, and Harry Oster. January 25, 1960. Hogan Jazz Archive, Tulane University, New Orleans. Sub-series 26-Z, Item 7, ID: 927–28. Accessed July 13, 2017. http://musicrising.tulane.edu/listen/detail/607/Zeno-Interview-1960-01-25.

Zeno, Alice, and George Lewis. Interview by William Russell and Richard B. Allen. December 10, 1958. Hogan Jazz Archive, Tulane University, New Orleans. Sub-series 26-Z, Item 6, ID: 926. Accessed July 14, 2017. http://musicrising.tulane.edu/listen/detail/606/Alice-Zeno-Interview.

Zeno, Alice, and George Lewis. Interview by William Russell and Richard B. Allen. November 14, 1958. Hogan Jazz Archive, Tulane University, New Orleans. Sub-series 26-Z, Item 5, ID: 922–25. Accessed July 14, 2017. http://musicrising.tulane.edu/listen/detail/608/Zeno-Lewis-Interview-1958-11-14.

Zimmerman, Keith, and Kent Zimmerman. *The Art of Jazz: Monterey Jazz Festival, 50 Years*. Monterey, CA: Monterey Jazz Festival, 2007.

SELECTED DISCOGRAPHY

Bonano, Sharkey. *Sharkey Bonano At Lenfant's Lounge*. Sounds of New Orleans, vol. 8. Storyville Records: STCD 6015, 1991.

Bonano, Sharkey. *Sharkey and His Kings of Dixieland*. Jasmine Records JASCD 669, 2008.

Barnes, Emile. *The Louisiana Joymakers Introducing DeDe & Billie Pierce*. American Music Records AMCD-13, 1995.

Barbarin, Paul. *Paul Barbarin and His New Orleans Jazz*. Atlantic Records LP SD 1215, 1955. Reissued on Collectables Records: CD COLCD 6912, 2008.

Barbarin, Paul. *Paul Barbarin and His New Orleans Jazz Band*. GHB Records BCD-2, 2013.

Barker, Danny. *New Orleans Jazz Man and Raconteur*. GHB Records BCD-535, 2015.

Castellanos-Taggart, Marguerite, with Edna McLaughlin. *Bayou Ballads of the Louisiana Plantations*. RCA Victor M-728 (2130–2132), 1941.

Collins, Peter. *Music of Basile Barès*. Centaur, 2007.

Desmarest, Henry, Composer. *Manuscrit des Ursulines de la Nouvelle-Orléans*. Le Concert Lorrain, direction Anne-Catherine Bucher. France: K617134, 2002, ℗ 2001.

Dodds, Warren "Baby." *Baby Dodds Trio/Jazz A' La Creole* [sic]. Circle Records 78 rpm album set S-13, 1947. Reissued on GHB Records BCD-50, 2000.

Le Poème Harmonique, directed by Vincent Dumestre. *Plaisir d'amour: chansons et romances de la France d'autrefois*. France: Alpha 513, 2004.

McCalla, Leyla, and the Special Men. *Eh La Bas*. Special Men Industries, 2019.

Miles, Lizzie, and Sharkey's Kings of Dixieland. *A Night in Old New Orleans*. Capitol Records LP T 792, 1956.

Miles, Lizzie. *Complete Recorded Works in Chronological Order*, Vol. 1, 1922 to 1923. Document Records DOCD-5458.

Miles, Lizzie. *Complete Recorded Works in Chronological Order*, Vol. 2, 1923 to 1928. Document Records DOCD-5459.

Miles, Lizzie. *Complete Recorded Works in Chronological Order*, Vol. 3, 1928 to 1929. Document Records DOCD-5460.

Miles, Lizzie. *Lizzie Miles*. American Music Records AMCD-73, 1994.

Miles, Lizzie. *Creole Special by Lizzie Miles and Her New Orleans Boys*. Circle Records 78 rpm Special No4/Jazz Singer, N.Y. (NO-70), 1946. Reissued on *Lizzie Miles*, American Music Records AMCD 73, 1994.

Miles, Lizzie. *Moans and Blues*. Sounds of Our Times Recordings. Cook Records 1182, Smithsonian Folkways Recordings, 1956.

Miles, Lizzie. *Hot Songs My Mother Taught Me.* Sounds of Our Times Recordings. Cook Records 1183, Smithsonian Folkways Recordings, 1956.

Miles, Lizzie. *Torchy Lullabies My Mother Sang Me.* Sounds of Our Times Recordings. Cook Records 1184, Smithsonian Folkways Recordings, 1956.

Morand, Herb. *Herb Morand's New Orleans Band—1950—Herb and Paul Barbarin's Band—1951.* American Music AMCD 106, 1999.

Nicholas, Wooden Joe. *Rare and Unissued Masters 1945–1949.* American Music Records AMCD 136, 2013.

Ory, Kid. *Kid Ory at the Green Room*, Vol. 2. American Music Records CD AMCD 43, 1992.

Ory, Kid. *Kid Ory Creole Jazz Band 1944/1945: The Legendary Crescent Recordings Sessions.* GHB Records BDC-10, 1995.

Ory, Kid. *Kid Ory and His Creole Jazz Band 1922–1947.* Document Records DOCD 1002, 1996.

Ory, Kid. *The Complete Kid Ory Verve Sessions.* Mosaic MD8–189, 1999.

Ory, Kid. *The Complete Kid Ory Columbia Session 1946.* American Music Records AMCD-121, 2007.

Pierce, Billie and DeDe. *Gulf Coast Blues.* Arhoolie Production 488, 1971 and 2000.

Pierce, DeDe. *DeDe Pierce with Billie Pierce in Binghamton, N.Y.*, vol. 1. American Music Records AMCD-79, 1996.

Pierce, DeDe. *DeDe Pierce and His New Orleans Stompers in Binghamton, N.Y.*, vol. 4. American Music Records AMCD-82, 1994.

Scobey, Bob. *The Great Bob Scobey and His Frisco Band.* Vocals by Clancy Hayes and Lizzie Miles, Vol. 1. Jazzology Records JCD 275, 1996.

Scobey, Bob. *The Great Bob Scobey and His Frisco Band.* Vocals by Clancy Hayes and Lizzie Miles, Vol. 2. Jazzology Records JCD 285, 1997.

Van Wey, Adelaide. *Street Cries and Creole Songs of New Orleans.* Folkways Records, Smithsonian Center for Folklife and Cultural Heritage LP FW02202/FA 2202, 1956.

Don Vappie and the Creole Jazz Serenaders. *Swing Out.* Vappielle Records VR-0502, 2005.

Don Vappie and the Creole Jazz Serenaders. *Creole Blues.* Vappielle Records VR-0503, 2005.

Don Vappie and Jazz Creole. *The Blue Book of Storyville.* Le Jazzetal JCD 22, 2019.

Various artists. *Zodico: Louisiana Créole Music.* Rounder Records 6009, 1976.

INDEX

Abbott, Lynn, 85, 183n47
Acadia, 10, 11
Acadians, 12, 18–19
acculturation, 126, 192n5
"Achin' Hearted Blues," 91, 185n70
"Act to Regulate the Conditions and Forms of the Emancipation of Slaves, An," 166n37
adaptation
    of clawhammer, 65
    in colonies, or the New World, 126, 193
    of songs and *cantiques*, 45, 54, 56, 119
affranchissement, 14. See also *coartación*; emancipation; manumission; self-purchase
affranchitte, 30
Africa, 11, 14, 29, 38, 111, 118–19, 174n63, 192n2
African(s)
    acculturation/creolization/*Créolité*, 126, 127, 128, 192nn2–3, 193n11
    countries of origin, 11, 13–14, 166n26
    descent/ancestry/heritage, 20, 50, 51, 53, 66, 74, 81–82, 166n36, 167n38, 169n1
    enslaved, 3, 4, 8, 11, 14, 50, 62, 125, 128, 169n10
    origin of jazz/influence/elements, 3, 27, 29, 32, 33, 38–40, 44, 47, 55, 59, 62, 114, 119, 163n3, 169n4, 171n28, 171n31
African American(s)
    enslaved/civil rights/segregation, 9, 20, 21, 30, 61, 62, 63
    identity/culture, 93, 98, 126, 128, 164n11, 165n13, 171n31, 181n21, 191n14, 193n12
    music/recordings, 50, 53, 56, 66, 73, 78, 83, 95, 192n2

Afro-American Folksongs (Krehbiel), 129, 132, 172n39, 173n49
Afro-Creole culture, 38
Afro-French Creoles (community/music), 28, 59, 81, 98, 169n1, 190n6. See also French Creoles
agréments, 53
"Ah! vous dirai-je, maman," 116
Aimé, Valcour, 173
"Aine/Inne, dé, trois." *See* "Caroline"
Albanese, Antonio (Antoine Albanèse), 176
Alexis, Albertine Hilaire, 133, 189n47
All Star Jazz Group (Kid Ory's), 94, 185n6
Allen, Richard, 23, 103, 106
Allen, William Francis, 28, 41, 132. See also *Slave Songs of the United States*
Almerico, Tony, 183n56
Almoravides Empire, 192
Alpaugh, Marie Magdalene, 51, 175n11
alteration (microtonal/pitch), 27, 35, 36, 90
American Music label, 94
American sector, 19
ancestry, 20, 181n24
    African, 74, 81, 111, 128, 167n38
    Creole, 67
    French, 64, 74, 81, 128
    French Canadian, 74
    German, 81
    Native American, 81, 84, 163n6
    Spanish, 74, 81, 128
Anglo-American(s), 5, 9, 12, 14, 19, 81, 82, 128, 169, 180n6
    bipartite racial classification, 19–21
Ansermet, Ernest, 90, 184

INDEX

Antilles/Antillean, 128, 192n1. *See also* Caribbean
Antoine, Caesar Carpentier (Captain), 67
Arguedas, Jeanne Wogan
    Congo Square, 45–48, 173n61, 174n63
    life, 4, 21, 23–24, 64, 170n17, 189n48
    plantation songs/street cries, 33–35, 95–96, 118, 133
    voodoo songs, 37, 171n28
Armstrong, Louis, 3, 71, 76, 87, 93, 179n1, 184n66, 185n69
    and Kid Ory, 73, 81, 82 188n34
arrangement, 37, 76, 79, 95
    of Creole songs, 95, 104–6, 110, 113–14, 117, 118n34, 118n40
    written/stock/head, 71, 103, 188n33
arranger, 6, 65, 73, 75, 77, 78
artisan-class, artisanship, 13, 71
assimilation, 18, 126
assimilationist ideal, 11
"Au clair de la lune," 190n64
"Au Sang qu'un Dieu Va Répandre," 56–57, 144
Augustat, Bouboul, 101–2
"Auprès de ma blonde," 190n64
"Aurore Bradaire"/"Aurore Pradère," 32, 41

Babouille, 39, 40, 47
Baby (dancing master), 61
Baby Dolls, 103, 182n42
Baker, Josephine, 185n71
ball, 5, 19, 23, 30, 31, 43, 60–63, 85, 129–33, 177n8, 177n10, 178n11
ballad, 28, 41, 95
"Ballade Creole," 32
ballroom, 61, 62, 177n8
Bam, 86, 183n47
Bamboula
    dance and song, 33, 39, 40–41, 44, 45, 130
    drum, 45, 96, 172n41, 174n63
"Bamboula: Danse des Nègres," 41, 64
bandleader, 6, 73, 77, 81, 82, 87
banjo
    in early jazz, 72, 91, 104
    players, 171n23, 183n56, 184n65, 185nn68–70 (chap. 5), 185n5 (chap. 6), 186n7, 188n34, 188n43, 189n51, 191n1
    in precursors, 31, 39, 40, 44, 178n20
"Banjo, The," 64–65, 178n20
banjoist, 100. *See also* banjo: players
Baquet, Achille, 76
Baquet, George, 76, 89, 98, 99, 186n20
Barbarin, Isidore, 71
Barbarin, Paul, 102–3, 109
Barbarin, Rose, 121
Barbarin family, 171n23
Barès, Basile, 5, 39, 63–64, 178n17
Barker, Danny, 35, 103, 131, 171n23, 180n9, 182n42
    "Eh La Bas," 109–11, 187n24, 189n51
    "Les Ognons," 116–18
Baron, John, 61, 62, 63, 66, 178n15, 179n26
Baron, Robert, 192n6
barrel (as drum), 30, 32, 186n14
Baroque music. *See* French Baroque music
Barth, Wilhelmina, 85
Basie, Count, 81
"Basin Street Blues," 183n57
bass
    in Creole songs, 114, 117
    in early jazz, 72, 102, 104
    players, 87, 99, 182n37, 185n69 (chap. 5), 185n4 (chap. 6), 186n7, 186n20, 188nn37–38, 188nn41–43, 189n51, 190n59, 191n1
bassist, 82. *See also* bass: players
bassoon, 75
Bayou St. John, 60, 187n30
Beaumont, Joseph, 109, 112, 115
Bechet, Leonard, 89, 103, 179n5, 180n6, 187n23
Bechet, Sidney, 6, 72, 73, 76, 77, 85, 88–92, 93, 103, 118, 180n6, 180n9, 184n60, 184nn65–67, 185nn68–70
    "Les Oignons," 118, 190n69
Bell, Caryn Cossé, 9
"Belle Layotte," 32, 41
Benbow, Edna, 85
bend notes, 91
Bernabé, Jean, 128, 193n11

INDEX

Bernhard, Duke of Saxe-Weimar, 178n11
Beroche, Elie, 67
Berquin-Duvallon, 178n11
Bethell, Tom, 164n8, 180n9
Bhabha, Homi, 127
Bienville, Jean Baptiste Lemoyne de, 11, 66, 164n3, 165n18. *See also* Governor
Bigard, Alex, 179n3
Bigard, Barney, 71, 76, 77, 90, 179n3, 180n9, 186n7, 188n41
"Bill Bailey, Won't You Please Come Home?," 183n57
Bizot, Celestin, 67
Black Atlantic, 127
Black Code, 15, 38
Black Flowers/Black People, 91
Black Rose, The, 87
"Blanche Touquatoux," 111–15, 188n38, 190nn58–59, 190n61
Blesh, Rudi, 94, 116, 163n5, 191n77
Blue Five, The, 90, 184n65, 185n69
blue notes, 27
blues, 3, 29, 169n2
    and Jelly Roll Morton, 78–81, 180n6, 182n30
    and Lizzie Miles, 73, 84–88
    and Lorenzo Tio, 76
    and Sidney Bechet, 72, 89–91
"Blues for Marili," 182n41
blues scale, 169n4. *See also* scale
boat songs, 27
Bob Scobey and his Frisco Band, 106, 188n43
Bocage, Peter, 77
Bolden, Buddy, 78, 102
Bonniol, Jean-Luc, 125, 192n1
Borders, Ben, 182n37
Borneman, Ernest, 114, 163nn4–5, 169n4
Bossu, Jean-Bernard, 164n4
Bouqui et Lapin, 178n18
Bouté, Charles-Henri, 176n28
Brandon, Elizabeth, 54, 55, 56, 177n33
brass bands 68, 75, 76, 89
Braud, Wellman, 82
breaks (in music), 78, 83, 90, 104

Brothers, Thomas, 71, 89
Brown, Sterling, 93
Brunious, Wendell, 189n51, 191n1
Bucher, Anne Catherine, 52
Buck, Jack, 188n43
Buckner, Teddy, 188n42
Bucktown, 86
Butler, Benjamin F. (General), 68
Butler, Philomène, 108, 189n48

Cable, George W., 33, 37, 39–42, 43, 46, 62, 67, 95, 132, 186n12
"Cadja, Ma coupé ça," 47
Caffery, Joshua Clegg, 29
Caillot, Marc-Antoine, 30, 60–61
Cailloux, André (Captain), 67
Cajun cultural identity, 18
calas (*Belles/marchandes de*/vendor), 35–36, 41–42, 43, 116–18, 170n22, 171n23, 171nn25–26. *See also* "Les Ognons"
California, 195, 191n74
Calinda, 30, 32, 39, 41–42, 44, 45, 46, 47, 111, 129–33, 169n9, 173n55, 174n62
call and response, 3, 28, 105–6, 110–11, 117–18, 119
Calypso song, 111
Camp, Red, 183n56
Campanell, Barthelemi, 67
Campanella, Richard, 173n60
Canada, 11, 57, 116, 190n64, 191n78
Canary Islands, 12
can-can, 100, 187n23
Cancans Kisinieres "Cooks Gossip," 187n23
"Can't Help Loving That Man of Mine," 183n57
cantiques, 5, 27, 54–59, 85, 98, 111, 164n8, 175n20
Capuchin, 49, 50, 175n6
Carey, Mutt, 182n37, 186n7, 188nn37–38, 188n41, 190n59
Caribbean
    colonies/islands, 11, 111, 165n4
    creolization in, 125, 127, 192n3
    enslaved coming from, 11, 14
    rhythms, 3, 29, 65, 78, 104, 119, 163n5

society/culture, 10, 13, 18, 167n53
    See also Antilles; rhythm
Carnival, 5, 23, 60–61, 62, 96, 102–3
"Caroline," 32, 41
Carondelet, François Louis Hector, Baron de, 45–46. See also Governor
cask, as an instrument, 40, 44
Cata/Chacta, 39
Catalan, Léonore, 177n33
Catalon, Inez (Enes Catalan), 58, 157, 177n33
Catholic
    Church/religion/faith, 3, 5, 12–13, 27, 49–52, 57
    Creoles, 5, 59, 81
    song/hymns, 55, 59, 85
    See also cantiques
census (1727, 1860), 5, 15, 16–17
Century Magazine, 39
Césaire, Aimé, 128, 193n13
"C'était N'aut' Can-Can, Payez Donc"/"C'est l'aut Can-Can," 99–100, 115, 187n23, 191n77
Chamoiseau, Patrick, 128, 193n11
"Chanson de Lizette," 64
chanson française, 3
chansons morales, 5, 52
"Chant du Vié Boscugo," 42, 129–33, 172n45
Chariot, Louis, 67
Charles, Josephine, 51, 175
"Chere Mo l'Aimer Toi," 45
Chicago, 10, 73, 82, 83, 87, 88, 114, 182n29, 183n55
Chilton, John, 180n9, 184n60
choir, 50, 57, 66
Chopin, Frédéric, 64
chorus, as a group of singers, 32, 41, 44, 52, 66. See also singers; vocals; voice
Christian, Buddy, 184n65, 185nn68–70
Christian, Marcus, 170n22
Circle Records, 94
Civil War
    and military music, 67–68
    and race relations, 15, 20, 44, 73, 168n55, 191n73
    and the Tio family, 74

socio-racial classes before and after, 9, 14, 18, 19, 30, 60, 63, 73, 128
    See also Congo Square; Creole (word)
Clarence Williams' Blue Five, 90, 184n65, 185nn69–70
Clarence Williams' Trio, 185n70
clarinet
    in Creole songs, 105–6, 113–14, 117–18
    in early jazz, 72, 102, 104
    players, 71, 87, 99, 118, 182n37, 185n70 (chap. 5), 185n4 (chap. 6), 186n7, 188n34, 188n37, 188nn41–43, 189n51, 190n59, 191n1. See also clarinetist
    stylistic school of playing, 77, 181n18
    the Tios and Bechet, 74–76, 88–91, 185m70
clarinetist, 23, 72, 73, 74–76, 92, 101, 102. See also clarinet: players
Clark, Emily, 15, 50
classical music, 5, 29, 63–66, 78
Claude Luter Orchestra, 92, 118, 190n69
clawhammer, Gottschalk adaptation of, 65
coartación, 15. See also affranchissement; emancipation; manumission; self-purchase
Code Noir, 13, 14, 15, 38, 50
Cohen, Robin, 8, 9
Coleman, Will H., 42–43, 129, 193n2
collective playing, 28, 72, 90, 104, 105–6, 113–14
collectors, 93–94, 98, 185n1
Collier, James Lincoln, 81, 169n2, 191n70
Columbia (Records), 76, 94, 116
Comité des Citoyens, 21, 182n30
Company of the Indies, 5, 30, 60. See also La Compagnie des Indes
composer, 5, 6, 29, 41, 53, 56, 60, 63–66, 73, 77, 78, 81, 102, 163, 176n28
Compton, Glover, 87
concert, 60, 61, 63, 64, 68, 74, 84, 85, 95, 99, 178n15
Concert and Ball, 85
Confiant, Raphaël, 128, 193n11
Congo dance, 39–40, 43, 172n41
Congo Square, 4, 5, 23, 24, 171n31

after the Civil War, 44–48
and Gottschalk, 64
Sunday gatherings, 38–44, 171n27, 172n39
Congo/Angola, 13, 14
Constitution, State of Louisiana, 20–21, 73, 167n47, 168n55
contrafacta, 52–53
Cook, Emory, 88
Coonjai/Counjaille, 32, 39, 41, 108
Corb, Morty, 168n42
Corn Feast, 38
cornet
  in early jazz, 72, 91, 104
  players, 82, 87, 99, 102, 182n37, 184n65, 185n69, 186n20, 188n38
cornetist, 82, 89, 90. *See also* cornet: players
cotillion, 62
countermelody, 82, 83, 91, 104, 105, 113–14, 118
cowan, 101, 102, 103, 119
cowbells, 103
"Crazy Blues," 87
Creecy, James R., 35, 39
Créole
  bière/beer, 44
  comedy, 61
  danses, 44, 47
Creole (word), 4, 8, 10, 20, 73, 83, 163n1
"Creole Bobo," 116
Creole cultural identity, 3, 4, 6, 10, 12–13, 18, 19, 20, 21, 73, 83, 93, 128
Creole French (language), 3, 23, 24, 38, 84, 87, 191n75
Creole Love Call, 10
"Creole Rebels," 89, 180n6
Creole Rhapsody, 10
Creole Serenaders, 116
"Creole Slave Songs" (Cable), 33, 37, 67, 95, 172n39, 178n18
"Creole Song (C'est l'Autre Can-can)." *See* "C'était N'aut' Can-Can, Payez Donc"
Creoles of Color, 9, 14, 18, 19 20, 21, 61, 63, 65, 67, 71, 73, 163n6, 164n11. *See also* Free Blacks; Free People of Color; *Gens de Couleur Libres*; People of Color

creolism, 20
Créolité, 128, 193n11
creolization, 4, 6, 8–10, 13, 54, 65, 74, 78, 103, 125, 127, 128, 164n5, 192n3
creolizing situations/location, 125
creolophone, 14
Crescent Records, 94
Cuba, 10, 12, 15, 23, 29, 126
Cubans, 81, 95, 126

Daily Picayune, 38, 43, 44
Damas, Leon Gontran, 128
dance band/orchestra, 63, 72, 74, 75, 76, 98, 100, 180n17
dance halls, 45, 61, 62, 72, 78, 85, 99
"Dance in Place Congo, The" (Cable), 39, 40, 42, 95, 132
dancing/dances, 3, 4, 23, 24, 82, 85, 98, 112, 126, 129–30
  in early jazz, 71, 78, 99 102, 119, 174n65, 181n28, 182n36, 182n42, 185n71, 187n23, 188n36
  in precursors, 29, 30–31, 32, 55, 67, 68
  See also Congo Square; European music/dances; Voodoo
"Dans un Brigatoire (Purgatoire)," 58, 154, 156
"Dans un Jardin Solitaire," 56–57, 141–49, 176n29
danse Créoles, 44, 47
"Dansez Calinda," 42, 45, 47, 129–33
Darenbourg, Joe, 190n59
"Darktown Strutters' Ball," 183n57
Darnell, Howard, 186n7, 188n37
Debergue, Michel, 67
Decca Records, 94, 111
Decou, Walter, 185n4
deculturation, 126
Dédé, Edmond, 63
Deggs, Sister Mary Bernard, 51, 175n11
Delachaise (Mesieur/Street), 45–46, 172n60
Delaunay, Charles, 92
Delille, Henriette, 51, 89
Delille/Delisle, Louis Nelson "Big Eye." *See* Nelson, Louis

"Denise Lacage," 108, 189n47
Desarzant, Anastasie, 109, 189n50
Desdunes, Mamie, 81, 180n6, 182n30
Desdunes, Rodolphe, 114–15, 128, 182n30, 190n62
Desmaziliere, Eglantine, 189n50
"Dí que sí," 65
Diderot, Denis, and Jean le Rond d'Alembert, 164n4
Dixie Park, 85
Doby, Francis/Frances, 30, 41
Dodds, Johnny, 87, 93, 188n34
Dodds, Warren "Baby," 72, 79, 87, 94, 111, 113, 164n10, 181n28
Dominguez, Paul, 102
Domínguez, Virginia, 8, 16–17, 164n3
Dominique, Natty, 72
"Don't Tell Me Nothin' 'bout My Man," 88
Doré, Charles (early fife player), 66
double consciousness, 127
double entendre/double meaning, 43, 117, 119, 189n52
Doublet, Antoinette Hazeur, 74–75
downtown (Creole/musician), 11, 21, 72, 78, 79, 82, 102, 111, 179n2, 180n6, 188n33
drums
  in early jazz and Creole songs, 72, 104, 105–6, 110
  on plantation and Congo Square, 30, 32, 37–38, 39, 40, 41, 45, 96, 174n63
  players, 66, 72, 78, 87, 94, 99, 111, 179n26, 182n37, 185n4, 186n7, 186n20, 188n37, 188nn41–43, 189n51, 190nn59, 191n1
  religious and military music, 49, 66, 67, 179n27
  See also Bamboula; barrel; *petit tambour*
drummer, 5, 66, 72, 87, 111, 179n26, 182n42. *See also* drums: players
Du Bois, W. E. B., 127, 193n9
Dubuclet, Laurent, 65
Duhé, Lawrence, 87
Duke Ellington Orchestra, 10, 74, 77, 81, 91
Dumas, Francis E. (Major), 67
Dumont de Montigny, Jean-François Benjamin, 15

Eagle Band (Bunk Johnson's), 76, 89, 184n60
early jazz, characteristics of, 72, 104
early jazz revival. *See* revival
"Eh La Bas," 79, 101, 102, 104–11, 188n38, 188nn41–43, 189n44, 190n54. *See also* "Mon Cher Cousin"
Ellington, Duke. *See* Duke Ellington Orchestra
Ellison, Mary, 67
emancipation, 14, 20, 189n48. See also *affranchissement*; *coartación*; manumission; self-purchase
"En Avant Grenadiers"/"En Avan' Grenadié" [*sic*], 64, 67
engages, 18
England, 90, 91, 98
Ertegun, Nesuhi, 94
"ethnic absolutism," 127
Eureka (French-speaking colony in Mexico), 180n14
Europe, 62, 63, 73, 91, 93, 192n2
European(s)
  and double consciousness/*Créolité*, 127, 128, 192nn2–3, 193n11
  education/beliefs/codification, 18, 126, 167n23
  music/dances, 3, 5, 28, 29, 60, 61, 62, 78, 99, 169n4, 188n36
  parentage/colonizer, 8, 11, 125, 164n4
Evans, Freddi, 38, 40, 172n39, 172n41, 174n65
Exner label, 94

"fake" (improvise)/fakers, 71, 179n5
Farragut, David G. (Admiral), 68
Federal Writers' Project, 23, 30, 191n73
Fénelon, François Salignac de La Mothe, 56–57, 144, 146, 148–49
Fête du Blé, 38
fiddle, 30, 31, 37, 178n11
Fiehrer, Thomas, 163n5
field hands, Original Creole Band dressed as, 98, 100
field hollers, 9, 27, 169n2
fife, 5, 66, 67, 179nn26–27

Fihle, George, 71
first families, 18, 74
First Nations, 11. *See also* Indian(s); Native American(s)
fish fries, 71, 119
flexibility, lyrical/formal/in Creole songs, 45, 58, 110, 111, 119
Flint, Timothy, 43
folk music
    Black/Black American, 6, 9, 27, 54, 120, 169n2
    Franco-American, 6, 120
    Louisiana-French, 59
foot (stomping/percussion/tapping/beating the ground with), 37, 45, 46, 55, 96, 176n23
"foreign French," 12
Fortier, Alcée, 38, 42, 171n30, 173n61, 190n62, 191n76
Fortunette, Bouboul, 102. *See also* Augustat, Bouboul
Foster, Pops, 116–17, 190n67
four in a bar/four beats in a bar, 91, 102, 117
France, 18, 19, 55, 57, 66, 78, 176n28, 187n23
    Hachard's letters, 49–50, 174nn3–5
    musicians touring in, 87, 91–92, 98, 116, 118
Franco-American folk music, 6, 120. *See also* Louisiana-French folk music
Free Blacks, 30, 167n2. *See also* Creoles of Color; Free People of Color; *Gens de Couleur Libres*; People of Color
Free People of Color, 12–13, 14–19, 20, 44, 50, 66, 74, 164n11. *See also* Creoles of Color; Free Blacks; *Gens de Couleur Libres*; People of Color
free-floating signifier, 4, 10, 73, 83, 125
Freeman, 85
French, Albert, 183n56
French Baroque music/vocal technique, 53
    and Black American folk music, 54
    See also Ursuline manuscript
French Canadian(s), 11, 18, 74, 164n11, 165n18
French Creole(s)
    as a community (enslaved/aristocracy), 3, 4, 14, 19, 82, 98, 128

culture/three-tiered society, 9, 10, 19, 120
    See also Afro-French Creoles
French culture, in Louisiana, 5, 10, 60, 73
French Empire/colonies, 5, 10–11, 67, 165n14
French ethos, eighteenth-century, 11–12
French horn, 5
French language, 3, 12, 18, 21
    ban of, 73, 98
French Opera House, 63, 109
French Quarter/district/part of town, 14, 79, 171n31, 174n2, 179n2. *See also* Vieux Carré
"Frère Jacques," 190n64
funerals, 9, 35, 71
Furetière, Antoine, 164n2

Gaillard, Raymond, 67
galop, 62
Garden District, 79, 81
Garland, Eddie/Ed, 87, 182n37, 186n7, 188nn37–38, 188n41, 190n59
Garrett, Charles H., 181n28, 190n55
Garrison, Lucy McKim, 28, 41, 132. See also *Slave Songs of the United States*
Gates, Henry Louis, 191nn73–74
Gaudin, Juliette, 51
Gayarré, Charles, 61
gender, 9, 103
Gens de Couleur Libres, 13, 15, 18, 20, 71, 78, 128, 164n11. *See also* Creoles of Color; Free Blacks; Free People of Color; People of Color
German(s), 11, 12, 18, 21, 22, 64, 66, 81, 171n31
Gershwin, George, 190n61
Giddins, Gary, and Scott DeVeaux, 163n6, 169n3
Gillespie, Dizzy, 81
Gilroy, Paul, 127
Ginell, Cary, 94, 182n41, 185n4, 185n6, 186n7
Gioia, Ted, 163n5, 169n3, 182n38, 192n2
Gipson, Jennifer, 53, 175n17
glissando, 82, 91
Glissant, Édouard, 164n5
Golden Rule Band, 100–101
Good Hope plantation, 28, 32

"Good Man Is Hard to Find, A," 183n57
Goodman, Benny, 81
Gore, Laura Locoul, 14, 60, 166n32
Gottschalk, Louis Moreau, 5, 29, 32, 41, 63–65, 178n20
Gottschalk Peterson, Clara, 40, 95, 132, 178n18
Gould, Virginia Meacham, 51
gourd, as an instrument, 37, 40, 45, 186n14
Governor, of Louisiana, 13, 31, 43, 46, 61, 66, 165n18, 168n54, 170n14
"Grand Dieu du Ciel/Paradis l'Aura," 58–59, 158–59, 161, 162
"Grand Orchestra," 40
"Grande Polka des Chasseurs a Pied de la Louisiane," 63
Griffiths, David, 84–85, 88, 183n43
growl, 88, 89, 91, 119
grupetti, 56, 176n26
guitar
    in Creole songs, 114, 117
    in early jazz, 72, 102, 104
    players, 74, 78, 99, 171n23, 180n11, 186n7, 188n37, 190n59
guitarist, 100, 102. *See also* guitar: players
Gushee, Lawrence, 78, 98–100, 165n13, 181n20, 181n24, 188n36
guttural tones, 28

habanera, 4, 29, 64, 65, 78, 81, 104, 190n55
habitations, 169n10
Hachard, Madeleine, 49, 174nn4–5
Hadlock, Richard B., 89, 190n65
Haggerty, Frank, 188n42
Haiti, 10, 11, 78. *See also* Saint-Domingue
Haitian Creole song, 29
Haitian Revolution, 23, 127
Hall, Gwendolyn Midlo, 166n26, 192n2
Hall, Manuel, 102
Hall, Minor, 87, 186n7, 188n37, 188n41, 190n59
Halpert, Herbert, 23, 170n17, 170n21, 171n28, 173n60, 173n61, 174n63, 189n47
hand (clapping/percussion/making the beat with), 34, 37, 39, 45, 55, 96, 101, 176n23

Hanger, Kimberly S., 15
Hardin, Lil, 87, 188n34
Hare, Maud Cuney, 67, 95, 186n14, 190n66
Harlem Renaissance, 128
Harlem Trio, The, 91
Havana, 13, 63
Hayes, Clancy, 188n43
Hazeur, François Marie Joseph, 74
Hazeur, Louis, 67, 74, 181n18
Hazeur, Marguerite Athenaïs, 74
Hazeur, Mathilde, 74–75
Hazeur Doublet, Antoinette, 74–75
head arrangement, 71. *See also* arrangement
Hearn, Lafcadio, 39, 172n38, 178n20
Henderson, Fletcher, 81
Henry, Irma, 190n66
Herskovits, Melville J., 118, 126, 127, 192nn5–6, 193n7
"Hesitating Blues," 86
Hicks, Edna, 85
Higuera, Fred, 188n43
Hobson, Vic, 102
Hodges, Johnny, 91
Holmes, Isaac, 38, 171n30
home music-making, 5, 57–58, 62, 68, 74, 95, 187n30
Hoodoo, 187n23
Hot Five. *See* Louis Armstrong's Hot Five
"hot" jazz, 76, 82, 83, 89, 93, 94, 100, 180n16, 185n1
Hughes, Langston, 193n12
hunting horn, 5
hybridity, 8, 127

"I Got Rhythm," 68, 190n61
"I Hate a Man Like You," 88, 183n54
Iberville, Pierre Lemoyne d', 11, 164n3
"Il était une bergère," 190n64
improvisation
    in Creole songs, 104, 114, 118, 119–20
    and early jazz musicians, 71, 72, 76–77, 82, 88, 90, 102, 103, 184n66
    in precursors, 27, 28, 32, 35, 36, 37, 41, 43, 45, 46

indentured servant, 18
Independence/Independent Band, 102, 187n26
Indian(s), 23, 30, 49, 84, 171n31. *See also* Native American(s)
Indian market, 23
Indianapolis Sunday Star, 100
inflection, 3, 53, 56, 88, 119
Ingersoll, Thomas N., 13–14, 175n7
insult songs, 192n70
interculture/intercultural phenomena, 9–10, 165n10, 180n8
interlude, 117–18, 190n68
interracial marriage/union/choir/relation, 13, 15, 50, 168n56
Irish, 12, 21, 31, 66
Irvis, Charlie, 185n69
Isleños, 12
Italian(s), 21, 168n56

Jackson Square, 5, 66
Jamaica, 12
Janis, Harriet, 94, 118, 189n52, 190n68, 191n70
"Jass and Jassism," 187
jawbone, as an instrument, 32, 39, 40, 44
Jazz a la Creole sessions/album/LP, 94, 116, 118, 163n1, 189n52, 190nn67–68, 191n70
Jazz and Heritage Festival in New Orleans, 84
Jazz Man label, 94, 185n4
Jazz Man Record Shop, 84, 94, 185n6
Jazzmen, 93–94
"Je M'en Vais Finir Mes Jours Avec la Madeleine," 55, 137, 140
"Jelly Roll Blues, The," 78–80
Jelly Roll Morton and His Red Hot Peppers, 81, 84, 117
"Jelly Roll/I Ain't Gonna Give Nobody None of This Jelly Roll," 183n57
Jews, 12, 21, 166n23
"Jew's harp" [*sic*], 40
Jim Crow laws, 20, 72, 179n4
"Joé Férail"/"Joe Féraille," 28–29

Joe "King" Oliver's Creole Jazz Band, 10
John Robichaux Orchestra, 75, 76, 82, 89
Johnson, Bill, 99, 186n20
Johnson, James P., 116–17, 190n67
Johnson, Jerah, 11, 171n31, 179n4
Johnson, Ollie "Dink," 99, 182n37, 186n20
Johnson, Willie Geary "Bunk," 76, 85, 89, 93–94, 182n30, 185n4
Jones, Leroy, 191n1
Joplin, Scott, 65
Juré songs, 55
Justice, Andrew, 53, 175n18

"Kansas City Man Blues," 90, 184n65
Kein, Sybil, 108, 187n30, 191n75
Kelly's Band, 68
Kennedy, Emmet R., 36, 171n24
Keppard, Freddie, 77, 87, 89, 98, 99, 186n20
Kid Ory and his All Star Jazz Group, 94, 185n6
Kid Ory's Creole Jazz Band, 73, 82, 104, 188n37, 188n39, 190n59
King, Grace, 22
King Oliver and His Dixie Syncopators, 83–84
King Oliver's Creole Jazz Band, 10, 76, 83, 87
Kinzer, Charles E., 67, 72, 74, 77, 179n27, 180nn10–11, 180n14, 180n17, 181n18, 184n60, 196n17
Kmen, Henry A., 61, 62, 177n8, 177n10, 178n11
Krehbiel, Henry E., 40, 42, 47, 129, 132, 172nn38–39, 172n48, 173n49, 178n20

La Clé du Caveau, 56–57, 147, 176n28, 176n30
La Compagnie des Indes, 18, 30. *See also* Company of the Indies
La halle sauvage, 23
La Louisiane, 4, 11, 165n18, 192n2
la manière (ornaments), 56, 176n26
La Menthe, Ferdinand Joseph. *See* Morton, Jelly Roll
"La Misère" (Misery), 102, 113, 115

La Nouvelle-Orléans, 5, 174n3, 178n13
"La Paloma," 78
"La Passion de Notre-Seigneur J. S." 144, 148–49, 176n30
La Revue du Monde Noir, 128, 193n12
La Revue Nègre, 91, 185n71
La Rose Noire, 87
La Salle, Robert-René Cavelier de, 11
"La Savane (*Ballade Créole*)," 32
"La Vie en Rose," 121, 163n2
"La Vierge Marie/Paradis l'Aura," 59, 160, 162
Labranche, Mélazie, 23
Labranche Plantation, 4, 23, 48, 95, 108, 173n61
Lachance, Paul F., 14, 166n32
"Lady Luck Blues," 91
"L'alouette," 190n64
Lambert, Lucien, 63
Lambert, Sidney, 63
Lamothe, Ferdinand Joseph. *See* Morton, Jelly Roll
lancers, 62
Landreaux, Elizabeth Marie. *See* Miles, Lizzie
Landry, Irma, 59, 162
Laprerie, Jean-Philippe, 66
Larrieu, Emellian, 67
Larrieu, Etienne, 67
Las Siete Partidas, 15
Latin American songs, 78
Latin jazz, 81
Latin tinge, 163n5
Latrobe, Benjamin, 39, 171n27, 171n35
L'Avenir, 53
lawn parties, 71, 119
"Le Bananier: Chanson Nègre," 64
Le jeu du mouchoir (Drop the handkerchief), 170n12
Le Jeune, Emilie, 95, 186n14
"Le Mancenillier," 64, 178n18
Le Page Du Pratz, Antoine Simon, 29, 169n9
"Le roi Dagobert," 190n64
Le Villageois/The Villager, 42, 172n45

LeBlanc, Pierre, 189n50
Leçons des Ténèbres, 50, 174n5
legato, 84
Lemmon, Alfred E., 175n13
"Les Ognons"/"Les Oignons," 36, 102, 116–18, 171n25, 190n67. See also *calas*
Les Sœurs de la Sainte-Famille, 51
Levin, Floyd, 184n64
Levine, Lawrence W., 95
Lewis, George, 185n4
Lincoln Park, 78, 85
literacy. *See* musical literacy
Locke, Alain, 193n12
Logsdon, Joseph, 9
"Lolotte," 32, 64, 178n18
Lomax, Alan, 29, 77–78, 81, 100–101, 115, 180n9
Lomax, John, 29, 171n25
Long, Edith, 172n48
"Long Head Bob," 103
Los Angeles, 81, 82–83, 94, 99, 102
"Los Campanillas," 64
Louiguy (Louis Guigliemi), 163n2
Louis Armstrong's Hot Five/Hot Five and Hot Seven sessions, 73, 83, 184n66, 188n34
Louis Nelson and His Palm Court Jazz Band, 109, 189n51
Louis "Papa" Tio's Large Ensemble, 97
Louisiana, colonial, 8, 125, 166n36
Louisiana Purchase, 9, 10, 12, 14, 15, 19, 78, 127
Louisiana Quartet, 64, 65
Luter, Claude, 92, 118, 190n9

"Ma mourri"/"Tant sirop est doux," 64
"Madeleine au Tombeau," 55–56, 135, 139
"Maison Denise," 189n47
"Make Me a Pallet [on the Floor]," 84
Malaga, 12
"Mamie's Blues," 81
Mammie Cavie (old maid Cavie), 33, 47, 170n17
"Mandy Make Up Your Mind," 91
Manetta, Manuel, 72, 76, 87

manumission, 14, 15. *See also affranchissement*; *coartación*; emancipation; self-purchase
"Maple Leaf Rag," 65
Marable, Fate, 71
march(es), 3, 62, 64, 66, 68, 78, 86, 181n28
marching band, 74, 104
Mardi Gras, 5, 10, 60–61, 103, 108, 119, 182n42, 187n30
   men cross-dressing, tradition of, 60, 103, 108, 182n42, 187nn30–31
   songs, 78, 102
Mardi Gras Indians, 78, 181n21
"Marianne," 111
"Marie, Je Souviens Ti"/"Enfant de Jésus-Christ," 58, 153, 156
"Marie-Madeleine, Laisse-Moi Passer," 57–58, 151–57
Marimba brett, 40
"Marlborough s'en va-t-en guerre," 190n64
Marrero, Lawrence, 185n4
Martin, Gilbert, 55, 58, 59, 139–40, 156, 162, 176nn22–23, 176n32
"Mary Ann," 111
Mass, 5, 49, 50, 52, 56, 176n29
Massy, Sister Claude, 175n15
Maxwell Sheet Music Collection, 62, 95
Mayfield, John, 184n65
Mazureau, Étienne/Stephen (attorney general), 46, 173n60. *See also* "Michié Mazureau/Mazuro"
mazurka, 62–63, 99
mbira (thumb piano), 40
McCants, Sister Dorothea Olga, 190n57
McCormick, Hal, 188n43
McCraken, Bob, 188n42
McCusker, John, 81, 82, 182n32
melisma, 28, 35, 36, 53
Merlin, Pierre, 92
métissage/mestizaje, 9, 127
Mexico, 75, 193n7
"Miché Banjo," 32, 41, 43. *See also* "Musieu Bainjo"
Michel, Marianne, 163n2

"Michié Mazureau/Mazuro," 45–46, 111, 119, 130–33, 173nn60–61
"Michié Préval," 32, 41–43, 45–46, 111, 119, 129–33, 172n48, 173nn60–61
micromusic, 4, 9–10, 120, 164n7, 165n10, 169n2
microtonal alterations/variations, 27, 36
Miles, J. C., 85–86
Miles, Lizzie, 6, 73, 84–88, 94, 117, 119, 183n43, 183nn55–56
   bilingual songs, 88, 183n57
   "Eh La Bas," 106–7, 111, 187n24, 188n43
military marches. *See* march(es)
military music, 3, 62, 66–68
Miller Surrey, Nancy M., 166n26
Millien, Achille, 55–56, 135, 139, 176n26
Million Dollar Baby Dolls, 103, 182n42
minstrel shows/songs, 75, 95
Minstrels (J. C. Miles Band and/Georgia), 85, 97
minuet, 32, 61, 62
Miserere, 50, 174n50
Mitchell, Louis, 87
Mitchell-Kernan, Claudia, 191n74
"Mo Marché sur Grand Chemin"/"Quand Mo Té Dans Grand Chemin," 35, 170n17
"Mo Pas l'Aimé Ça"/"Ai Ai Ai Mo, Pas Lemmé Ça," 101–3
Mobile, AL, 8, 11
mode, 54, 56, 58, 158
"Mon Cher Cousin," 106–9, 111, 189n47. *See also* "Eh La Bas"
Monroe, Mina, 43, 95–96, 129, 133, 173n61, 174n65, 186n14
Monterey Jazz Festival, 88
Montreal, 116
"Mood Indigo," 77
Morden, Marili, 84, 94, 182n41, 185n6
Morris, Thomas, 184n65
Morton, Célestine, 58, 159, 162, 177n34
Morton, Jelly Roll, 6, 65, 73, 77–81, 84, 99, 100–101, 115, 164n10, 180n6, 181n20, 181nn23–24, 191n77
   and His Red Hot Peppers, 81, 84, 117

Library of Congress recordings, 77, 81, 94, 182n29
and Lizzie Miles, 87–88, 117
Spanish tinge, 3, 29, 65, 163n5
Moten, Bennie, 81
motet, 50, 52, 174n5
"Moulin Grillez di Cannes," 33
Municipality (First, Second, Third), 19, 43
"Muscle Shoals Blues," 183n50
Music Inside Out (radio show), 121
music teacher. *See* teacher
musical literacy, 62, 68, 72, 82, 99, 165n13
solfège/sight-reading/theory, 71
"Musieu Bainjo," 41. *See also* "Michié Banjo"
"Muskrat Rumble," 83

Napier, Bill, 188n43
Nardal, Paulette/Nardal salon, 128
Native American(s), 11, 12, 38, 50, 81, 163n6, 166n36, 169n10, 171n31, 174n4, 181n21. *See also* Indian(s)
Négritude, 128, 193n13
Negro spirituals, 3, 5, 27, 32, 54, 55, 175n20, 176n23
Nelson, Louis "Big Eye," 89, 98, 186n20, 189n51. *See also* Louis Nelson and His Palm Court Jazz Band
neoculturation, 127
Neumann-Holzschuh, Ingrid, 172n45, 189n47, 193n1
"New Orleans Blues," 78
"New Orleans Hop Scop Blues," 185n70
New Orleans jazz style, characteristics of, 72, 104
New York City, 10, 76, 77, 87, 94, 179n1, 180n17, 184n63
Nicholas, Albert "Nick," 71, 76, 77, 116–18, 190n67
Nickerson, Camille, 28, 96–98, 120, 186n19, 191n76
Nickerson, William, 97
Nolan, Charles E., 51
Noone, Jimmie, 77, 93, 186n7
Nordskog, Arne A., 83
Nordskog label, 83, 182n38

notation, 27, 28, 77, 89, 191n75
notes inégales, 53, 175n18
Nouveau Theatre, 63
Nouvelles poésies spirituelles et morales, 52–54, 65, 175n13

oboe, 60, 67, 75
"Off and On Blues," 91
"Ojos Criollos (Les Yeux Créoles): Danse Cubaine," 65
OKeh label, 76, 87
Oliver, Joe "King," 10, 81, 82, 83, 85, 87, 165n3
one-drop rule, 20, 82
oom-pah pattern, 64
opera, 5, 19, 60, 61, 63, 78, 95, 109, 178n15
Original Creole Orchestra/Band, 98–100, 165n13
Original Dixieland Jazz Band, 76
ornaments (*la manière*), 56
Orson Welles Almanac (radio show), 94, 185n6
Ortiz, Fernando, 126–27, 193n7
Ory, Cecile Tregre, 111, 113, 115, 190n59
Ory, Edouard/Edward "Kid," 6, 48, 73, 82–84, 85, 94, 116, 180n6, 180n9, 182n32, 182n36, 190n64, 191n77
"Blanche Touquatoux" 111, 113–15, 188n38, 190nn58–59, 190n61
"Eh La Bas," 104–7, 111, 188nn38–39, 188nn41–42
See also All Star Jazz Group; Kid Ory's Creole Jazz Band; "Ory's Creole Trombone"; Ory's Sunshine Orchestra
"Ory's Creole Trombone," 83, 104, 182n37, 188n34, 188nn37–38
Ory's Sunshine Orchestra, 82, 182n37, 188n34
Oster, Harry, 23, 54–55, 56, 57, 59, 59, 139, 143, 164nn8–9, 175n20
"Ou Som Somroucou," 64, 178n18

Palao, Armontine, 98, 186n21
Palao, James/Jimmy, 87, 98–99, 186nn20–21

Palm Court Jazz Band, 109, 189n
"Pan Patat"/"Pam Patat," 36, 171n24
Panique, Nicholas Augustin, 54, 55–56, 58, 139–40, 143–44, 146, 156–57, 176n25, 176n32
Pan's pipe, 40
parade, 9, 45, 46, 67, 68, 71, 103, 181n21
"Paradis l'Aura," 58–59, 158–62
Paris, 64, 87, 91, 92, 126
parish(es), 5, 19, 23, 30, 32, 33, 48, 49, 50, 52, 173n61, 176n22, 176n25. See also paroisse Vermillon
parks, 78, 85
parlour music, 9
parody, 52, 56, 119
paroisse Vermillon, 54, 175n19, 177n34. See also parish(es)
partie de masques/party of maskers, 60
"Pasquinade," 65
passepied, 61, 177n3
passing/pass for White (*Passé Blanc*), 108–9. See also Toucoutou
"Pauv' Piti Mam'zelle Zizi," 64, 178n18. See also "Lolotte"
Pavageau, Alcide, "Slow Drag," 189
Pavie, Theodore, 38, 171n30
Pénavaire, Jean-Grégoire, 56
People of Color, 45, 51, 60, 164n11. See also Creoles of Color; Free Blacks; Free People of Color; Gens de Couleur Libres
percussion, 39, 45, 55, 81, 176n23
Perez, Manuel, 71, 85
Pergolesi, Giovanni Battista, 176n28
Peterson, Clara Gottschalk, 40, 64, 95, 178n18
petit tambour, 44
phrasing, 27, 55, 88, 89
Piaf, Édith, 3, 163n2
pianist, 64, 65, 72, 73, 77, 81, 87, 95, 180n6. See also piano: players
piano
  in Creole songs, 95, 96, 98, 105–6, 114, 117–18
  in early jazz, 72, 91, 104
  players, 74, 78, 85, 87, 88, 182n37, 183n56, 184n65, 185nn68–70 (chap. 5), 185n4 (chap. 6), 186nn7, 186n14, 188n34, 188n37, 188nn41–42, 189n51, 190n59, 190n67, 191n1
  in precursors, 62, 63, 65, 66, 68, 95, 178n20
Picou, Alphonse, 71, 89, 101–2
Picou, Ulysse, 102, 119
Pierce, Billie, 106
Pierce, Dede, 106, 189n44
Piron Orchestra, 76, 180n17
pitch (alteration/inflection), 4, 35, 36, 88, 90
plaçage, 15, 167n38
Place Congo, 4, 38, 44. See also Congo Square
Place d'Armes, 5, 66
plantation act/formula/economy, 18, 98, 125
plantation songs, 3, 4, 29–32, 95
play songs, 27
Plessy, Homer, 21, 168n55
Plessy v. Ferguson, 21, 98
polka, 3, 62–63, 187n23
polyrhythm, 3, 27, 64, 66. See also rhythm
popular songs, 9, 88, 95
ports de voix/portamento, 56, 176n26
Pouinard, Alfred, 28
Powell, Shannon, 121, 191n1
Pozo, Chano, 81
Préval, Gallien (judge), 43, 172n48, 173n61. See also "Michié Préval"
Prévos, André, 57
prison songs, 27, 169n2
producer, 65, 83, 94, 98
Protestant(s), 12, 54
public rights, 20, 167n55
Purchase. See Louisiana Purchase

quadrille, 3, 4, 62–63, 163n5, 187n23
Quadroon, 15, 62, 164n11, 167n38, 177n10
"Quan Patate La Cuite"/"Tan Patate la Chuite," 41, 45, 64
"Que ne Suis-je la Fougère," 56, 147, 176n28, 168n30

Quebec, 10, 54, 57, 116, 176n30
   Diocese of, 11, 176n30
"Qui Veut Qui Dit Toi Que Mo T'Apé lé Là-Bas?" (Who Told You I Was Going Over There?), 102
"Qui Veut Qu'y Volé Ma Bouteille?" (Who Stole My Bottle?), 102
quills, as an instrument, 40

raddy, 84, 182n42
Raeburn, Bruce, 81, 165n13, 166n23, 180n17, 181n22, 182n30, 185n1, 186n10, 187n22
rag, 65, 66, 86, 89, 99, 163n5
ragtime, 3, 5, 64, 65, 76, 78, 84, 86, 88, 99, 100, 178n19, 188n36
rasp, 28, 88
ratty, 76, 89, 180n16, 182n42
Reason, Lionel, 188n42
Reconstruction (post–Civil War), 20, 32, 73, 181n24
Redd, Alton, 186n7
Redeemers, 20, 168n54
refrain, 33, 37, 56, 68, 112, 117, 173n61, 190n62
reinterpretation, 126, 127, 192n6
religion, 3, 9, 12, 49, 126
religious music, 95, 175
"Ramoné la Cheminée," 36
"Rémon," 32, 41
Rena, Henry "Kid," 87
"Réponds-moi (Dí que sí)," 65
revival, of early jazz, 6, 73, 84, 88, 92, 93, 94, 98, 106, 116, 118, 119, 186n10
Revue Romande, 90
rhythm
   binary, 28
   Caribbean/Afro-Latin/Afro-Spanish, 3, 29, 65, 78, 79, 104, 119, 163nn4–5
   from tresillo to swing, 114
   syncopation/syncopated, 3, 27, 28, 59, 65, 66, 72, 76, 119
   three-over-two/three-over-four, 27, 29, 64, 66
   two-beat versus four-beat, 188n36
   See also habanera; *notes inégales*; polyrhythm; "Spanish tinge"; swing; tresillo

"Rhythm changes," 114, 190n61
rhythm section, 72, 102, 104, 106, 110, 113–14
riffs, 78
Rimington, Sammy, 189n51
ring shouts/ring dances, 3, 27, 55
ring-around song, 116
Robinson, Jim, 185n4
Rogers, Ernest, 185n4
Roussel, Kyle, 191
routinier, 72, 179n5
"Rowers Song," 33
rubbing songs, 35
Russell, William "Bill," 23, 93–94, 181n28, 185n5
Russell, William H., 31, 170n14

Sabbath, 30, 41, 169n9
Sadler, Cora, 36, 171n25, 171n29
Sager, David, 83
Sailes, Jesse, 188n42
Saint-Domingue, 8, 11, 12, 14, 23, 29, 40, 62, 64, 67, 84, 172n39, 178n12. See also Haiti
"Salee/Sali Dame," 110, 118, 190n54, 191n77
salle de bal, 61
San Francisco, 87, 88, 104
Sarebresole, Paul, 66, 179n23
sarrusophone, 91, 184n67, 185n69
satire/satirical songs, 32, 41, 43, 45, 109, 115, 119, 173n49
Saxon, Lyle, 41, 54, 108, 115, 174n62, 182n42, 190n57, 190n62
saxophone, 73, 75, 76, 88, 90, 91, 184n67
saxophonist, 65, 73, 74, 91
scale, 27, 34, 36, 169n4
Scarborough, Dorothy, 34–36, 170n20
schottische, 3, 62–63
Schuller, Gunther, 79, 163n5, 169nn2–3, 185n70, 191n77
Scobey, Bob, 106, 188n43
Scott, Bud, 186n7, 188n37, 188n41, 190n59
Scott, Rebecca J., 21, 167n53, 168n55
Seck, Ibrahima, 14
second-class citizen/citizenship, 98, 128
segregation, segregationist, 9, 11, 20–21, 52, 72, 73, 179n4, 181n24

self-purchase, 15. *See also affranchissement*; *coartación*; emancipation; manumission
Senegal, 23, 128
Senegal River Basin/Senegambia 13, 14, 192n2
Senghor, Leopold, 128
Separate Car Act, 21, 182n30
Seroff, Doug, 85, 183n47
Severin, Chris, 191n1
Shannon Powell Traditional Jazz Band, 121, 191n1
"She Walked Right Up and Took My Man Away," 183n50
show tunes, 88, 103
sight-reading, 71. *See also* musical literacy
signifier, 4, 10, 73, 83, 125
signifying song, 118–19
sig'fication, 119
Simeon, Omer, 77, 186n7
singer-songwriter. *See* songwriter/songster
singers, 3, 65
　in *cantiques*, 54, 55, 56, 58, 59, 175n20
　in early jazz and Creole songs, 6, 73, 83, 84, 91, 95, 96, 102, 106, 111, 118, 119, 185n71
　in precursors, 28, 32, 41, 43, 54, 67
　See also chorus; vocals; voice
Singleton, Zutty, 186n7
Sisters of the Holy Family, 51
situations créolisantes, 125
Slave Songs of the United States (Allen, Ware, and Garrison), 3, 28, 32, 43, 119, 132, 172n41, 178n18
Slobin, Mark, 9, 164n7, 165n10, 169n2
slur, 28, 54, 55, 58
smear, 82, 83, 89, 106
Smith, Mamie, 87, 91, 185n68
Snaër, Samuel, 63
social class, 9, 12, 21, 62, 72
Société Philharmonique, 5, 63
"Society Blues," 83
Soeur Saint-Stanislas/Sister St. Stanislaus. *See* Hachard, Madeleine

solfège, 71. *See also* musical literacy
solo, 28, 32, 52, 88, 94
　in Creole songs, 104, 105–6, 113–14, 116, 117–18
　in early jazz, 76, 78, 91, 102, 184n66, 185n70
soloist, 82, 83, 84, 88, 90, 184n66
songs of allusion, 118–19
songs of derision, 27, 118, 191n70
"Songs of Wood and Waters," 33
songwriter/songster, 65, 83, 102
sons tremblés, 56, 176n26
Sousa, John Philip, 3
sousaphone, 104
Spain, 11, 12, 50, 66, 91, 192n2
Spaniard(s), Spanish (colonizers), 3, 8, 18, 163n4
Spanish regime/Empire/rule, 10, 12, 13, 15, 18, 62, 66, 74, 166n36
"Spanish tinge," 3, 29, 65, 78, 81, 104, 111, 113, 114, 163n5
Spikes Brothers, 83
Spikes' Seven Pods of Pepper Orchestra, 182n37, 188n34
Spitzer, Nicholas, 57, 58, 65
St. Cyr, Johnny, 89, 100–101, 187nn23–24, 188n34
St. Joseph's Day, 181n21
St. Louis Cathedral, 64, 66, 174n2
St. Mary's Academy, 51
stanza, 33, 37, 42
Starr, Frederick S., 40, 65, 171n29, 172n39
"Steal Away to Jesus," 119
Stearns, Marshall W., 118, 163n5, 189n52, 191n77
Steiner, John, 77, 181n18
Stephens, Stanley, 189n51
Stewart, Jack, 65, 164n5
stock (written) arrangement, 71. *See also* arrangement
storytelling nature, of Creole songs, 45, 119
straight 2/4 and 4/4 time, 114
street cries/street vendors, 27, 35–36, 116, 118, 170n22
string band/group, 97, 102, 103, 186n17

strings (stringed instruments), 37, 39, 65, 67
Stuart, David, 94, 185n6
subculture, 9, 165n10
Sunday gatherings, 4, 29, 38, 48, 64
Sunshine label, 83, 182n38
Sunshine Orchestra (Ory's), 82, 182n37, 188n34
superculture, 9, 165n10, 169n2
"Sur le pont d'Avignon," 190n64
"Sur un Orchestre Nègre," 184n63
"Suzanne Belle Femme," 97–98
Sweatman, Wilbur, 182n38
swing/swinging, 27, 54, 88, 104, 113–14
syncopation. *See under* rhythm
syncretism, 8, 192n6

tag, 111, 115
tambourines, 103
"Tan Patate la Chuite"/"Quan Patate La Cuite," 41, 45, 64
"Tandis que Babylone" (psalm), 53
"Tant sirop est doux," 64
Taylor, Eva, 185n69
T-Bone Walker, 84, 182n41
teacher (music), 6, 52, 63, 73, 74, 75, 77, 186n19
Textes anciens en créole louisianais (Neumann-Holzschuh, ed.), 42, 129, 172n45, 189n47, 193nn1–2
Theard, Marie, 171n29, 189n47, 190n66
theaters, 61, 63, 91, 112
Théâtre de la Gaîté, 61
Théâtre des Champs-Élysées, 91
Théâtre d'Orléans, 61
theory of music, 71. *See also* musical literacy
third space, 127
Thompkins, Gwen, 121
Thompson, Butch, 189n51
three-over-two/three-over-four. *See under* rhythm
three-tiered society, 10, 19, 20
thumb piano (mbira), 40
Ti Balai, 31
"Tia Juana"/"Tee Wanna," 78
Tiersot, Julien, 108, 189n48

"Tiger Rag," 99
timbre, 3, 28, 56, 163n4, 176n26
Times-Democrat, 37
Times-Picayune, 187n22
Tin Pan Alley tunes, 114
Tinker, Edward Larocque, 36, 171n24
Tio, Antoinette, 74, 180n11
Tio, Lorenzo, Jr., 74, 76, 77, 89, 102, 180n6
Tio, Lorenzo, Sr., 75
Tio, Louis "Papa," 72, 75, 76, 77, 89, 97
Tio, Louis R. (Papa's nephew), 72, 74, 76
Tio, Marcos, 74
Tio, Thomas, 74, 181n18
Tio and Doublet String Band, 97, 186n17
Tizol, Juan, 81
"Tombeau, Tombeau Marie-Madeleine," 55–56, 134–40
tom-tom, 39
tone, as notes, 55, 56
tone/tonal quality, 28, 54, 77, 88, 89
Tony Almerico's All Stars/Parisian Room Band, 183n56
"Toucoutou," 109, 111–15, 119, 189n50
Toussaint, Allen, 65
"Tout Pitit Négresse," 34
transculturation, 126
transmutations of culture, 126
Tregle, Joseph G., Jr., 8, 20, 164n3
Tremé, Emile, 67
Tremé, Félix, 67
tremolo, 56
tresillo, 29, 64, 78–79, 104, 109–10, 113–14, 178n19, 190n55, 190n60
triangle, 39, 40
Trist, Hore Browse, 31
trombone
  in Creole songs, 104, 106, 113–14
  in early jazz, 72, 83, 84, 182n36
  players, 78, 99, 101, 182n37, 184n65, 185n69 (chap. 5), 185n4 (chap. 6), 186n20, 188n34, 188n37, 188nn41–43, 189n51, 190n59
  slide/smear/tailgate/valve, 82, 83, 104, 106, 182n36

trombonist, 73, 81, 91. *See also* trombone: players
Trotter, James M., 63, 178n17
trumpet
   in Creole songs, 105–6, 110–11, 113–14
   in early jazz, 72, 102, 104
   players, 92, 93–94, 185n4, 186n7, 188nn37–38, 188nn41–43, 189n51, 190n59, 191n1
tuba, 104
"Twinkle, Twinkle, Little Star," 116

uptown (Anglo-American, musician), 71–72, 76, 78, 79, 81, 82, 89, 103, 111, 164n10, 179n2, 179n5 180n6, 180n16, 188n33
Ursuline manuscript, 52–54, 65, 175n13
Ursuline(s), 5, 19, 49–52, 57, 66, 174n4, 175n15, 176n30
Usner, Daniel H., 8
USSR, 73, 91

vaudeville, 85, 87–88, 98, 103, 147
Vaz, Kim Marie, 103
Venet, Seva, 191n1
Verges, Alphonse "Al," 66
Verges, Joseph "Joe," 66
Verve (Records), 94, 105, 114, 116
Viator, Étienne, 190n58
vibrato, 33, 53, 54, 56, 58, 77, 88, 91, 119
Victor, 76, 94, 183n54
Vieux Carré, 36, 66. *See also* French Quarter
Vigne, Jean, 182n42
Vincent, Edward/Eddie, 99, 185n20
viola, 97
violin, 39, 60, 87, 97, 186
violinist, 56, 76
vocals
   in Creole songs, 105–6, 110, 111, 113–14, 116–19
   vocalists, 33, 88, 91, 185nn68–70, 188nn41–42, 189n51, 190n59
   See also chorus; French Baroque music; singers

voice
   in Creole songs, 88, 106, 110, 117–18
   in precursors, 28, 32, 33, 34, 35, 36, 41, 45, 46, 52, 56, 66, 95
   See also chorus; singers
Voodoo, 24, 27, 32, 37–38, 41, 47, 172n39, 174n62, 187n23
"Vous Conné Tit la Maison Denis," 108

Walker, T-Bone, 84, 182n41
walking bass, 177
Wallace, Sippie, 91, 185n70
waltz, 62–63, 130
War of 1812, 67–68, 74
Ware, Charles Pickard, 41, 132. See also *Slave Songs of the United States*
Warner, Charles D., 47, 174n62
washboard, as an instrument, 35
Washington, Fred, 182n37
Wehrmann, Henri, 66, 189n47
Welles, Orson, 84
West Africa, 11, 118–19, 169n4, 192n2
West Indies, 8, 14, 38, 119, 172n41, 173n49, 191n78
White, Amos, 87
White supremacy, 14–15, 19–21, 166n36, 168n54
Wilber, Bob, 89
Wilbur Sweatman and his Jass Band, 182n38
"Wild Cat Blues," 90, 184n65
Wilkinson, Christopher, 180n9
William Marion Cook's Southern Syncopated Orchestra, 90
Williams, Clarence, 90, 184n65, 185nn68–70
Williams, Norwood, 99
Wilson, Buster, 186n7, 188n37, 188n41, 190n59
Wilson, Mary Louise, 59
Wilson, Theresa (Paul Barbarin's sister), 102–3
Wilson, Wash, 119, 191n73
Winther, Christian, 191n1
Withers, Frank, 91
Wogan Arguedas, Jeanne. *See* Arguedas, Jeanne Wogan

Woodland Plantation, 48, 81
work songs, 3, 27, 33–35, 191n70

Young, Austin (Lester Young's uncle), 185n4

Zagala, Mathilde, 62, 64, 95, 178n13, 178n19, 178n20
Zardis, Chester, 189n51
Zeno, Alice, 63, 116, 171n24, 187n30
    cantiques, 57–58, 156–57
    Congo Square, 44, 47, 173n55
    life, 4, 21–23, 164n8
"Zoli Pon," 47
zydeco, 55

ABOUT THE AUTHOR

Caroline Vézina holds a BFA specialized in Jazz Studies from Concordia University in Montreal (1996) and a MA in Music and Culture from Carleton University in Ottawa (2014). During the last semester, she was an invited scholar at Tulane University in New Orleans where she presented her work in an article published in the *Jazz Archivist*, then the newsletter of the Hogan Jazz Archive, in 2015.

Before going to graduate school, she taught music to children and adults for seven years. Inspired by a lifelong interest in geography and history, she then worked in two of Canada's national historic sites, where she used her skills as a teacher and researcher to create, implement, and deliver guided tours and various interpretive activities. Her keen interest in diverse peoples and cultures led her to travel extensively in Central America, Europe, New Zealand, Australia, and the United States, visiting New Orleans for the first time in 2008.

Following graduation, she split her time between Montreal and New Orleans researching the music of the French Creole for five more years as an independent scholar. This gave her the opportunity to visit many cities and historic sites, and to explore the French heritage of Missouri and Illinois, once part of the French Empire in America.

But most of all, her passion for poetry and music has endured, as she is now completing an online certificate in songwriting at the Berklee College of Music.

www.ingramcontent.com/pod-product-compliance
Lightning Source LLC
Chambersburg PA
CBHW022007220426
43663CB00007B/997